Alverno College

Presented by

Robert G. Pitman

Director of Theatre Alverno
1963-1978

Academic Dean of Alverno College
1974-1978

A Guide to the Plays of

BERNARD SHAW

by the same author

HARLEY GRANVILLE BARKER
(Rockliff and Harvard University Press, 1955)

BERNARD SHAW'S LETTERS TO GRANVILLE BARKER
(Theatre Arts Books and Phoenix House, 1956)

A Guide to the Plays of

BERNARD SHAW

by C. B. PURDOM

London
METHUEN & CO LTD
36 Essex Street WC2

First published in 1963
© *1963 by C. B. Purdom*
Printed in Great Britain by
The Shenval Press Ltd.
London, Hertford and Harlow
Catalogue No. 2/2567/1

'Either I shall be remembered as a playwright as long as Aristophanes and rank with Shakespeare and Molière, or I shall be a forgotten clown before the end of the century.'

Contents

Preface

STARTED twenty years ago during his life-time, and at last completed, this book is a descriptive and critical account of Bernard Shaw's work as a playwright. It is as a dramatist that his name will live. When I first encountered his plays at the Court Theatre in 1904 they were a revelation that opened a window into my mind. The excitement and exhilaration of spirit of those days I have never lost, and every new Shaw play that followed had its own excitement. I have tried to convey something of that personal experience in writing about the plays in these pages as well as aiming at giving the results of reflection and considered judgment.

The leading ideas contained in the plays are discussed because they are relevant to the work of the dramatist, and I have thought it well to say something upon their original productions because they were mostly done under his direction. I sometimes think that if Shaw were to be reincarnated as a dramatic critic he would only too often be as scathing of the treatment of his plays upon the stage today as was G.B.S. when writing of the Shakespeare productions in the London theatre sixty years ago.

Acknowledgment is made to the Public Trustee and the Society of Authors for the use of copyright material.

C. B. PURDOM

Welwyn Garden City
Hertfordshire

PART ONE

The Man

The Man

'I DREAD to think of the biographers waiting for me to go,' said
Bernard Shaw towards the end of his life. He wrote no auto-
biography, and while he left a good deal of material for biography,
and took a hand in many of the biographies written during his
lifetime, it was rather to maintain and magnify the figure he chose
to present to the world than to reveal the true man. The mask in
which he appeared in the public eye was often that of a mounte-
bank and scoffer, an irresponsible joker and trifler. The real man
was sensitive and generous, interested in people and deeply concerned about the future of mankind, a hard worker in everything
he undertook, and especially serious as a playwright.

It is true of everyone, of course, that he has a mask, for few
people's real selves are revealed even to those who know them
best; but this is an unconscious mask, not deliberately created, the
result of involuntary self-disguise. Shaw's mask, however, was
consciously created; for that reason when he chose to appear
without it he exposed himself as few men have done, and those
glimpses of the real man enabled us to get to know him as few
men are known. Shaw's sensitiveness was due to his apprehension
of that fact. Indeed, the mask that so delighted him in his hey-day
made him more and more uncomfortable as he grew old, for he
could not escape from the 'monster' the public thought him to be.
In a 'Warning from the Author' attached to a special popular
edition of his complete plays published when he was well over
ninety, he said:

I must warn you, before you attempt to enjoy my plays, to

clear out of your consciousness most resolutely everything you have ever read about me in a newspaper. Otherwise you will not enjoy them: you will read them with a sophisticated mind, and a store of beliefs concerning me which have not the slightest foundation either in prosaic fact or in poetic truth. In some unaccountable way I seem to cast a spell on journalists which makes them recklessly indifferent not only to common veracity, but to human possibility. The person they represent me to be not only does not exist but could not possibly exist.

It is not my object to compete with the biographers, though I think it necessary to offer in these opening pages a brief sketch of his long life in relation to his work as dramatist.

(2)

George Bernard Shaw was a native of a city that has been nursery and training place for men of the theatre for many generations. He was born on Saturday, 26 July 1856, at No. 3 Upper Synge Street (now 33 Synge Street), Dublin, a five-roomed house, with a basement kitchen. Two sisters had preceded him there. His father, George Carr Shaw, son of a Dublin stockbroker who made a failure of his life, had been a civil servant, and retired on a pension of £60 before Bernard, named after his father and grand-father, was born. George Shaw had already sold his pension and become a corn merchant, but proved to be as unsuccessful as a man of business as his own father; he was in fact a cheerful ne'er-do-well given to drink. Shaw's mother was Bessie Gurley, grand-daughter of a country squire; she was much younger than her husband. Shaw was more than a little proud of his genteel origin, in that respect being a true Irishman. The Shaws were originally a Hampshire family, a member of which, Captain William Shaw, settled in Kilkenny after the battle of the Boyne. Both parents

4

(1)

were Protestants, and Shaw was baptised in the faith of the Church of England in Ireland, believing that God was a Protestant and that Roman Catholics went to hell. He was sent to school to the Wesleyan Connexional School, afterwards Wesley College, and elsewhere, and was miserable at school as he afterwards copiously explained.

Shaw said he had three fathers: 'my official father, the musician, and my maternal uncle'. He gives an account of his father and his early years in the preface to his first novel *Immaturity* when it came to be published in his old age, and said much more about his parents and sisters in *Sixteen Self Portraits*, published in 1949. 'The musician' was George Vandaleur Lee, a teacher of singing, who, being much taken with Mrs Shaw, got the Shaw household to move to his own rather better house, 1 Hatch Street, not far from Synge Street, thus arousing more than a little scandal. To this fantastic man Shaw undoubtedly owed a great deal, including a method of voice production from which he greatly benefited and used afterwards not only in his public speaking but in his work with actors on the stage. He owed to Lee much more, for the latter had a cottage on Torca Hill, above the little town of Dalkley, which Lee lent to Mrs Shaw and her family. The cottage overlooked Killiney Bay in the front and Dublin Bay at the back. There Shaw spent many happy weeks for many summers, and there his feeling for Nature was aroused: the sunlight and cloud, the grass and dew, the soft Irish air and the expansive landscape, fed the romantic spirit which never deserted him.

The young Shaw had numerous aunts and uncles, and the uncle who fathered him was the Rev William George Carroll, curate of St Bride's, Dublin, who taught him Latin; another uncle, Walter Gurley, who was a ship's surgeon, and had a Rabelaisian wit, perhaps taught him more. When Shaw was approaching sixteen the home was broken up, for his mother would not live with the wastrel father any longer, and Lee having gone to London she took herself off with her two daughters to England, first to Ventnor, Isle of Wight, because her younger daughter, Agnes, was consumptive (she died there in March 1876), afterwards to London, where she kept herself as a music teacher. On her departure, Shaw senior, we learn, became a rabid teetotaller.

The Shaw family was a musical one. His father, who read nothing but newspapers, played the trombone; his mother was a fine singer and pianist; his elder sister, Lucinda Frances (known as Lucy Carr), an operatic singer; and Shaw's love of music came from what he learned at home. He had opera in his cradle, and his first ambition was to sing in opera. Left much to himself as a boy, he ran the streets of Dublin, and lived largely in his imagination. He spent many hours in the Dublin Art Gallery – 'the only real education I got in Ireland' – and read Shelley and Dickens with great attention. When his mother deserted the loveless home, his father and he went into lodgings at 61 Harcourt Street, and Shaw left school to become office boy to a firm of land agents in Dublin. There he remained for four and a half years. Many of his evenings were spent at the theatre, which he had frequented from his earliest years whenever he had the money for a seat. He saw every new play and especially every Shakespearean actor that came to the city, and every other actor of renown, among them Barry Sullivan in Shakespeare's tragedies and the young Henry Irving in *The Two Roses*. His profound and exact knowledge of Shakespeare was based upon these visits to the theatre, and many of the plays he knew by heart.

(3)

At the age of nineteen, in April of the year 1876, his sister Agnes having just died, he followed the example of many of his countrymen and shook the dust of Ireland off his feet. One of his colleagues in the Dublin office had set his mind alight by saying one day that every young chap thought he was going to be a great man. Apparently the idea had not previously occurred to Shaw, but when it entered his head he knew that there was no prospect of realizing greatness in Dublin, therefore he went to London intending to become a great man either as a musician or painter. He joined his mother and elder sister where they were living at 13 Victoria (renamed Netherton) Grove, a cul-de-sac off the Fulham Road (the house has since been demolished), exchanging the noise and dust of Dublin streets for the overwhelming noise and greater dust of London. Fulham was a district of small houses, and even at that time had decaying large houses with ample gardens; but it was beginning to be overcrowded, there were slums and much unemployment. As everywhere the public houses were open all day, there was squalor and drunkenness. But in London Shaw found an atmosphere of great personal freedom, the individual could do what he pleased, without comment, unlike in Dublin, and no one took any notice of the shy young man.

He had no idea of conquering London but intended to look for work, for his mother had no thought of supporting him, which at first was not pressing, as she and the family had just received a small legacy. His mother's musical friend, Lee, having taken an appointment as music critic to a weekly paper, *The Hornet*, handed over the work and the emoluments to the young Shaw, who delighted in this opportunity of expressing himself, and from November 1876 to July 1878 he wrote criticisms and other articles for that paper under the name of Lee. Then, other literary employment failing, he succeeded in getting a job in the way-leave department of the Edison and Bell Telephone Company, which he held until that company was absorbed by another in 1880, when he gave up 'working for his living'. He was not indolent; but he had made up his mind that work in an office was at an end. He was then twenty-three, a tall, thin, red-haired, beardless, shabby fellow. Having tried it out he had decided to make his name as a writer, for writing came naturally to him: 'I never felt inclined to write,' he said, 'any more than to breathe.'

He was methodical and wrote articles on all kinds of subjects, which he sent to one magazine or newspaper after another, all of them were rejected. So he set himself to be a novelist, writing in his small hand five pages a day in an exercise book. A novel was completed, which no publisher would look at, but, in the next four years from 1880 to 1883, he wrote four more. All were rejected; afterwards he succeeded in getting all, except the first, published serially in little magazines from 1884 to 1887, which brought him little except more friends.

Shaw became a vegetarian at twenty-five, following Shelley's example, and was already a teetotaller, having before him the awful parental example. The same year, in 1881, he had a mild attack of smallpox and gave up shaving, hence the beard. He had gradually got to know many of the reforming spirits of the time, among them the business man, James Leaky, who was interested in phonetics. Leaky had taken him two years earlier to the Zetetical Society, which met in Great Queen Street, a debating society formed to discuss freely all subjects, religious, philosophical, and political. The young Sidney Webb was a member, also Ebenezer Howard, afterwards founder of the garden city movement, in which Shaw always retained a lively interest. At the Zetetical Society, as afterwards at the more famous Dialectical Society, which he joined the following year, he found himself to be a horridly nervous public speaker, and deliberately set out to overcome this drawback by speaking on every possible occasion. To his friend Leaky he also owed an introduction to a retired opera-singer, Richard Deck, pupil of the famous Delsarte, who taught him how to articulate his words in public speaking; the result was that added to what he had learned from Lee he became one of the most fluent, cogent and attractive public speakers of his time. Under the influence of these societies, and his own disposition, he was seldom able to refrain from public speaking whatever the occasion or subject.

In the early 'eighties there was constant and increasing unemployment in London and much social distress of a kind altogether unfamiliar today. Shaw was deeply impressed by the widespread poverty, being not far from poverty himself, though not one of the lower orders. He was working like a lunatic at his writing when the family moved to 36 Osnaburgh Street, St Pancras, having in the year before, in 1881, found it necessary to move from Fulham to rooms at 37 Fitzroy Street (both houses now demolished). These enforced moves provided an altogether different setting for his life from that of the all-pervading meanness of Fulham, for this part of St Pancras was a district of larger houses in which many artists and professional people lived, close to the centre of things, saving him the dreary horse-bus ride whenever he wanted to come into town. That year, too, he heard Henry George lecture, which made him an enthusiastic land reformer; afterwards he read Karl Marx, in a French version at the British Museum, and, he says, 'From that hour I became a man with some business in the world.' Indeed, he became a socialist, and his life had reached a turning point. At the meetings of Hyndman's Democratic Federation he argued with the Marxists, who he found had mostly not read Marx. At Osnaburgh Street he wrote *Cashel Byron's Profession*. He was twenty-six. He was attending boxing contests at the St James's Hall and elsewhere and became the friend of boxers. This proved to be his one popular novel, though he came to dislike it. His fifth novel, *An Unsocial Socialist*, completed in 1883, was intended to be the opening of 'a vast work depicting capitalist society in dissolution', but no publisher would

9

have it and his novel writing was ended, though from time to time he wrote and published a short story.

At the Henry George Land Reform League he had met J. L. Joynes, who introduced him to his brother-in-law, Henry Salt, then an assistant master at Eton. Salt and Shaw became greatly intimate, Shaw being attracted by Salt's unconventionality, vegetarianism and love of Shelley, and not a little by his wife, Kate, a fervent musician and dark-haired beauty. When Salt with Joynes both left Eton, the Salts settled in a little cottage at Tilford, in Surrey, where they lived the simple life. Shaw became a frequent visitor; there he met Edward Carpenter among other prominent social democrats, and there, too, he brought George Moore, who did not like it at all, also Sidney Webb.

Shaw's other friends included A. H. Macmurdo and Thomas Davidson, he who founded the Fellowship of the New Life – 'to promote the general social renovation of the world' – which Shaw joined. Havelock Ellis, a student at St Thomas's Hospital, was also a member. Out of that Fellowship the year after, in 1884, Shaw and others broke away to form the Fabian Society, to the meetings of which he enticed Sidney Webb. The two threw themselves wholeheartedly into the new society's activities, Shaw writing its first manifesto. Shaw's friendship with Webb and later his wife is rightly to be regarded as one of the memorable friendships of history, for these three great personalities were associated for fifty years in the most important public affairs. In the interests of their own brand of socialism, Shaw became a persistent street corner orator and political pamphleteer. His economic and political essays show how thoroughly he gave himself to the mastery of these subjects. His love for Shakespeare brought him to the New Shakespeare Society, and he became very friendly with its founder F. J. Furnivall, joining, too, the same scholar's Browning Society. He was already a member of the

Shelley Society, where he had met Henry Arthur Jones. By the
time he was twenty-eight his life had intense activity, and, more
important, it had direction. Soon, his pecuniary anxieties were
over, for in 1885, the year his father died, he earned just over
a hundred pounds by his pen, and from then onward was able to
keep himself by taking on any journalistic work that turned up.
Early in 1887 the family moved again, to 29 Fitzroy Square, the
rooms on the second floor of which remained Shaw's home until
he was married.

(4)

The first direct connection Shaw had with the theatre was on
6 November 1886, when to help his dramatist friend, Edward
Rose, he read the part of Chubb Dumpleton in a copyrighting
performance of *Odd To Say the Least of It* at the Great Queen
Street Theatre.

The change in his fortunes had come about largely through
William Archer, with whom he had got acquainted somewhere
about 1884. They had sat next to each other in the Reading Room
of the British Museum, without speaking, until they were introduced by Henry Salt. Archer got him on to the reviewing staff of
the evening paper, the *Pall Mall Gazette*, then edited by W. T.
Stead, and through Archer, too, Shaw became art critic for the
weekly review, the *World*. The two men were very different, but
developed deep affection for each other, which had an effect upon
them both, and upon their work throughout their lives. Archer
was a good friend, for he got Shaw many journalistic jobs. In
1888 Shaw became leader writer, afterward music critic, for the
Star, T. P. O'Connor's new London evening newspaper, in
which, under the name of Corno di Bassetto, he added to his
fame as socialist orator that of the most exciting writer on music
the London press had known. A. B. Walkley was the dramatic
critic. After two years, he went back to the *World*, as music

critic, where he continued for four more years, when he resigned. At the beginning of 1895 he started his three and a half years' career as dramatic critic on Frank Harris's *Saturday Review*, for which he received six pounds a week, a post he held until in May 1898 Harris sold the paper.

These were all material factors in the making of Shaw as dramatist. But there were others of importance, in particular the extension of his friendships. He had got to know William Morris, who had read the instalments of *An Unsocial Socialist* in Joynes's monthly magazine *To-Day*. This, the last of Shaw's novels, was the first to reach the public eye, and had so favourable an effect upon the magazine's sales that it was followed by *Cashel Byron's Profession*, after which the magazine closed down; but its publishers succeeded in getting the novel published as a book, so that *Cashel Byron* became Shaw's first book. By this time, Miss Annie Besant had got interested in the young Shaw, and serialized his two earlier novels in her magaine *Our Corner*.

Morris had been greatly taken with Shaw's writing, and with the man himself and his sparkling energy, and he became a frequent visitor at Kelmscott House, Hammersmith Mall, also to the Morris's home in Gloucestershire; there he fell in love with May Morris, but was too shy to mention it, so that she married someone else. At the Morris's he got to know Florence Farr, and met W. B. Yeats. His reddish beard became well grown, and, whether visiting or lecturing, he invariably wore the familiar snuff-coloured tweeds made in St Pancras. Shaw then and always paid much attention to his body, to cleanliness, to exercise, to food, and to his physical health and appearance. He treated his body as the instrument of his mind and sought to maintain and perfect it for his work; for that reason he dressed for maximum bodily advantage and often flouted convention. His vegetarianism had a similar origin.

More and more time was devoted to the serious study of economics, and he joined the Economic Circle conducted by Philip Wicksteed at his home at Hampstead, to which leading professors of economics belonged: out of that circle came the Royal Economic Society. Shaw, grounded in Marx, became a Jevonian economist, and remained so all his life. His practical interest in public affairs led to his being co-opted on to the St Pancras Vestry.

Fitzroy Square and the neighbouring streets were then a cosmopolitan part of London, the home of English and foreign artists, musicians and actors, as well as refugees from Tzarist Russia and elsewhere. Artists have now left it, but it remained as cosmopolitan as ever until rebuilding after extensive war damage rapidly changed its one-time Bohemian character, some of which survives in the many small restaurants in Charlotte Street, and round about. When the vestries were wiped out and borough councils were created, Shaw sat as a St Pancras borough councillor until 1903, a period of municipal service spread over six years, during which time he was an assiduous attender at committees, neglecting no part of his duties.

(5)

During the period we have just surveyed Shaw had reached the turning point in his life. It happened in this way. In 1890 the Fabian Society had wanted a lecture on Ibsen. Shaw had seen twice the London performance of *A Doll's House* the year before, and had been engaged in rigorous defence of the dramatist on the outcry that arose. Also he had written and published a sequel to it, not in play form but as a short story, and more important he had listened a lot to Archer and Philip Wicksteed, so he offered to give the lecture. This afterwards became *The Quintessence of Ibsenism*, published the year of the lecture, the first book in

English about the Norwegian dramatist. The writing of this book provided the model for the prefaces to his own plays that were to come. In it he discussed, as was usual with him, questions not directly relevant to the plays. What was more important, how-ever, was that Shaw's attention was turned to the drama as a means of expression of the ideas crowding his mind, and when a year later the Independent Theatre was about to be started by J. T. Grein, Shaw quickly completed a play upon which he had been unsuccessfully collaborating with William Archer seven years earlier, which had led Archer to decide that Shaw was no dramatist, a view from which Archer never departed, and one that at the time Shaw accepted. That play was *Widowers' Houses*, announced as 'An Original Didactic Realistic Play', and performed by Grein's society on 9 December 1892, at the Royalty Theatre, with Florence Farr as Blanche. The theme was declared by the playwright to be 'middle-class respectability fattening on the poverty of the slums as flies fatten on filth', and the play's two performances aroused furious controversy, for to attack the respectability of the middle-class as Shaw had done was to strike at the backbone of Victorian England, and to put on the stage an unladylike heroine was to undermine the very foundations of Victorian drama. 'The most daring play submitted of late years to a metropolitan audience', said one critic. Others found it 'silly', 'despicable', 'revolting', 'fractious', 'sordid', and 'in no sense a drama'. Indeed, it was agreed by all except the enthusiastic Grein that the play proved Shaw to be, as Archer had discovered, no dramatist; but Shaw did not care. He had tasted the delights of dramatic authorship, and realized the sense of mastery of the theatre; from that moment he did not turn back. Although Archer declared that in producing the play the Independent Theatre had 'proved its utility and justified its existence', he never lost his utter dislike of it. Shaw wrote to him after his attack:

. . . A more amazing exposition of your Shaw theory even
I have never encountered than that *World* article. Here am I,
who have collected slum rents weekly with these hands, and
for 4½ years been behind the scenes of the middle-class landowner – who have philandered with women of all sorts and
sizes – and I am told gravely to go to nature and give up
apriorizing about such matters, by you, you sentimental Sweet
Lavendery recluse.

All the same, thirty years later Archer was still saying 'oh, but it
is bad, bad, bad!' so little do men shift from their opinions.

The play was published the year after its production, when
Shaw wrote his first preface, and said:

> It is not my fault, reader, that my art is the expression of my
> sense of moral and intellectual perversity rather than of my
> sense of beauty. My life has been spent mostly in big modern
> towns, where my sense of beauty has been starved, whilst my
> intellect has been gorged with problems.

These words were a manifesto by the dramatist, to be borne in
mind when his future work is considered, for Shaw never turned
from the ideas and experience of these years.

A year later he wrote *The Philanderer*, an unpleasant satire,
which many of his friends hated, for it came very near home,
providing an early example of how uncomfortable a playfellow
Shaw could be. William Archer called it an 'outrage upon art
and decency'. The play was not performed for twelve years. Of it,
Shaw later said: 'The first half of the first act of the Philanderer
is the only scene in my plays founded not too disagreeably on
something that actually occurred. . . .' This referred to an infatuation with Mrs Jenny Petterson, one of his mother's pupils, much
older than himself, whom he had got to know in 1884, when he

was twenty-eight. A few months later he wrote his third play, *Mrs Warren's Profession*, provoked thereto mainly by Mrs Sidney Webb, who disliked intensely the previous play and urged him to write about an unromantic hardworking woman; so he returned to the manner of his first play and wrote on the subject of prostitution due to the 'underpayment and ill treatment of women who try to earn an honest living'. The play was intended for the Independent Theatre, but, as Shaw knew quite well would happen, the censor refused to pass it, so it could not be performed and Grein never succeeded in making arrangements to get it done privately. When the play was sent to the Lord Chamberlain in March 1898, and permission to perform it for copyright purposes was refused, Shaw asked the censor to indicate what portions of the play were objected to so that they might be deleted, but the censor refused to say. Afterwards an abbreviated text was submitted omitting the second act, with Mrs Warren 'converted into a female Fagin', and a licence was granted, but except for copyrighting purposes this has never been publicly performed. Shaw was always very particular about the copyrighting of his plays, for which at that date a public performance was necessary; and he was quite right. The complete play was first performed by the Stage Society in January 1902, and is now often to be seen, the ban upon it having been raised in 1925.

Shaw, unlike many men, flourished on opposition, and the result of banning the play was that he immediately completed two more, making both pleasant plays so that the censor should not touch them. The first was written because the 'New Drama' had to exist. There was a theatre for it, provided anonymously by that enthusiast for drama and feminism, Annie Elizabeth Horniman, though so far as the public and Shaw himself were concerned the promoter was his intimate friend, Florence Farr, and as a play had to be found quickly Shaw wrote *Arms and the Man*, one of his most popular plays, an attack upon the romance of war. The illustrated weekly *The Sketch* had a page drawing by Bernard Partridge (who played Sergius) of Shaw rehearsing on the stage of the Avenue Theatre, which has often been reproduced. An unsigned article, probably by the playwright, in the same paper (25 April 1894) contained the following remarks:

> The work, then, is infinitely amusing but hardly a play. ... Of course the critics were all puzzled, so, too, the audience. ... It is impossible to get away from the fact that it was vastly entertaining, and that, even if one laughed derisively at times, one felt also hearty admiration for the immense cleverness and audacity of the writer. Like his Major Saranoff, the daring author has won his battle by neglecting the rules of his art, or rather, perhaps, by ignoring rules of which he does not know much. ... I have not for a long time laughed so heartily, and consequently, I feel far more grateful to Mr Shaw for his play than he will feel to me for my notice.

The work that was 'hardly a play' ran for eleven weeks, from 21 April, and Miss Horniman lost a lot of money, for there were almost empty houses, the receipts averaging £161 a week. Afterwards it was taken on tour for six months, but the play's popularity was still to come. A fifth play, *Candida*, was started towards the end of the year, but because Shaw had offered it to his actress-socialist friend, Janet Achurch, who played it in the provinces, he would not allow it to be done in London for six more years for he thought Miss Achurch merely 'kicked it around the stage'. On Shaw's insistence she had been engaged by Richard Mansfield early in 1895 to play the part in New York, but after putting it in rehearsal the actor abandoned the play saying 'I couldn't have made love to your Candida'; for he liked neither the play nor the lady.

Richard Mansfield had produced *Arms and the Man* in New York soon after its London production, having seen one of the performances there and being taken with the character of Bluntschli. The production had much critical praise but did not draw, though the actor kept it in his repertory. When Shaw wrote for him in 1895 *The Man of Destiny*, he would have none of it.

During this year in a letter to the actor Charles Charrington, husband of Janet Achurch, Shaw laid down what should be regarded as a fundamental principle: 'You cannot be an artist until you have contracted yourself within the limits of your art.' He was in fact continually preoccupied with the theory and practice of his own art, and among his casual contributions to magazines and in his letters, as well as his criticisms, is to be found possibly the best exposition of the playwright's art to be found in the literature of the subject. He claimed always that he was a classical dramatist who perfected the form of drama for the actor in the theatre.

Shaw started on *You Never Can Tell* in the summer of 1895 when Cyril Maude asked for a play, though it was not completed until the following year. He thus carried out his programme, having written six plays by the time he was forty: 'I made a rough memorandum for my own guidance that unless I could produce at least half a dozen plays before I was forty I had better let playwriting alone' (*Plays Unpleasant*, p. *v*.). He was fully convinced of his powers as a dramatist and knew that he had found his true vocation; from that time he had not a single doubt. He intended *You Never Can Tell* for a place on the fashionable West End stage, which he believed to be his proper field, and Cyril Maude proposed it for the opening of his season at Haymarket Theatre in 1897. Difficulties arose at once, however, for none of the company understood Shaw's humour. Miss Winifred Emery first chose the part of Dolly, because of its sparkle, but having heard

Shaw read the play immediately agreed to play Gloria, because of its romance, but Maude himself was not happy. He had cast himself for the waiter, William, though Shaw wanted him to play the hero, and after a fortnight's rehearsal Shaw withdrew the play.

William Terriss, famous actor of melodrama, had suggested to Shaw that he should write a piece for him, so Shaw, with Mansfield in America also in his eye, wrote *The Devil's Disciple*, the same year, 1897. According to Shaw, Terriss went to sleep when it was read to him, which means that the actor could not make head or tail of it, and the idea of producing the play was dropped until Mansfield made a success of it in October that year. Terriss, however, was never to play Dick Dudgeon for he was murdered outside the Adelphi Theatre in December. There can be no doubt that Shaw enjoyed himself immensely in writing this piece, for he took a stock theatrical form, giving it his own characteristic content, turning it upon its head, and putting into it a rare quality of writing. Furthermore, it enabled him to introduce an exquisite English character in General Burgoyne to sharpen the satire with a razor edge.

This by no means inconsiderable dramatic activity coincided with his work as a dramatic critic, and with unabated activities in the Fabian Society. Socialism was in the political air and Shaw was deeply breathing it. Keir Hardie had formed the Independent Labour Party in 1893 on a programme largely prepared by Shaw. Blatchford's *Merrie England* appeared the same year. Shaw was writing tracts and articles and lecturing throughout the country, and wrote the important manifesto *The Sanity of Art*.

How hardworking he was is shown in a letter to Ellen Terry on 29 January 1898:

Oh Ellen, Ellen, what a week! nay, a fortnight! Three first

nights, the county council election meetings, four vestry committees, one Fabian committee, a pamphlet to write about the Southwark police business (just completed), an adaptation of a novel to make to secure the dramatic rights for an ancient revolutionary comrade (female Nihilist), the Julius Caesar article, and one frightful headache.

The headaches were an affliction from which Shaw suffered throughout his life. The adaptation was of a book entitled *The Gadfly*, by Mrs Voynich: nothing further is known of it.

(6)

That year, 1898, he published the volumes *Plays Pleasant* and *Plays Unpleasant*, for if the plays were not to be seen on the public London stage they should at least be read. He also completed *Caesar and Cleopatra*, written for Richard Mansfield, who turned it down, saying that he could not play Caesar. Shaw had also had Johnston Forbes-Robertson in mind, but the actor, though admiring the play, was afraid of it; he did, however, play it in New York eight years later. Shaw published *The Perfect Wagnerite* the same year, but, what was more important, in that year, at the age of forty-two, he gave up dramatic criticism and married a lady of some fortune, Charlotte Frances Payne-Townshend, who was a year younger than he. Charlotte was a member of the Irish family of Townshends to which belonged the Dublin firm of land-agents for which Shaw had worked as a boy. She had written to the Webbs to say she would like to use her wealth to establish a man in his career, and Mrs Webb had told her that Shaw needed somebody to look after him or his genius would be lost. That was the beginning. They often saw each other and had constant correspondence, and when Shaw was laid up Charlotte went to see him in his mother's apartment in Fitzroy Square, and was so horrified at the way in which he was living that she wanted to take him away at once to her cottage at Hindhead. Shaw agreed to go only if they got married. So married they were at the West Strand registry office, on 1 June 1898; Graham Wallas and Henry Salt being the witnesses. Shaw has given an amusing description of the event; but he had someone to look after him at last. Charlotte had an apartment at 10 Adelphi Terrace over the newly established London School of Economics, of which, through the Webbs, she was a financial supporter. There they lived, with a house in the country, for nearly thirty years. The marriage was as near perhaps, as could be, perfect, except that it was on the basis of no physical sexual intercourse, to which Charlotte was averse, so that they had no children: 'we found a new relation in which sex had no part', Shaw explained afterwards. It is perhaps worth noting that Kate Salt, wife of Henry, who had been for some years Shaw's 'unpaid typist-secretary' until his wife took over the work, had also refused to consummate her own marriage. Charlotte was a woman of character and wholly devoted to her husband. She believed however that his real genius was as a socialist and she never more than barely tolerated his activities in the theatre. Although she let him have his way, she would have wished him to reduce or bring to an end his playwriting, for her own heart was in what the Webbs were doing, and she desired most of all that her husband's talents should be turned in that direction. Fortunately she had no success. But she did succeed in providing him with a home, for Shaw's home throughout their lives was hers: as often as possible he went out of the house to write. At times, and very early in their marriage, he found her solicitude for him a strain.

The year after marriage, Shaw started on his play for Ellen Terry, *Captain Brassbound's Conversion* – 'the only thing on earth in my power to do for you', he said – and a period in his career

21

as a dramatist closed. When he sent her the play, the actress wrote to say that she did not consider the part suitable for her; but Shaw now knew exactly what he could do: 'I have encountered no limit but my own laziness to my power of conjuring up imaginary people in imaginary places, and finding pretexts for theatrical scenes between them.' Henceforward, he was to devote himself not to casual pieces for the theatre and to writing for actors or actresses, however much he loved them, but to his proper task for the theatre, that on which he started with his first play; for he says in a letter to Ellen Terry '. . . it is time to do something more in Shaw-philosophy, in politics and sociology. Your author, dear Ellen, must be more than a common dramatist.' He meant that his playwriting must find its inspiration in serious political and social themes.

Although Ellen was saying that the play was not for her, and that if she played it the public would say she was not acting, she really wanted it, and had the idea of producing it with Laurence Irving and the Lyceum Company and taking it to America, if Henry would agree. Shaw proposed terms, telling her it was a money question. 'Remember', he wrote, 'that I am a most mean man about money.' She gave a copyright performance at Liverpool, but went no further at that time.

Shaw had first written to Ellen Terry in 1892, when he was a music critic, on the subject of a concert at which she recited and a young friend of hers sang. In that letter he said he would not walk a hundred yards to hear the girl sing again. This brought a letter of thanks from the actress; the correspondence between them was resumed in 1895, and the famous letters started.

(7)

London had its first opportunity of seeing *The Devil's Disciple* in September 1899 when Murray Carson gave eleven evening and two afternoon performances at the Prince of Wales' Theatre, Kennington, of which the *Daily Telegraph* said, representing the point of view of the middle-class playgoer of the time:

> Shakespeare simply made his characters humbug one another, whereas the magician Shaw can make his play humbug the actors, the actors humbug the audience, and, greatest miracle of all, the audience humbug themselves. . . . During the acts people were congratulating one another that Mr Shaw had cast off his fantastic manner and attempted a really sensible play. . . . Then . . . from . . . genuine emotion, he switched the plot off to sheer farce, while the pit and gallery looked at each other in blank amazement, and felt that they had been 'done'.

Earlier that year the Stage Society had been founded (the previous 19 July) on the initiative of Frederick Whelen and other Fabians, the object being to give at least six performances each year on Sunday evenings of serious plays not tolerated by the commercial theatre. Charlotte was put upon the reading committee and at once took her husband away for his first sea cruise on the Mediterranean. When they returned the society's first production, *You Never Can Tell*, took place on 26 November, produced by the comedian, James Welch, who played the Waiter and was on the society's managing committee. It was performed on a Sunday evening at the Royalty Theatre, which caused a sensation and disturbed the police, for not for hundreds of years had a play been performed in a London theatre on a Sunday. But being private the performance was found to be legal and was an enormous success, firmly establishing the society. Shaw was also firmly established as a London dramatist, though not yet in the public theatre.

What was almost equally important was that the society brought him into contact with a young actor named Granville

Barker. The two men had not met before, though Barker had been on the stage just short of ten years, and was still no more than twenty-two. His play written in collaboration with Berte Thomas, *The Weather Hen*, had been performed on 29 June 1899, at Terry's Theatre, but there is no record that Shaw had seen it. Neither had he seen Barker as Richard II in William Poel's production of Shakespeare's play the following November. Henry Arthur Jones, who did see him, wrote to Shaw to say that Barker was just the actor for Eugene Marchbanks in *Candida*; but it seems that Shaw did not notice Barker until he saw him at the third Stage Society 'meeting' on 25 February 1900, when Barker played Erik Bratsberg in Archer's version of Ibsen's *The League of Youth* at the Vaudeville Theatre.

Shaw recognized the young man's quality immediately, and the outcome was that *Candida* became the play at the sixth meeting, on 1 July at the Strand Theatre, with Barker as Eugene. This was a great occasion, for Shaw had found an actor who acted beautifully and intelligently, and imaginatively *was* the character. The delighted young Barker naturally wanted the play put on for public performances, but Shaw would not have it, for reasons that Barker was able to appreciate. But the friendship between the two men grew and became one of the most fruitful and notable in the early twentieth century English theatre. They both loved walking in the country and cycling, and spent much time together, their interests coinciding not only in theatrical matters, including epecially the idea of a National Theatre, but in politics and literature.

Forbes-Robertson got the dramatist to rehearse *The Devil's Disciple* in July, which the actor took on tour together with *Hamlet* and *Othello*. Writing to Ellen Terry to tell her what was happening Shaw said, 'It goes without a hitch and we are off in two hours to lunch, remarking, if you please, that the play is quite easy. . . . The only dreadful thing is that as far as I can see there are only two men in the company who can act.' He writes later to say that the performances were a success.

By the end of the year *Captain Brassbound's Conversion* was performed by the Stage Society with Janet Achurch as Lady Cicely, Laurence Irving as Captain Brassbound, and Granville Barker as the American Captain Kearney. Ellen Terry had a box at the performance and saw Shaw for the first time. There was talk of doing *The Philanderer*, which came to nothing because a Julia to suit Shaw couldn't be found. Barker was on the committee of the society and often at the Shaw's, for Charlotte was very fond of the brilliant, serious, but not well-cared-for young man.

(8)

This year, 1900, Shaw was busily occupied by politics, taking a share in the foundation of the Labour Representation Committee, and writing for the Fabians the important pronouncement entitled *Fabianism and the Empire*, provoked by the South African War. He also brought out his third volume of plays, *Three Plays for Puritans*. To preserve the stage copyright, he made a stage version of his pugilistic novel under the title of *The Admirable Bashville* in the 'childishly easy and expeditious' form of blank verse: the novel had much publicity in America and dramatized versions had been produced without Shaw's authority.

There is no more of theatrical interest to be recorded until 6 January 1902 when the first performance of *Mrs Warren's Profession* took place. Because the play was censored it was impossible to find a theatre, so the performance was given on an improvised stage at a club, secured under great difficulties. Mrs Warren was played by Fanny Brough, and Granville Barker became the first Frank, being subjected to a fusillade of criticism from the dramatist. The play was violently attacked: no one had a good word to say for it in the papers except Max Beerbohm.

Shaw was hard at work upon another play, but in the meantime the Stage Society decided to put on *The Admirable Bashville*, which Barker produced, Shaw giving him endless advice. The piece had been produced on the previous 14 December 1902 at an amateurs' theatre by Shaw's Irish Journalist friend, Conal O'Riordan, with a company of fellow journalists including W. R. Titterton and Cecil Chesterton, which gave Shaw some idea of its stage qualities. *Man and Superman* was finished and published next year. Barker wanted it at once for the society, but there was no actress for Ann Whitefield in sight. The published volume had a long Epistle Dedicatory to A. B. Walkley, and an appendix containing Maxims for Revolutionists, and made Shaw a best seller. That was after he had offered the book to John Murray, who found it too dangerous for him, so Shaw had it printed himself and arranged with another publisher to take it on com- mission, a practice he followed for the rest of his life.

He was speaking in Glasgow in September that year, and wrote while there to say that Patrick Geddes 'wants me to go to Dun- fermline next week to discuss immediate measures for the breeding of the Superman; and perhaps I shall accept his invitation'. Geddes was a biologist, a remarkable and unconventional Scots- man, and the two men admired each other greatly. In his Glasgow speech Shaw displayed the clarity of thought and the uncom- promising political sagacity that made him an uncomfortable companion for party politicians:

. . . a Socialist society cannot take the Free Trade point of view. We are necessarily anti-Free Trade, anti-Manchester, anti-Laissez-faire, anti-Cobden and Bright, anti all the Liberal Gods.

Since Richard Mansfield had produced *The Devil's Disciple* in New York, six years earlier, Broadway had seen no more new Shaw until the young Arnold Daly tried out *Candida* for a series of matinees, with such success that the play was given a run at the end of 1903, and next year was taken on tour, with *The Man of Destiny*, and played in the principal cities in the United States. And the year after *You Never Can Tell* was given a five months' run on Broadway by the same actor. This was the foundation of Shaw's theatrical fortune and of his sustained vogue in the United States.

(9)

The year 1904 was an important one for Shaw in London too. In April the determined Granville Barker was at last successful in arranging for six public matinees of *Candida*, with a cast of which Shaw approved, at the Royal Court Theatre, then being managed by J. E. Vedrenne for J. H. Leigh. The matinees were a success and led to the partnership between Vedrenne and Barker, which was to make the Court Theatre famous. They took a lease of the theatre from Leigh, who gave them more than moral support, and decided to start with Tuesday and Friday matinees in the following October. Shaw would not listen to the suggestion that the management should open with *Man and Superman*, for the reason already stated, but promised a new play, entitled *Rule Britannia!*

In the spring, Shaw, having resigned from the St Pancras Borough Council the year before, stood as a candidate for the newly formed London County Council, as a Progressive, but his outspokenness in a violently contested election resulted in rejection. He had offended his own Party, especially the passive resisters and the temperance reformers, and afterwards declared that the only people who voted for him were those who had never voted before. The Shaws now went to live at Harmer Green in Hertfordshire, where Barker was a frequent visitor, Charlotte urging him to come because he needed feeding up. She took her husband off to Scotland for a holiday in the summer when he was hard at work on the new play. He decided that its production had to be delayed for the assembly of Parliament, as it was a political play, and that the title should be *John Bull's Other Island*. So the play became the second production of the Vedrenne-Barker management on 1 November, Barker playing the part of the Irish priest. The play had to be cut because of its great length, Shaw leaving the cutting to Barker, professing afterwards to be not a bit pleased with the result. 'The theme is a huge one,' he wrote, 'and it can't be cut down to Court size.' Although the play was an enormous success, the audience's enthusiasm being unbounded, Shaw considered six matinees to be enough.

It was put on again for nine more matinees the following February, after *Candida* had been rapturously revived for eight matinees and two evening performances, and after a great disappointment over the failure to get satisfactory audiences for Laurence Housman and Granville Barker's Christmas play, *Prunella*, 'for grown-up children'. His Majesty, King Edward VII, had a command performance of the Shaw play on the evening of 11 March, of which the oft-told story is related that the King broke the chair on which he was sitting because he laughed so much. His Majesty was not alone in his laughter, for the play proceeded on a sea of merriment. It started the regular evening performances at the Court on 1 May. In the meantime, *How He Lied to Her Husband* was done at matinees, a short piece Shaw had written at the request of Arnold Daly in the middle of completing the Irish play. On 2 May *You Never Can Tell* came on for nine matinees, and when the *John Bull* ended *Candida* went into the evening bill for three weeks, followed by *You Never Can Tell* in the evening for another three weeks.

28

On 23 May, *Man and Superman* at last reached the stage, for an Ann had appeared in the person of Lillah McCarthy. The actress had called upon Shaw, as she tells in her memoirs *Myself and My Friends*, after some years' experience of playing with Wilson Barrett, and as soon as he set eyes on the handsome dynamic young woman he knew she was what he wanted. The play was a triumphant success. In the part of Jack Tanner, as everybody knows, Barker was made to look like the bearded Shaw. As usual, A. B. Walkley, in *The Times*, said the play was not a play, but admired it none the less; and it was heartily praised by nearly all who saw it. Its merits have been endorsed many times since. The following September when it was produced under Charles Frohman's management in the United States by Robert Loraine a fortune was made by manager and actor, to say nothing of Shaw's own share, but the treatment the play then received was farcical rather than that of high comedy. Shaw never saw it, of course.

(10)

The first season at the Court ended early in July, when the theatre was closed. Shaw was taken on holiday to Ireland by Charlotte, and Barker went on holiday to Greece with his friend Gilbert Murray. Plays by Maeterlinck, Euripides, Yeats, Schnitzler, Hauptmann, Housman and Barker, as well as by Shaw had been given, none hitherto known on the London public stage. The experiment had amply justified itself; Shaw was established as a London dramatist, and a new standard of acting and stage production had been set. The plays had been announced as produced (or, as we should say now, 'directed') by Granville Barker, but, as always, Shaw was the virtual producer of his own plays. He was not without dependence upon Barker, however; the two men worked together in the closest association and understanding, though their methods were largely different.

Shaw's way with his plays, then and afterwards, was first to read the play to his friends; when it was cast to his satisfaction, he read it to the company. This reading was an education in acting, for he characterized each part and gave a performance no one could afford to miss. When rehearsals started he would indicate positions and allow the players to do their best with their parts. He sat in the auditorium making few interruptions; but after the first week he would come on to the stage and go over the parts where he thought necessary. He had the ability to demonstrate exactly what he required. He would, however, often exaggerate in both speech and movement, telling the player not to imitate him, which the latter usually found difficult not to do. The more unable the actor was to get what Shaw wanted the more he would exaggerate.

For that reason it can be argued that Shaw's productions of his own plays were sometimes at fault, owing to his not giving up hope of the actor. This was not true, however, of plays at the Court Theatre where Barker was always at hand. There can be no doubt that Shaw gained much from him and I am sure that he was the ideal producer of Shaw's plays when Shaw was not about.

Rehearsals always started promptly and finished promptly, usually early in the afternoon, for Shaw did not believe in over-working actors. If they appeared tired or negligent he would dismiss the rehearsal. He had infinite patience, but overlooked nothing, though, as I have indicated, he often put up with much less than he asked for. He made copious notes, some of which have been preserved, and would afterwards send notes or postcards to the players on particular points. He was probably one of the most-liked producers who ever worked on the stage, especially when actors were not quite up to the mark, without in the least relenting in his efforts for what he wanted. He was, however, extremely strict. On one occasion at the Court Theatre Louis Calvert came in declaring that it was a crime to rehearse on such a beautiful day, they would be much better off playing golf, so Shaw immediately dismissed the rehearsal saying he would not rehearse when an actor had such ideas about his work. He thought players should give up everything to the parts they were working at. He even insisted that an actor rehearsing a part should be guarded as a prize-fighter is guarded by his trainer, surrendering every diversion to concentrate upon his task.

He knew how to praise even when a part was by no means played according to his ideas, if he were satisfied the actor was doing his best. Shaw's high praise of some leading players is on record, but it need not be assumed that when he wrote enthusiastically to a player he is to be taken literally. His real opinion may have been quite different; but he wrote for the occasion and to help the player. Except for Granville Barker's Eugene Marchbanks, and a few parts performed by other players, it is to be doubted if he was ever fully satisfied with the acting his plays received.

Shaw did not usually see his plays after the first performance unless there was a change in the cast or some other special reason why he wanted to do so. One can understand why. The demands his method of producing made upon him can be seen from what he once told Cyril Maude:

This system of putting up plays for six weeks is certainly a wonderful success pecuniarily, for the plays don't die and the business doesn't slack; but it is the very devil in point of rehearsal. I spend months every year producing when I ought to be writing.

As I have told the story of the Vedrenne Barker management

elsewhere[1] I do not propose to repeat it here; though not wholly concerned with Shaw, it made the Shavian drama a cult of the twentieth century intelligentsia, and Shaw became, according to Beatrice Webb, 'the adored one of the smartest and most cynical set of English society'. Features were made of the matinees on afternoons when other theatres were not open, and the short evening runs limited to three weeks, afterwards extended to six weeks. Shaw was relentlessly opposed to the long run system, for he considered that it killed plays that could otherwise be kept alive on the stage for which they were written. His plays certainly drew the largest audiences at the Court, but they were taken off at the height of their popularity – Barker consenting but Vedrenne thinking they were all mad – despite the knowledge that the plays replacing them would bring nothing like the same return.

(11)

Shaw's intentions for the new autumn season, 1905, were a new play on which he had been working for some time, also *Captain Brassbound's Conversion* with Ellen Terry, and while in Ireland he was writing to Barker about the casting of both plays. The new play was *Major Barbara*, for which Shaw got the co-operation of the Salvation Army, a fact that removed the objections the censor might otherwise have taken to it. It had the normal six matinees starting on 28 November, with Annie Russell in the name part. Shaw called it 'a discussion', and the critics took him at his word and said it was not a play. But they enjoyed it none the less, though some professed to be shocked. Shaw was by no means pleased with the performance, for the players achieved neither the gaiety and sparkle he intended nor the sharpness of the comic spirit that he most valued.

[1] See *Harley Granville Barker* (Rockliff, 1955) and *Letters of Bernard Shaw to Granville Barker* (Phoenix House, 1956).

On the following 20 March 1906 Ellen Terry appeared at last in *Captain Brassbound's Conversion*. Although it was something of a triumph to have brought it off, Shaw had another uncomfortable experience of a play to which the actors gave far less than he, rightly, thought it called for. Barker took the major part of the production work, Shaw looking on, but the actress was tired and unable to do her best. In fact, the production was ragged, and nothing of the usual brilliance of the Court Theatre was present. Ten days after the matinees ended it went into the evening bill for twelve weeks, after which the actress took it on tour. On the whole this was one of the Court Theatre failures: it certainly lost the management a good deal of money.

When this play was to be performed the previous year, in 1905, at the Lessing Theatre in Berlin, Shaw had made it a condition that the play should be produced by Gordon Craig, which was accepted; but the management had difficulty in getting the producer's designs, and, on their appealing to Shaw, the reply was received from Craig that he must be placed in complete control without regard to the views of the author, with the result that the arrangement immediately broke down.

The Shaws moved from Harmer Green to the Old Rectory, Ayot St Lawrence, early in this year, 1906, which was to be his home for the rest of his life. He also got his mother out of the Fitzroy Square rooms, and bought a house for her near Gloucester Gate. While Ellen Terry was occupying the theatre they went to Paris for Shaw to be sculptured by Rodin, and Barker and Lillah McCarthy got married. Afterwards the Shaws went away to Cornwall for a long holiday, and he wrote to Barker to say that he could definitely announce a new play entitled *The Doctor's Dilemma*. He wanted both Barker and Lillah, though Barker tried to get out of playing. 'It is a rotten play' wrote Shaw encouragingly to him in September. As usual, it was given eight matinees starting on 20 November, and put into the evening bill for six weeks only until the last day of the year. Entitled a tragedy, it was exquisitely played and had a great reception. This was another play 'suggested' to its author. One day in the summer in which it was written, Charlotte was told a story by Granville Barker of a doctor who had been treated for tuberculosis at a London hospital; this started a discussion upon doctors preserving the lives of people irrespective of whether they were worth preserving or not. 'There's a play in that!' said Mrs Shaw. Shaw agreed. His original idea, it seems, was to write about a worthless artist saved by doctors with the artist's wife in the leading part to be played by Lillah McCarthy, the play called *Jennifer*. The doctors, however, ran away with Shaw, and though the story is about the artist and his wife, the doctor became the leading character. The play is not an attack upon the medical profession, for the doctor 'is made of the same clay as the ignorant, shallow, credulous, half-educated, pecuniarily anxious people who call him in when they have tried in vain every bottle and every pill the advertising druggist can persuade them to buy'. The public wants 'a cheap magic charm', said Shaw and forces the doctors to give it what it wants. What Shaw condemns is any claim by medical men to knowledge they do not possess. Speaking from his own experience, he says in the preface that 'many unlearned amateur pathologists and hygenists . . . are safer guides than the Harley Street celebrities who laugh at them, their secret being that they have had the gumption to guess that it is the mind that makes the body and not the body the mind'.

During the play's short run Shaw at last got *The Philanderer* on to the stage, for Lillah McCarthy was the Julia he wanted. But he was unlucky; at the dress rehearsal she was taken ill and had to be rushed off to hospital, so that the understudy had to take the part. It was, therefore, a failure, Shaw being very put out, for he thought it 'the best of my plays'.

34

There was no new play by Shaw, and the tenure of the Court Theatre was coming to an end. The dream scene from *Man and Superman*, called 'Don Juan in Hell', was put on as the last matinee production, with *The Man of Destiny*, while *Man and Superman* was being played in the evenings. It was a perfect close to the Court management and no one who attended these last performances will ever forget them.

(12)

Though the Vedrenne-Barker management had produced in rather less than three years, from 1904 to 1907, the plays of seventeen authors, including the first plays of Galsworthy, it was the Shaw plays that were the leading attraction: only two other plays paid their way. During the period, 988 performances were given of thirty-two plays, of which 701 were of eleven plays by Shaw. With the exception of *John Bull's Other Island*, *Major Barbara*, and *The Doctor's Dilemma*, these were plays already written, most of them already performed by the Stage Society and others. This was Shaw's golden age as a dramatist, and, had the management continued, who can say what would have resulted from it? As the Court Theatre though cheap to run was inconveniently situated and poverty-stricken in its stage, a move was made in 1907 to the Savoy Theatre in the Strand. It was a fatal move.

Before this took place some friends arranged a complimentary dinner to the managers on 7 July at the Criterion Restaurant when Shaw, in a speech towards the end of the evening, replying to the toast of the Court authors, made a long and violent attack upon the press. He was much aggrieved that the critics did not enter into the spirit of what was being done by the management, and that they showed so little understanding of the revolution in playwriting as well as production and acting that had been started. There were exceptions, but the press as a whole gave no help to these efforts and, instead of being a guide to the public, confused and misled it, he said. And it was true that the standard of criticism generally applied to the Court productions was so low as to indicate what seemed to be actual contempt for the theatre. Though amusing, Shaw's attack was severe, and the loud applause it received showed that it was thought to be well deserved.

Among those who were present at the dinner was Archibald Henderson, who had come to London the previous month to meet Shaw to discuss the biography he was proposing to write, about which he had been corresponding for three years. Henderson was a teacher of mathematics, afterwards a professor, who first heard of Shaw when he went to a performance by students of a school of acting of *You Never Can Tell* in Chicago in 1903, and 'emerged from the theatre a changed man'. He wrote to Shaw the year after to propose that he should become his biographer. Shaw seems to have taken to the shy but persistent Henderson at once and laid himself out to give him all the help he could. Thus Shaw gained the most devoted biographer a man of genius ever had, not a Boswell, however, so much as a painstaking recorder of facts.

Shaw was the financier of the Savoy enterprise, though he called it folly, and refused to be a partner, but he had no new play for it. The venture did not start too well, for *The Devil's Disciple*, produced by Barker on 14 October, was not completely successful, Barker being brow-beaten by Shaw; and when his own play *Waste* was censored, intended for the following month, Barker suddenly and characteristically lost all heart. Nothing was gained when Forbes-Robertson brought to the theatre *Caesar and Cleopatra*, with which he had been touring, for a five weeks' season in November, which in Barker's gloomy and wholly justified view definitely lowered the standard of the theatre. *Arms and the Man*, which followed with Robert Loraine, Lillah McCarthy and Barker, should have been an ideal production, but Barker did not want to play a part he performed superbly, and Lillah hated playing with Loraine. Yet it was well up to the old Shaw-Barker standard and almost restored the fortunes of the management. If only a suggestion that Shaw should write a Christmas Pantomime had come to anything results might have been different; as it was the season ended on 14 March 1908 with the management in debt to the extent of some thousands of pounds. The magic that existed at the Court Theatre was not recaptured, except for the brief *Arms and the Man* run, and Shaw was left displeased. Barker was by now wholly disheartened by the conditions of the London theatre, and Vedrenne had established himself in the new Queen's Theatre in Shaftesbury Avenue.

(13)

Four years earlier, in 1904, Shaw had arranged with a young Frenchman Augustin Hamon and his wife to undertake the translation of his plays, the first to be given a French version being *Candida*, a production of which took place at the Théâtre du Parc in Brussels on 7 February 1907; not until April 1908 was the play done in Paris at the Théâtre des Arts. The Hamons translated many of the plays, and were enthusiastic admirers of the dramatist, but it cannot be said that the plays in the French form given to them by the Hamons made much appeal, at least at first, to Parisian audiences, perhaps because their wit lacked the cynicism the French so much enjoy. Augustin later wrote an understanding book about Shaw, *The Twentieth Century Molière*, published in Paris in 1912 and in London three years later.

Shaw continued to be busy with the Fabian Society in which

a crisis had arisen, also with a committee for the abolition of the censorship arising out of the banning of Granville Barker's *Waste*. In May 1908 he took part in a demonstration at the Lyceum Theatre on behalf of a National Theatre as a memorial to Shakespeare. Placed ninth on the list of speakers and called upon to address an audience depleted by the lack of eloquence to which it had been treated, he rose and said 'Ladies and gentlemen, if the subject is not exhausted we are', and sat down to the chagrin of those who had remained to hear him. He consented to serve on the committee which was appointed with the Lord Mayor as chairman; but despite Shaw's efforts, for he was an admirable committee man, the inefficiency made evident at the meeting pursued this committee then and indeed for long afterwards. Shaw's activities on behalf of the committee included drafting a letter to millionaires, to be sent personally by him enclosing the official documents. He asked each millionaire for 'a hundred thousand pounds if you can spare it', his accompanying memorandum stating that half a million pounds was required altogether. He based his argument upon the private enterprise at the Court Theatre, the success it had achieved, and the proof that without endowment the work it had done could not be continued. He opened the memorandum by an admirable statement of the case for a National Theatre, which has lost none of its force today:

I have been pointing out to the country for the last twenty years that our population is now an urban and not an agricultural population; that as the Church censuses show, urban population go to theatres instead of to places of worship; that the newspaper reports of civil and criminal trials, especially those dealing with divorce, murder, and suicide, prove that the morality of the town is becoming more and more a sensational and romantic morality inculcated in the commercial theatres;

and that our profusely endowed free libraries, however well stocked with high class literature, act mainly as circulating libraries of romantic and essentially theatrical fiction. To continue in the face of these facts a boundless endowment of libraries and charities whilst leaving the theatre to prostitute itself further and further on the plea that 'they who live to please must please to live' is really to abandon the most potent factor in the formation of our national conscience and character to the survivors in a competition in which the most scrupulous go to the wall. No European nation neglects this grave fact as England does.

Nothing came of it, however.

He was completing a new play in 1908 which Frederick Harrison, manager of the Haymarket Theatre, arranged with him to put on for a series of matinees jointly with Vedrenne and Barker, starting on 12 May. The play was *Getting Married*. Shaw took the most meticulous care over every detail of the production, including designing the posters, and paying close attention to publicity. He tried to make Barker play the leading part without success. He called the play 'an instructive conversation in one piece', and attacked the critics in advance. A brilliant piece of writing, admirably acted, it delighted all admirers of Shavian drama, otherwise it aroused violent opposition, which Shaw did not mind. The subject-matter was of constant interest to him, marriage being one of his favourite themes. The preface is a long attack upon the conditions of marriage, not an attack upon marriage itself; for Shaw was above everything a prudent man and declared that marriage is compulsory upon all normal people. But he was full of contempt for what the ordinary respectable British champion of marriage means by it, 'monogamy, chastity, temperance, respectability, morality, Christianity, anti-socialism,

D   39

and a dozen other things', even 'ownership of the person of another human being'.

Thus he castigated the conventional ideas of marriage – 'two persons who accept slavery to one another' – and what he says is so true that it is impossible to avoid the force of his onslaught. 'There is no shirking it,' he declares: 'if marriage cannot be made to produce something better than we are, marriage will have to go, or else the nation will have to go.' And though we may answer that marriage is what men and women make it, yet we have to admit that marriage exists for making men and women what they would not be without it. The conclusion Shaw comes to is that 'the solution of the problem of marriage is to be found in making the sexual relations between men and women decent and honourable by making women economically independent of men, and ... men economically independent of women'. Deeply interesting as this is to everyone, a very hot July and the fact that the play needed listening to kept the audiences small, and Shaw lost quite a lot of money.

Robert Loraine who played St John Hotchkiss wrote a protest to a friend at the time of its performance about misconceptions of Shaw's character, saying:

'Brilliance' is universally conceded to him; but buffoonery, clownery, moral laxity and, above all, *insincerity*, are charged against him ... I wonder when the world will discover that, so far from being insincere, he is a fanatically serious writer; that this cynicism is the view of a realist, his buffoonery the exuberance of high spirits; and that instead of moral laxity, he practises a code of such high honour few can attempt to approach it.[1]

[1]*Robert Loraine* by Winifred Loraine (Collins, 1938), p. 92.

Charlotte took the disgusted Shaw for a trip to the Continent, first visiting Sweden, where in Stockholm at a rehearsal of *Miss Julie* they met August Strindberg, who was then fifty-nine, seven years older than Shaw. Writing to William Archer on 17 July he said 'I achieved the impossible – a meeting with Strindberg – today. He said "Archer is not in sympathy with me". I said Archer is not in sympathy with Ibsen either; but he can't help translating him all the same, being accessible to poetry, though otherwise totally impenetrable.' On a postcard portrait of Strindberg he wrote to Granville Barker: 'This great man reached the summit of his ambition when he met the immortal G.B.S. at the Theatre Interne at Stockholm on 16 July 1908 at one o'clock in the afternoon. At 1.25 he said in German "At two o'clock I'm going to be sick". On this strong hint the party broke up.'[1] Shaw really thought Strindberg a great man. Three weeks later in Munich they saw a Reinhardt production of *Candida* which Shaw described as a 'devastating experience, and confirms my belief that Germany has everything to learn from Vedrenne and Barker'. The performance was got through in ninety minutes, with one brief interval!

A small satirical piece entitled *Press Cuttings* was written for the women's suffrage movement, but was banned by the censor. Also a short play for Frederick Whelan's After Noon Theatre at His Majesty's Theatre, *The Shewing-up of Blanco Posnet*, was banned. The outcome was that opposition to the censor among playwrights was re-aroused, and the Prime Minister, H. H. Asquith, who had succeeded Campbell-Bannerman in April the year before, appointed on 19 July 1909 a Select Committee of both Houses of Parliament to enquire into the working of the censorship. This was despite the fact that Asquith had been satirized in Shaw's women's suffrage play.

[1] *Letters of Bernard Shaw to Granville Barker* (Phoenix House, 1956), p. 130.

Shaw threw himself with characteristic energy and thoroughness into the censorship matter, and tells the story of his part in it in the long preface to *Blanco Posnet*. His statement, rejected by the Committee, is printed in the preface, and displays Shaw's polemical gifts at their best. Shaw's objection was that the censorship prevented immoral and heretical plays from being performed – he being a specialist in such plays – although such shocks to the prejudices and superstitions of public opinion 'are essential to the welfare of the nation'. By 'immoral' Shaw did not mean improper, but what was contrary to conventional manners. Indeed, he declared that the existing censorship 'unintentionally gives the special protection of its official licence to the most extreme impropriety that the lowest section of London playgoers will tolerate'. Shaw considered censorship to be a form of spiritual tyranny, which could only result in lowering the value of the theatre as a social influence, which Shaw contended it had done. He declared himself against censorship in any form, however enlightened, as he was bound to do on his own principles, and advocated that all plays should be freely performed, subject only to action being taken against those responsible for them should they offend the laws against disorderly housekeeping, blasphemy, indecency, and so forth. Despite his fierce language, it should be noted that Shaw was never much bothered by the censorship in his own work. Apart from *Mrs Warren's Profession*, *Blanco Posnet*, and the little suffrage play, his work had never been interfered with. He opposed censorship on principle. The enquiry received much publicity, the theatre managers in the main being in favour of retaining the censorship, the dramatists, almost to a man, being opposed to it. Following the committee's report, issued in November, an advisory committee was appointed to assist the Lord Chamberlain in the exercise of his censorship duties, and the censorship (though not the committee) continues to this day. In the course of time, however, the operation of censorship has been affected by changes in public taste and official authority is now lightly though unevenly felt.

(15)

Chesterton's book *George Bernard Shaw* appeared in 1909 and on the day of publication Shaw reviewed the book, saying it was 'the best book of literary art I have yet produced'. But privately he told its author that it contained a lot of nonsense about him. By this time the Vedrenne-Barker management which had been touring three of Shaw's plays was finally wound up, Shaw liquidating its debts with much expression of dissatisfaction though great good service had been done to him. There was, however, a move in London towards repertory, which Shaw, with Granville Barker, considered of vital important. Frederick Harrison's entry into the 'higher drama' had led him to consider, with finance from Lord Howard de Walden, a repertory season at the Haymarket. Herbert Beerbohm Tree was already taking part with his After Noon Theatre at His Majesty's, and J. M. Barrie succeeded in persuading Charles Frohman to come into the new movement with repertory at the Duke of York's. The Haymarket venture was originally intended for Granville Barker, but he had personal reasons for fighting shy of it and, by the time it was announced, he, with Barrie and Shaw, were committed to Frohman's enterprise. Barker was to produce and had a new play ready; Barrie promised one; so did Shaw. Barrie's domestic affairs prevented him doing what he intended, though he continued to give close attention to the Frohman Repertory. Shaw did his utmost to get G. K. Chesterton to contribute a play, and went so far as to prepare a scenario on the subject of St Augustine's return to England, but while Chesterton was attracted by the idea he did nothing with it. Shaw completed *Misalliance*.

The play was written after hearing Barker read his new play *The Madras House*, Shaw being moved then as so often in his writing by some comic impulse. Finished in November 1909, and produced the next 23 February at the Duke of York's, *Misalliance* caused more annoyance, perhaps, than any other Shaw play. Much had been expected of him; this outwardly frivolous piece outraged his friends, as well as many in the audience, and the criticis were prostrate with rage. Needless to say, it was a profound shock to the manager, and made him doubt his own sanity as well as that of those associated with him in the repertory. Frohman had every reason to look with favour upon Shaw because of the fortune made in the United States by *Man and Superman*, but this new play was a bomb-shell that destroyed all thought of a Frohman-Shaw combination that was being talked of. The play was given only six performances and quickly dropped out of the repertory.

On 11 May King Edward VII died and the blow to the London theatre finished the short life of the repertory on 17 June. Shaw was not at all pleased with the manager's behaviour, and contented himself by working on a little propaganda piece for the Shakespeare Memorial Theatre called *The Dark Lady of the Sonnets*, which was completed that month and performed at a matinee at the Haymarket on 24 November, in aid of the funds.

(16)

There was half an idea of continuing repertory at the Coronet Theatre at Notting Hill the next year, 1911, with Shaw urging Barker to revive *Misalliance*, but it came to nothing. At the beginning of the year Charlotte had taken her husband away from the theatre on a cruise to Jamaica. On their return he brought out a sixpenny edition of *Man and Superman*, with a special preface in which he declared that the play was ' a careful attempt to write a new Book of Genesis for the Bible of the Evolutionists; and . . . Bibles must be cheap'. A visit was paid to him by Lillah McCarthy, desperate to keep her husband in the London theatre (for he was saying he would go off to Germany, where the theatre was taken seriously), asking for help in taking a lease of the Little Theatre in the Adelphi, which had become available. She had already got £1,000 from Lord Howard de Walden, and Shaw added another £500 and the promise of a play.

The play was *Fanny's First Play*, a deliberate bid for public approval, which was not to be jeopardized by the name of its author. Shaw made the condition when he handed it to Lillah McCarthy that his authorship was not to be divulged, and that the play should be announced by an unknown playwright, spreading the suggestion himself that the author was probably Barrie. We should note that for all his love of publicity for his work, Shaw never went in for stunts, except on this one occasion. The play was, indeed, a great success when produced on 19 April 1911, and filled the theatre until the tenancy was ended, being continued the following year at the Kingsway Theatre. Of course, the secret soon came out, though for the discerning it never was a secret, and Shaw was much bothered by the play being allowed to work out its popularity in a run that seemed as though it would never end. This was entirely against his principles, but he allowed it to take place so as to help his friends. And he professed to consider the play to be of little consequence, 'a pot boiler', he said.

In October he was complaining to the Fabian Society about being asked to do so much lecturing. 'Of course,' he wrote to the secretary, 'the result of my speaking in any place now is that they pull in money.' He was perhaps the most attractive public speaker of the time. There took place in November the famous debate on religion at Cambridge with G. K. Chesterton, in which Shaw, as brilliant a talker as his opponent, proved the more effective debater. And in January the next year, 1912, after Hilaire Belloc's *The Servile State* had appeared, he debated with him, declaring that it was the task of every human being to serve, arguing against what Belloc called servitude and private property – 'there being no greater hell of private property in the world' than America – and uttering words that deserve to be recalled whenever Shaw is mentioned, that he 'hoped it might be said of him at the end of his career, "Well done, thou good and faithful servant".'

During 1911 he had been invited to join the council of the Royal Academy of Dramatic Art, which pleased him, and in which school for actors he took deep practical interest until the end. At the close of the year, having resigned from the executive committee of the Fabian Society, though remaining a Fabian, he started on a new play, *Androcles and the Lion*, a fable play, which was more or less finished the following February.

(17)

In the meantime, however, Shaw completed another play, finished in the early summer of 1912, but contemplated for many years past, for which he had Mrs Patrick Campbell in his eye. When the play was ready he paid a visit to read it to her, and, as he wrote to Barker a few days later, 'I fell head over ears in love with her – violently and exquisitely in love – before I knew that I was thinking about anything but business. . . . And I am on the verge of 56. There has never been anything so ridiculous, or so delightful, in the history of the world.' Shaw hoped that the play might be done at the Queen's Theatre by arrangement with Alfred Butt, and under the McCarthy-Barker management, where he thought at that time *Androcles* might also be produced, making, as he said, a 'double event' but it was not to be. The play did not appear until April 1914. But the love affair developed. The story of what took place between this man approaching sixty and the actress approaching fifty was told later, from her point of view, by the lady, and is contained in full in the correspondence Shaw allowed to be published forty years later (*Bernard Shaw and Mrs Patrick Campbell: Their Correspondence*. Gollancz 1952). It was a real love affair, as the volume of letters makes clear. Among his letters are some of the most exquisite and moving love letters ever written.

This was a serious event in Shaw's life. It greatly disturbed his wife, from whom Shaw kept nothing, at the same time doing everything to prevent her from being too much hurt. Charlotte in fact never got used to the adoring women he always attracted, and this affair with its theatrical atmosphere entirely absorbed him. I have no intention of dwelling upon it as were I a biographer I should have to do; but a matter is raised that has bearing upon Shaw as a dramatist, so that it must at least be noticed. I refer to the fact, which the correspondence seems to make clear, that Shaw was then for all practical purposes sexually impotent. There can be little doubt about the fact. It exasperated the lady and caused her to run away from him. The questions I have in mind are What caused this? and What is its relation to his playwriting? From the point of view from which I am writing the questions cannot be ignored. No doubt a psychological explanation is possible in answer to the first question. There can be no doubt that Shaw as a young man was wholly normal, for there is at least the story of his seduction at the age of twenty-nine by a married woman, older than himself, which became the foundation of his play *The Philanderer*, and there are his various intimate friendships with actresses and others in his early years. The young Shaw as well as the older, even the aged, Shaw was not only attractive to women, he liked them; but he was always highly fastidious. And as a fastidious young man he did not allow the ladies to go too far, nor usually, though not always, himself either. In his marriage, when he was approaching forty-two, a basis of sexual abstention was established to which Shaw remained faithful. This seems to have brought about an induced impotence in him, which may have been a defect from a natural point of view, but was certainly no defect in him as an artist, for it has a conscious origin. As a man in whom the emotional elements were controlled, Shaw provides an example of the lover presented in Plato's *Symposium*, who is not subject to carnal love. This is not something to deride, but to honour. To achieve that state does not lessen a man, either as man or artist, for it is a victory of the spirit, that is, of consciousness. Not everyone will agree with this, for not everyone is convinced of the supremacy of the spirit. By deliberately shutting himself out of the order of physical procreation and becoming incapable of reproducing himself physically, Shaw reproduced himself in his plays, which absorbed his creative energy. This is in harmony with his conception of himself as an instrument of Creative Evolution, the Eternal Mind. It is my contention that he made himself physiologically incapable in one direction for the sake of increased capacity in another. It made his personal position a comic one, that of a passionate man who could not procreate. The fact that, as I suggest, it was choice, not affliction, transforms the merely comic into lightness and joy. That is true not only of Shaw's life but of his work: in the Nietzschean sense the comedian dances.

That he put into his dramatic work an incredible amount of mental labour, with its severe demands upon bodily energy, there can be no doubt. He wrote rapidly – he wrote as he breathed, as he said himself – but with an intensity, concentration, and imaginative power of a most unusual kind. His playwriting was his life; his other activities extensive as they were became altogether subsidiary to it. I think for instance that the sick headaches which afflicted him from middle age, and the pernicious anaemia from which he was found to be suffering at the age of eighty-two, have some relevance to the subject.

(18)

The play over which the affair arose was *Pygmalion*, which he had started in March 1912 and completed in June, but not produced until April 1914, when Sir Herbert Beerbohm Tree put it on at his theatre, with Mrs Pat as Eliza Doolittle. It became the talk of London. Shaw's distraction and the ups and downs with the actor-manager over the production of the play were taking up much of his time, but he did finish the play for the Barkers, *Androcles and the Lion*, in which he wanted Lillah to play the principal part.

In March 1913 he smashed up his car near Dunstable when Charlotte was taking him away from feminine danger for a holiday to Ireland. Fortunately, apart from the shock, neither suffered a scratch. In Ireland they stayed with the Plunketts and Shaw wrote to Barker:

> Charlotte is in high spirits – almost in health. The domestic fiend of the last few months has become a green-eyed angel of the fireside. She actually gibes at her rival.

He wanted Barker to play Androcles. He was not sure of the play. 'It may prove simply an irritant', he said, 'I believe I was slightly mad last year', referring, as does the letter, to Mrs Pat. Lillah wanted to open the forthcoming season at the St James' Theatre with *Macbeth*, and much work was done upon the production, not altogether wasted work, so far as Barker was concerned, for it provided the basis for his subsequent *Prefaces to Shakespeare*, but Lillah was deeply disappointed. The fact was that the money available would not run to it. *Androcles* was put on instead on

1 September. There was much public irritation against this play fostered by the press, as Shaw anticipated, for it was regarded as an attack upon Christianity and became hotly denounced; it had even more defenders, however, who looked upon it as a serious religious tract, as indeed it was. Its ostensible aim, to please children, was overlooked, but the play did please their parents, getting reasonably good houses, which did not pay, however, and Lord Howard de Walden, who was financing the season, lost the money he had made over *Fanny*.

(19)

Shaw's interest in politics was by no means diminished. He had made a proposal in 1912 for a 'four power pact', a combination of England, France, Germany and America 'to impose peace on Europe'. The same year he published a 'Home Rule' sixpenny edition of *John Bull's Other Island*. Early in 1913 he was actively engaged in the founding of the new weekly to be called *The Statesman*, for which he with the Webbs and others found the money. Shaw had declared that he would confine his newspaper writings to this paper in future, but his contributions were to appear anonymously: an arrangement that did not last long when the paper appeared as *The New Statesman* in May, for the editor wanted the advantage of Shaw's name. He engaged in many other activities. On New Year's Day 1914 he had a featured article in the paper on *The Peace of Europe and How to Attain It*. The Shaws went for a holiday on the Continent in the summer.

When the world war broke out in August, Shaw proved himself to be no pacifist, but felt 'oppressed by my own ignorance', so he collected all the documents he could lay his hands on, and went to Torquay; at the end of two months he produced *Common Sense About the War*, issued as a supplement to *The New Statesman* on 14 November. This candid, unsentimental statement of the position, free from hatred of the enemy, aroused great controversy, and gave its author such a bad name as a pro-German and pacifist, that, for immense numbers of people, incensed by the war atmosphere to violent opposition to it, his name even as a dramatist was never cleared. The supplement was attacked by H. G. Wells with particular violence 'as distorting, discrediting, confusing'. His fellow playwright Henry Arthur Jones said, 'I never felt more angry with any man . . . I do not think I can meet him in future'. These remarks reflected common opinion. Yet the unabashed Shaw went on writing about the war and the ideas upon which it was ostensibly being waged, in the long preface to *Androcles and the Lion*, written in 1915, when his theme was, 'Why not give Christianity a trial?'

During the war the Shaws stayed frequently with a relative of Beatrice Webb in the neighbourhood of Presteigne in Radnorshire; he spent many hours in the peace of the country, tramping the hills. One who knew him wrote afterwards in *The Times*:

> . . . Once, when he was looking out at the hills which encircle the town, he suddenly remarked, with arms outstretched, 'No man ought to be in the government of this land who does not spend three months every year in the country – and in such country as this.' On another occasion he was paying the local tailor for some repairs which had been done for him. Instead of paying the amount asked for, he put down double the sum. The tailor pointed out what he thought was a mistake, and received the smiling reply, 'I earn my money more easily than you, Mr P——'

He turned to writing little plays, first *O'Flaherty, VC*, in late 1915, announced by the Abbey Theatre, but they shied off it, though Robert Loraine faced the British Expeditionary Force in France with it in February 1917. Shaw saw one of the performances himself, as he had been sent to the front by the Government to write a series of articles on the war for American consumption. There followed *The Inca of Perusalem*, and the same year, 1916, *Augustus Does His Bit*; finally *Annajanska*, to cheer up Lillah McCarthy in 1917. He then completed a long and as he considered his most important play to date, *Heartbreak House*, inspired by the lack of direction in government that led up to the war, rather than by the war itself, for he had started upon it some years earlier. He would not let it be produced, however, until the war was well over, and then first in New York.

(20)

When the war ended Shaw was pre-occupied with political questions, and though 'nobody was paying the slightest attention to my criticisms', as he said, he wrote for the Peace Conference a long pamphlet entitled *Peace Conference Hints*, which wound up with the words 'The old lion is triumphant on the crest of the mountain. But the crest of the mountain is also the brink of the abyss.' Of course, he aroused opposition, but less acute annoyance than before.

He was working on a long play, intended to be his masterpiece, a work so long that no theatre could afford to produce it, he said. This was *Back to Methuselah*: published in 1921, a cycle of five plays rather than a single play, of unequal length, a work of legend, realism, criticism, myth and prophecy, of which, said G. K. Chesterton, 'the Book of Genesis is a short summary'. He was sixty-five. None but a man who felt himself a master of his craft would have dared to attempt it. The theme was the extension of human life. Starting with Adam and Eve, the cycle finished 'as far as thought can reach'. This was the response of Shaw to the first world war: how can man overcome his own folly? The answer was that, given time, in the creativeness of his spirit he will make life worth while. Arnold Bennett records in his diary that he went to sleep during the first London performance at the Court Theatre in 1924 of the second play; he also records that it started at 8.37 and ended at about 10.15, so he did not consider that despite his quiet slumber he had had his money's worth. Had Shaw's work ended at this point his dramatic career would have been well rounded off, for the play was an admitted masterpiece. But having completed his great cycle, he did a good turn to his German translator Siegfried Trebitsch, by writing an English version of the latter's play *Frau Gittas Sühne*, under the title *Jitta's Atonement* (1922).

Then in 1923, in the full tide of creativity, came *St Joan*, which proved to be after *Fanny's First Play* the play that most pleased the great public, a play of which he declared that it wrote itself. 'Make your offerings at her [Joan's] altar, not at mine', he said. It contains all the characteristics of Shaw as a dramatist, his thoroughness, seriousness, sensitivity, fantastic sense of humour, ability to present characters, detachment, and theatrical skill. He was finally restored to public favour. The play was first performed in New York, three months before it was done in London. This practice of allowing his plays to be produced first abroad had been followed by Shaw for some time; it was intended to allow the foreign public to see them before they had been damned by the London critics.

St Joan appeared at the New Theatre, replacing *The Lie* by Henry Arthur Jones, taken off at the height of its success, which did nothing to lessen the acerbity between the two playwrights, though Shaw had no responsibility for what happened. On 17 April two years later it was performed in Paris by the Pitoëffs and though very successful aroused much controversy – 'I am too old to educate Paris', exclaimed Shaw.

(21)

There were no more plays for five years. William Archer had died in 1924. Shaw often visited Stratford-on-Avon, and in 1925 was the principal speaker at the Shakespeare birthday luncheon, when he described the Memorial Theatre as admirably adapted for every conceivable purpose other than that of a theatre. 'You must have a new theatre', he declared. Twelve months later the old theatre was burnt down.

He reached his seventieth birthday next year when he declared that he treated his literary eminence with a snap of the fingers compared with his work in helping to found the Labour Party. To a complimentary letter from Germany he made a reply which included the words:

> The sole notice taken on my seventieth birthday by the British Government was its deliberate official prohibition of the broadcasting of any words spoken by me on that occasion.

He was, however, awarded the Nobel prize for literature, first refused, afterwards accepted, when he made the money over to a fund to form the Anglo-Swedish Literary Foundation, for promoting the knowledge of Swedish literature in Great Britain. The first act by the foundation was to publish a translation of a series of Strindberg's plays; later, translations of other Swedish authors were assisted, and the Swedish sections of various English university libraries were supported.

He gave one of his last public lectures at Welwyn Garden City on the subject of drama. His aim was to encourage the amateurs in a town in whose future he was much interested, for he had once announced himself as a member of the Welwyn Garden City Theatre Society. Shaw was always well disposed to amateurs, provided they played in the interests of drama itself, not of some other cause. This perhaps was due to the fact that amateurs showed early appreciation of his plays, and when they were serious he looked upon them with favour.

For some years he had been engaged upon an immense socio-logical work: *The Intelligent Woman's Guide to Socialism and Individualism*, the completion of which in 1928 relieved him greatly and enormously pleased Charlotte. That year, on 28 January, Shaw was one of the pall-bearers at Thomas Hardy's funeral in Westminster Abbey. That year, too, the Shaws left Adelphi Terrace, and moved to Whitehall Court, and the same year Barry Jackson suggested organizing a Festival of Drama at Malvern for which Shaw promised a new play. This was *The Apple Cart*, which he finished after eight weeks' work. The play was a criticism of democracy and the lack of responsibility in governments, an extravaganza, exciting in its audacities and highly popular.

The next year, 1929, he started preparing the limited collected edition of his works, which afterwards appeared as a standard edition. The Malvern Festival opened this year, Shaw himself, in person, being the greatest attraction. He also made his first broad-cast speech, which was a great success. There was no new play until 1931, when he completed *Too True to be Good*. He had established a friendship with T. E. Lawrence a few years earlier, Mrs Shaw especially becoming very fond of the young man who had nothing to do with the theatre. The play was a dream of disillusionment, and no doubt owed something to Lawrence, who was perhaps more attracted to Shaw than Shaw to him. But it owed rather more to Dean Inge, who was with its author when both men and their wives were on a cruise to Greece, and Shaw had the play in his mind. The theme is that the game of accumulation, the money game, is not worth playing because riches divorced from everything that makes life worth living are worthless. There are strong religious elements in the play, which was not produced until the following year.

E

In July, Shaw, without Charlotte, went to Soviet Russia in company with Lord and Lady Astor, their son, David, and the Marquis of Lothian, where he had a long interview with Stalin. Most of the talking was done by others, Shaw listened. He afterwards visited Lenin's widow. A public reception was given him in Moscow on his seventy-fifth birthday, the hall being crowded with people: 'I was certainly treated as if I were Karl Marx in person', he said: the others being treated as nobodies. He turned up wearing a Norfolk jacket and a shirt without a tie, trying his best 'to look Bolshevik', without success. He said in a speech on that occasion 'England should be ashamed that it was not she who led the way to Communism'. He met Stanislavsky, but the Moscow Art Theatre was in recess: Shaw said afterwards that he could not remember a word that was said between them. On his return he broadcast to America on 11 October 1931 a long talk in praise of Soviet Russia, 'where the sun shines as on a country with which God is well pleased'. At a meeting at the Kingsway Hall the following November he said:

> Up to the present we have had Fabianism, social democracy, collectivism, socialism and so on. All that has gone. There is nothing now but communism.

Shaw's deep interest in communism was due to its being a new approach to social organization, a new way of living, and specifically to his conviction that it provided the opportunity for the equality of incomes, which he considered essential for a rational and healthy human society. He knew quite well that such equality did not exist in Russia, but the possibility of it – that is to say, the consciously organized economic order – was there, the possibility, that is, of giving more to one's country than one takes from it, whereas in capitalist society the possibility – that is to say, the way – was non-existent, except for the few who sacrificed themselves.

A few months later, at the end of the year, Shaw and Charlotte went for a tour of South Africa. There in the following February they had a motor-car accident, both being injured. While they were recovering he started to write a play, 'in the ordinary course of my business as a playwright', but found himself writing instead a short story, *The Adventures of the Black Girl in Her Search for God*. It is a religious allegory, concerned with the Bible, the teaching of Jesus and Islam and winds up with the reflection, 'Mere agnosticism leads nowhere.' The story was provocative, and Shaw was viciously attacked, but it became a best-seller.

It is worth noting here that as soon as it was able to do so the first Labour Government had offered Shaw the Order of Merit. He refused, for he wanted nothing from politicians whose incapacity for government he was constantly attacking. On several other occasions he was offered the same honour, but always replied in the same terms:

I need no publicity: I have already more than my fair share of it. I shall have my period of staleness and out-of-dateness for years after my death (it is beginning already) but an Order of Merit will not save me from this. If I am offered the O.M. my answer will be: Deeply grateful as I am for the award of the highest distinction within the gift of the Commonwealth, yet the nature of my calling is such that the O.M. in it cannot be determined within the span of a single human life. Either I shall be remembered as a playwright as long as Aristophanes and rank with Shakespeare and Molière, or I shall be a forgotten clown before the end of the century. I dare not anticipate the verdict of history. I must remain simply (signed) Bernard Shaw.

At the end of 1932 the Shaws went for a voyage round the world, and Shaw wrote the short piece, *Village Wooing*, which is set in an imaginary version of the Ayot St Lawrence village shop. A first visit was paid to the United States of America in the course of the trip during April when he gave a lecture to the American Academy of Political Science, afterwards published as *The Political Madhouse in America and Nearer Home*. This was a prelude to writing *On the Rocks*, 'a political economy' performed the same year, 1933, to which when it was published the year after he contributed his last important preface, on the theme of tolerance, which included a few pages of a play he might have written dramatizing part of the Gospel story. It was a severe play, received with respect.

The unrelenting Charlotte took her husband off in 1934 to New Zealand; in the course of the voyage there and back, he completed *The Simpleton of the Unexpected Isles*, an account of the Last Judgment, and substantially finished *The Millionairess*, in which he discussed what should be done with bosses. He had already written one of his little farcical pieces, *The Six of Calais*. The two plays were provoked by his travels, and by the earlier visit to Russia, and had related themes, in which his sense of the serious predicament of mankind was strongly expressed.

(23)

When they returned he was visited by the Hungarian film producer, Gabriel Pascal, who had recently come to London without a penny, but with the idea of getting Shaw's plays for the screen. Pascal was a man of immense confidence, who knew exactly what he wanted to do, and impressed Shaw with his sincerity; almost as good a talker as Shaw, and having the sense to show his empty pockets, he got his contract for *Pygmalion*, not at once but some time later, and was a made man. Shaw's attitude to films in general was influenced by the fact that his own experience was an unfortunate one, the earlier British filming of his plays though following the text did no sort of justice to them, and a scenario he had prepared for a German version of the same play, *Pygmalion*, was altered out of all recognition, none of the solemn undertakings given him being carried out, and he was furious with the result. He considered that dramatically there was no difference between stage and screen, except that the resources of the screen were enormously larger. But it had not occurred to the film producing companies, he declared, 'that drama is a skilled trade. . . . When a play by Shakespeare is to be adapted to the screen they send for the office boy. The office boy, not being Shakespeare, takes great pains to spoil Shakespeare's work in the conviction that he is improving it.' Pascal convinced him that he understood Shaw's point of view, as indeed he did, and the film, directed by Anthony Asquith, was shown in 1938, made a marked impression and gained popular approval, as it deserved. By that time Pascal and Shaw had become great friends.

Shortly after he had met Pascal in 1935 the Shaws went off again, this time to the Pacific, and *Geneva*, inspired by the League of Nations, was started, though not finished until 1938. These sea voyages in their effect upon Shaw's writing are not to be ignored. At sea, one's writing is at sea, and so it was with these four plays. Shaw found himself free from the discipline of playwriting and never recovered it. His work retained its brilliance but lost its form.

(24)

In the spring of 1937 when it was proposed to do *Cymbeline* at Stratford-on-Avon he had offered to write a new last act for the play; an offer gratefully accepted. But Shaw's blank verse did not please, for he made his young Guiderius say:

This kingly business has no charm for me . . .
I am to be forsooth, another Cloten,
Plagued by the chatter of his train of flatterers,
Compelled to worship priest invented gods,
Nor free to wed the woman of my choice,
Being stopped at every turn by some old fool
Crying 'You must not', or, still worse, 'You must' . . .
I abdicate, and pass the throne to Polydore.

The Georgian Stratfordians found an allusion to the abdication of Edward VIII in these lines, and Shaw's version was not used. It was performed later in London and included by him in his collected works, with a somewhat shame-faced preface. A skilful piece of work, it is not Shakespearean blank verse and does not improve the ending of the play, the difficulties of which are exaggerated.

After the last play he was in his eighties but did not consider himself to have retired. He had always gone to Malvern for the Drama Festival, but after 1937 decided to go no more; for, indeed, he was bothered by hero-worshippers, and, what was more serious, he had developed pernicious anaemia, which was not discovered until 4 June 1938. He was then very ill and had to rest for six weeks, but was restored by the usual injections of liver extract.

The amazing vitality of the man was shown when the play written for the Malvern Festival in the fateful year, 1939, was performed, *In Good King Charles's Golden Days*. This was a fine piece of historical satire, not fully dramatic, but theatrically effective; it proved to be his final completed play, and was well received. *The Times*, writing upon the published version on 12 August, said that 'most of our best authors of comedy today sit at Mr Shaw's feet', and went on to say:

What is the explanation? It is surely that Mr Shaw is a model dramatist in spite of his pre-occupation with so-called ideas, not because of them, and that the secret of his dramatist's impulse is in his irrepressible comic sense.

This was first class criticism; for the free play of ideas that always possessed him awakened freedom of thought in others.

Henry Salt had died on 19 April, but the great personal disaster of this year was that Charlotte became a permanent invalid, demanding much attention from her husband, which he did not neglect; the public disaster was the second world war. Few of the infirmities of old age greatly afflicted Shaw, neither sleeplessness, failing sight, nor hardening of the arteries, only increasing deafness troubled him. The regular treatment he received for the pernicious anaemia kept him entirely free from any effects of that complaint. He still used his bicycle, though of course he had long given up motor-cycling (started in 1919), also driving a car. In the evenings he would play and sing songs from the operas to Charlotte up-stairs in bed. He wrote to the Keebles on 27 February 1940 inviting them to luncheon, adding:

> The united ages of B.W., C.F.S., and G.B.S. amount to 247 years; but Beatrice is still as alive as ever.

(25)

He was still walking about the streets of London, rather frail-looking but as active as ever. In June he wrote a broadcast talk, which the BBC refused, in which he said, 'If I were a gambler, I should back the neutrals for the real win, with Russia and the United States neck and neck', which indicates how far he was from being a political fool. He said he would perhaps not write any more plays, but that year Gabriel Pascal filmed *Major Barbara*, in which Shaw took a lively interest and for which he wrote a number of additional scenes. The result was much praised, but was not the equal of the first Pascal film in casting or direction. Some lines written for it by Shaw, sung as a quartet, included the following:

> In this our hour of darkness
> We warsmiths of the cannons,
> Where do we stand today?
> We forge our own destruction:
> We shall be slain who slay.
> Then from the gods who fail us
> Ourselves must win the way. . . .
> To thee the god within us
> We trust the world to win us
> Creation, not destruction,
> Henceforth shall make us great.

Afterwards he thought he would try his hand at another play, 'just to see whether I could'.

Some interesting particulars about himself are contained in an article he was asked to write for the RAF in July 1942 in which he advised pilots not to 'eat a between-rib beefsteak and drink a bottle of Guinness on a serious job'. He further said:

> . . . it may surprise you to know that it is more than sixty years since I last ate flesh, fish or fowl. I have given up eating eggs, though I eat butter and drink buttermilk sometimes when I can get them. I am a six footer, and am told that my weight should be at least twelve stone ten. As a matter of unromantic fact it is nine stone, and stood at ten stone eight during the most active part of my life. Yet I find myself working as hard as ever, a bit deafish and dotty, as becomes my second childhood, but still in fairly good form as an author, playwright, biologist,

philosopher and political pilot, not to mention journalism as a sideline.

You will say, perhaps, that if ever a man needed a plentiful and stimulating diet I am that man. But on such gluttony I should have gone stale or died years ago. Dickens, who ate and drank generously, died before he was sixty. So did Shakespeare. I have lived longer than they did by about thirty years, and written my most famous books and plays during those thirty years.

The Shaws were mostly at Ayot St Lawrence, 'skulking down here', he wrote. In a short letter to Lillah (Lady Keeble) he referred to his wife:

Charlotte, after four years of torment diagnosed as lumbago, has now been thoroughly overhauled and pronounced incurable, the new diagnosis being osteitis deformans (Paget's disease). She is in her 86th year, I am in my 87th. We have no excuse for existing and are literally not fit to be seen, even if this village were reasonably accessible, which it isn't. We are deaf, doddering, obsolete, a wash out. . . .

Yet they came to London occasionally, even when the bombing was severe, and on one of these visits Charlotte died suddenly at Whitehall Court on 12 September 1943. She was eighty-six. Her death was a heavy blow to him, and at the same time a release, for she had demanded much care, which he gave her unremittingly.

Henceforward he was a man alone. He ceased to walk about the London streets, and spent all his time in Hertfordshire, in his remote home. He was engaged in settling Charlotte's affairs, in housekeeping for himself, in negotiations about filming another play, and in making a new and complicated will.

Throughout the war he was busy writing articles and letters on many different subjects, including the book published in 1944 to everyone's amazement, not less than his own, *Everybody's Political What's What?*, a declaration on the political situation by one who, as he said, was in his second childhood. Yet it had all the old brilliance and energy, though rambling and long-winded. In the same year *Back to Methuselah* was made the 500th volume in the Oxford University Press's 'World's Classics', for which Shaw wrote an admirable postscript (which alone makes the book worth having) in which he said that as a writer he regarded himself 'as an instrument in the grip of Creative Evolution'.

(26)

A third film was completed in 1945 by Gabriel Pascal, *Caesar and Cleopatra*, for which Shaw wrote sequences at the producer's request, and in which he took as close an interest as ever. It was an extravagant production, which received enormous publicity, but Pascal's over-confidence and egotism ran away with him, and the film did neither him nor Shaw any credit, and from its failure Pascal did not in fact recover.

When the 26 July 1946 arrived, his 90th birthday was celebrated by the publication of ten volumes of his works in the Penguin Library, 100,000 of each volume being printed, and quickly sold out. A volume of tributes appeared some weeks earlier, edited by his neighbour, S. Winsten, entitled *G.B.S. 90*, and many complimentary articles appeared in the newspapers. The National Council of Labour and all the Labour members of Parliament sent him greetings. On 28 August he was made an honorary freeman of the city of Dublin, and the St Pancras Borough Council made him a freeman of the Borough, but he was not well enough to attend the ceremony, having had a fall, but he recorded the speech he intended to make, which was broadcast. It was on a political theme, an attack upon the party system. A few days later, listening to the news on the radio, he heard of Granville Barker's death in Paris. They had not met for many years. The news made him very sad, for he had always hoped that they would come together again. A pathetic letter expressing his grief appeared in *The Times Literary Supplement* with a photograph he had taken of Barker as a young man.

(27)

He was still writing letters, articles, and prefaces, and a new play entitled *Buoyant Billions*, 'an intentionally unfinished comedy', was done with in 1947 and produced at the revived Malvern Festival two years later. The play reflected the themes of his own plays of the past, including money, poverty and the need for self-direction; it was the work of a man to whom nothing else but the future had become important. 'Forgive it,' he asked in the preface to the printed version, 'I can hardly walk through my garden without a tremble or two; and it seems out of all reason that a man who cannot do a simple thing like that can practise the art of Shakespeare.' He arranged for the young daughter of his neighbour, Winsten, to design the settings for the play. In 1947, too, Sidney Webb died, and Shaw urged in a letter to *The Times* that his ashes and those of Beatrice Webb should be buried in Westminster Abbey, which was done.

Among the collection of printed postcards Shaw had been in the habit of sending to correspondents who wrote to him about various matters (there are specimens of fourteen in the British Museum Library) was one issued in 1948 on the subject of vegetarianism. People were curious to know how he at his great age fared on such a diet. He explained that he had discovered that his diet included an excess of protein, and went on to say:

Until he was seventy he accumulated some poison that exploded every month or six weeks in a headache but blew it off and left him quite well after disabling him for a day . . . he now makes uncooked vegetables, chopped or grated, and their juices with fruit, the staple of his diet. . . . His objection to carnivorous diet is partly aesthetic, partly hygienic, mainly as involving an unnecessary waste of labour of masses of mankind in the nurture and slaughter of cattle, poultry, and fish for human food.

But he had no more interest in life except that of an amused spectator, though he went on writing. Two more little pieces were performed and published. He completed his will at last, and offered his house to the National Trust, which was accepted, though a proffered endowment of the property was declined. Another play, which he called 'a comedietta', *Why She Would Not*, was prepared for the printer in 1950, and it looked as though he would live for ever; but working in his garden in September that year he fell, as he had done before, but this time fractured his thigh, and was taken to the Luton and Dunstable Hospital. His spirit remained high; but though he had wished to become a centenarian, for the joke of the thing, he now wanted only to die, to be no longer a nuisance to anyone. So he was brought home. One of his last visitors was his fellow Dubliner, Sean O'Casey, who has written tenderly of these last days in *Sunset and Evening Star* (Macmillan, 1954). On Thursday, 2 November, on the gate of his house at Ayot St Lawrence a notice was posted which read:

Mr Bernard Shaw passed peacefully away at one minute to five o'clock this morning, 2 November. From the coffers of his genius he enriched the world.

The world mourned his loss, and in New York the lights of Broadway were put out the night following. The entire press was full of praise of his memory, and though *The Times* said only that 'his work has passed into English dramatic literature', other papers said more truthfully that he was 'The greatest figure in English drama after Shakespeare'; yet the not yet dead animosity was shown by the *Daily Telegraph*, which printed a tribute from its dramatic critic, who doubted that Shaw's plays would live, and the editor devoted a leading article to an actress who had never played in any of Shaw's plays. A tribute was issued from 10 Downing Street by the Prime Minister (Mr Attlee).

His remains were cremated at Golder's Green on 6 November. The ceremony was private; there was music, chosen by Shaw himself, consisting of the hymn at the beginning of the overture to *Hänsel and Gretel*, 'Libera me' from Verdi's *Requiem*, and extracts from Elgar's *The Music Makers* and the *Nimrod* variation. As no request had been made for the ashes by any responsible national body they were scattered, as Shaw wished, with those of Charlotte, in the garden of their home at Ayot St Lawrence by the doctor who had attended him.

(28)

'Shaw's Corner' was opened to the public by the National Trust in March the following year, Dame Edith Evans performing the ceremony. For some weeks the crowds that came to the house seriously disturbed the village. A special bus service was run from Welwyn Garden City, but after some months public curiosity was satisfied, the crowds vanished, and the number of visitors became so small that the receipts from their admission fees, approximately £400 in 1955, barely paid for the upkeep of the property. Indeed, except for lovers of Shaw, the house had no interest, and except for his study and the garden hut in which he worked, the contents were removed and the house let to a tenant who agreed to keep these rooms available for the public two days a week. Latterly, Ayot has tended to become a place of pilgrimage, and sometimes, at least at the week-ends, small crowds invade its peace, curious about Shaw and his home.

When the will was published, it was disclosed that Shaw had left no less than £367,233, the largest fortune by any dramatist in history; but as income was still accruing, the final valuation was not made until ten years later when the amount was settled at £716,000, of which the copyrights accounted for £433,000. In a will of fourteen pages he appointed the Public Trustee as his executor; after various bequests the rest of his fortune was left for an inquiry into the use of the twenty-six-letter alphabet, and the means of establishing a new phonetic alphabet of forty letters, the inquiry to be limited to twenty years. The ultimate residue to go to the National Gallery of Ireland, the British Museum, and the Royal Academy of Dramatic Art, one-third to each. Up to April 1961 the three residual legatees had each received a total of £260,000 and funds are still being distributed.

He had bequeathed to the British Museum all papers in his possession (apart from business papers and diaries) of which he did not own the copyright. These consisted chiefly of letters addressed to Shaw, something like 5,000 items, though he had been in the habit of destroying much of his private correspondence. He also directed that his literary manuscripts should be sold for the benefit of his estate, which was effected during 1960 (when the estate was finally settled), and the whole was purchased by the British Museum for the sum of £55,000 which is included in the above-mentioned final valuation.

Though it is not surprising that the terms of the will relating to the alphabet aroused much adverse comment, it was entirely reasonable from Shaw's point of view, for he had been deeply interested in the defects of the existing alphabet throughout his life and regarded spelling reform as of the utmost importance to the Western World. After much public controversy and some

litigation, for there was doubt about the validity of these pro-
visions of the will, it was found possible to devote £8,300 from
the estate to carry out Shaw's wishes relating to the new
alphabet, and a public competition was inaugurated in 1958 by
the Public Trustee for designs for it. The result announced at
the end of 1959 was that of 467 entries received none was considered to merit adoption. The prize of £500 was shared equally
among four 'semi-winners'. An attempt has been made to 'co-
ordinate the best features' of these four alphabets to produce
something workable and a bi-alphabetic edition of *Androcles and
the Lion* was published in 1961.

An unwise appeal for £250,000 for a memorial and for the
maintenance of his Ayot St Lawrence house was made by a
national committee immediately upon Shaw's death, but met with
so little response, only £407 being subscribed, that it was quickly
abandoned. Why, indeed, should people subscribe to the memory
of one who had left so large a fortune? Another too hastily projected scheme for a Shaw Memorial Theatre at Welwyn Garden
City had the same fate. A theatre in Shaw's name should certainly
be built, and Welwyn Garden City, in which he took much
interest, and near which he lived for so long, should no doubt
provide a site for it. But these efforts were too conventional, too
unShavian, to deserve support. His works are his memorial,
otherwise the epitaph he once wrote himself would be appropriate:

HIC JACET
BERNARD SHAW
Who the devil was he?

(29)

This brief summary of Bernard Shaw's long life has been given
for the sake of the enjoyment of his plays, for it is well to under-

stand in reading them or participating in their performance (especially as a member of the audience) the individual tone of his work, and the fact that his plays are a whole and his life and work were one. Shaw might have been a painter or a musician, or he might have remained a critic, or become a novelist (as he almost did), or perhaps the statesman that he sometimes imagined he should have been, and that his wife so devotedly wished that he was, but he found his right vocation as a playwright. He was not forced into being a playwright; indeed the world as well as his wife was against it, and he had evidence enough that his plays were not wanted, but he knew that to write plays was the meaning of his existence. He was never confused or uncertain, for he had no doubt of his vocation. He once said, 'The matter was never really in my hands.' In that conviction he worked for more than fifty years.

It is significant that he was never conceited about his plays, and, in fact, unless he had to do so avoided seeing them performed. Yet in writing them he knew he was carrying out the will of what he called the Life Force, an instrument of Creative Evolution, and his great concern was that other men should so regard themselves. From moment to moment he knew what he had to do, and displayed the courage of one who knew why he exists. That Shaw thought himself to be the organ of genius that surpassed himself shows him to have been a true artist in the traditional sense. He worked as a playwright subject to a discipline beyond his own immediate interests. In that sense he worked as Michelangelo worked: an idea of the nature of work not easy for us to contemplate who work according to our own pleasure or profit or taste or fancy or disbelief or mere habit.

At all times his appearance testified to his state of mind. His confident, erect carriage, his energy and light, dancing movements, his expression always alive, eager and absorbed, were evidence of inner conviction. As he grew old and became fragile, walking as though a strong wind might blow him away, unsteady on his feet and inclined to fall, he still remained physically and mentally active, working to the last, leaving an unfinished play, and cutting away at trees in his garden, which was the occasion of his fatal accident. In those latter days, as many people have testified, he had the light of saintliness upon him. It was not for nothing that he was named Bernard, for the great Saint Bernard of Clairvaux was also famed for his wide interests and winning style of writing. The aim of all Shaw's plays – there is no exception – is for the sake of spiritual activity in the beholder.

The secret of Bernard Shaw, which accounts for his work and gives it significance, may perhaps be found if we think of that Hertfordshire house of his – Shaw's Corner, as he called it in some derision – a commonplace, tasteless, late Victorian building, furnished by Charlotte for domestic comfort, in which he lived so long. Everyone who saw it was astonished that it should be the home of genius. Shaw sometimes said that neither he nor Charlotte liked the house; but they went on living there. It was a home in which she took care of him, a working-place, where he could be quiet, and see his friends when so disposed, and no one in the village took any interest in him. Though so near to London, Ayot St Lawrence is in the depths of the countryside, isolated, without even a bus service. There Shaw lived without identifying himself with his surroundings. Detachment was in fact his secret.

It was the secret not only of his life but of his plays. He did not live in that dull house, except for bodily necessities; likewise, he attached himself to no possessions, not even lightly, not even to his plays, for they are the works of a completely detached mind. He lived in his imagination. All he did was an expression of this detached being; his political and social activities, no less than his plays, all expressed a disinterested and free mind. It is not that he stood outside his plays and their characters. The true artist works from within himself: he starts with vision not with the outer object. He does not create a semblance of the world, but transfigures it. Instead of assembling what exists outside himself, finding in it pattern or meaning, he perceives an inner reality and presents it in the form of the world. To do this the artist must be detached, not involving himself in his surroundings or the material of his art, or even in himself.

With Shaw there was not merely the mask, to which I referred at the beginning – the deliberately created false personality, the public figure. He was as detached from his mask as he was from the rest of his surroundings. He never for one instant supposed that the mask was the man. Neither should we suppose that the mask was the plays; for his work was no mask – it was the truth.

(30)

This detachment gave him throughout his life an insubstantial quality, of which everyone who knew him was conscious. It made him appear contradictory and unpredictable. He could not be pinned down, or hurt, or damaged by even the fiercest attack or opposition, and appeared to elude capture even in an argument. In a sense he was never wholly there. Precise, detailed, and accurate as he proved to be in his public debates on the platform or in the press, he was never caught out. This often caused great annoyance. The conclusion is that the real Shaw was not the socialist, the egalitarian, the spelling reformer, nor the dramatist. He was an instrument, and his was an impersonal life.

This conscious non-identification, except with the mysterious Self outside himself, was Shaw's outstanding characteristic, and as a dramatist puts him in a class by himself. It accounts, too, for his living to so great an age and his mental activity to the end. It explains why he was able to get his plays listened to – witness his great fortune – without accommodating himself to the taste or demands of the time. On no account would he disguise nor diminish the novelty of the truth that was in him. It was this essential disinterestedness that got him a hearing, despite the annoyance he aroused, for he was so clearly single-minded. Enemies called it egotism, but it was his singularity to be devoid of egotism: the egotist was the unreal mask. No one who looks upon himself as an instrument for what is beyond himself can be an egotist. He can only be a humble servant, as Shaw declared himself to be, 'an amanuensis or an organ blower', he said. He was never anybody's man but a hand of that which he had no objection to being called Providence, or God. That is what put him at loggerheads with the established professionals of his day in science, philosophy, art and politics, even in the theatre, though less there than anywhere, and made his work unsettling for everyone, for what he said could not be laughed away, even amidst the laughter he aroused. Often he outraged people, but he was never offensive. 'I am always shocked by what I write', he said in his old age. A Catholic critic has written of the artist as one who is in guilty rivalry with God, but to Shaw the artist was man as God would have him, obedient to the creative will.

(31)

Nearly all modern art, especially in painting, poetry and music, is little more than the very clever and technically expert effort of artists to work for or to speak to themselves. They do not know what they think and are trying to find out, to convince themselves. Their desire for knowledge is partly sensual, partly metaphysical, and the symbols of colour, shape, sound, or word are valid only for themselves. They have in mind no user of their art, no public, and whoever picks up anything from it may count himself

73

to be lucky, but it does not concern the artist. This seems, to me, to be true of Pablo Picasso and Paul Klee, of T. S. Eliot and Dylan Thomas, to go no further.

With such artists who consider the subjects of their work to concern nobody but themselves, Bernard Shaw had nothing in common. He aimed at understanding, and his plays were written to convey what he understood. His technique as a playwright was devoted to enabling the public to share his vision. He wrote plays to delight audiences and to change their minds. He was not a private but a public man. This was a necessary element in his vocation, for drama exists only as a public art. Participation is the soul of drama, for an audience is essential, and Shaw was never disrespectful to the audience and seldom criticized it. He found fault with the actors and with the critics, sometimes with himself, never with the public. He did everything to make his plays pleasing, while saying exactly what he wanted to say, for he never cringed to the public, while regarding himself, as he said in his very old age, 'your very faithful servant'. If the actors performed reasonably well, and provided the critics did not too grossly mislead the public, he thought any play of his would be enjoyed unless he himself had not written it well.

Shaw's political, economic and linguistic theories were funda-mental to his art. As a dramatist he was interested in people, in the theatre, and in language, and while the theories he held had no control over his art, they had an intrinsic place in his athletic mind, ever on the stretch, and therefore in his art. His plays are living drama because of the kind of man he was, and because he was in immediate and present contact with his time. He was as familiar with the every-day speech at street corners as with the elegancies of drawing rooms, and as much at home in the political con-troversies of the moment as with discussions upon Shakespeare or Wagner or Velasquez. Everywhere he looked he saw comic significance, and as a dramatist he holds eternal converse with Aristophanes, Shakespeare and Molière.

It is from this point of view that I invite consideration of the Shavian drama.

A Note on Biographies

With most of the biographies of himself in his lifetime Shaw had much to do, for he was always willing to read what was said about him, and, it must be confessed, not unwilling to allow writers to misrepresent him, so that all biographies are in various degrees unreliable. Shaw's own autobiographical references in the prefaces to the collected and standard edition of his early novels, together with the volume *Sixteen Self Sketches* (London, Constable, 1949), are of the greatest value. The following are the chief biographies, the most important is the 1956 volume by Archibald Henderson whom Shaw treated as his official biographer. His book is a vast factual record by a man who devoted a large part of his life to its preparation.

ARCHIBALD HENDERSON
George Bernard Shaw: Man of the Century. New York, Appleton, 1956.

ST JOHN ERVINE
Bernard Shaw. London, Constable, 1956.

HESKETH PEARSON
Bernard Shaw: his Life and Opinions. London, Methuen, 1961.

FRANK HARRIS
Bernard Shaw: An unauthorized Biography Based on Firsthand Information. With a Postscript by Bernard Shaw. London, Gollancz, 1931.

MAURICE COLBOURNE
The Real Bernard Shaw. London, Dent, 1949.

ERIC BENTLEY
Bernard Shaw. London, Robert Hale, 1950.

Biographical material is contained in the following works:

S. WINSTEN
Days with Bernard Shaw. London, Hutchinson, 1948.
Shaw's Corner. London, Hutchinson, 1952.

R. F. RATTRAY
Bernard Shaw: A Chronicle. Luton, Leagrave Press, 1951.

BLANCHE PATCH
Thirty Years with Bernard Shaw. London, Gollancz, 1951.

C. B. PURDOM (ed)
Bernard Shaw's Letters to Granville Barker. London, Phoenix House, 1955.

E. J. WEST (ed)
Advice to a Young Critic and other letters by Bernard Shaw. New York, Crown Publishers, 1955.

ALAN DENT (ed)
Bernard Shaw and Mrs Patrick Campbell: Their Correspondence. London, Gollancz, 1952.

CHRISTOPHER ST JOHN (ed)
Ellen Terry and Bernard Shaw: A Correspondence. London, Constable, 1931.

E. J. WEST (ed)
Shaw on Theatre. New York, Hill & Wang, 1958.

PETER TOMPKINS (ed)
To a Young Actress: the Letters of Bernard Shaw to Molly Tompkins. London, Constable, 1961.

DAN H. LAURENCE (ed)
How to Become a Musical Critic. London, Hart-Davis, 1961.

There are many articles and descriptive books on Shaw's ideas and activities in various spheres, some of which contain biographical material; there is also the following volume which is concerned with the plays:

R. MANDER and J. MITCHENSON
  Theatrical Companion to Shaw. London, Rockliff, 1955.

PART TWO

The Dramatist

I. The Comic Genius

The year after the young Bernard Shaw came to London, George Meredith delivered his famous lecture *On the Idea of Comedy and of the Uses of the Comic Spirit* at the London Institution. The opening words were:

> Good comedies are such rare productions that, notwithstanding the wealth of our literature in the comic element, it would not occupy us long to run over the English list.

It is unlikely that Shaw heard the lecture or paid any attention to the newspaper reports of it, though we know that he read it afterwards, for he reviewed an edition of it in *The Saturday Review* in March 1897. Meredith's essay can, however, appropriately be recalled in considering Shaw as a comic genius. Although Meredith made reference to comedy in general he was especially thinking of comedy in dramatic form, and raised the question why comedy writers are so rare, for while the 'comic element', as he pointed out, is by no means rare – existing in our society at every level and at every period (Meredith himself being an example) – comic playwrights are another matter.

Why that should be so the lecturer explained by saying that comedy is 'addressed to the intellect', intended for 'that assemblage of mind whereof the comic spirits has its origin'. A matter of intellect, therefore; and in a special sense a civilized activity, depending upon a civilized society consequently limited by the smallness of the possible audience. For while to arouse laughter is easily done, the laughter of comedy is not any kind of laughter, it involves thought, and as at any time the number of people disposed to think are few, and of those who attend the theatre very few, the number of comedies is few. That was Meredith's argument.

He distinguished between comedy, humour, irony, and satire, comedy being different from and superior to other forms of comic writing because 'the laughter of comedy is impersonal and of unrivalled politeness, nearer a smile; often no more than a smile'. To be a writer of comedy, it is necessary, he said 'to have a sober liking of your kind and a sober estimate of our civilized qualities'. Comedy arises from the application of common sense to the perception of human follies. It was Meredith's frequent use of the term 'common sense' that Shaw found most fault with in his review, for he could not perceive an audience for comedy in the English state of mind and English pride in its common sense, and declared that in Meredith's sense the 'English playgoing public . . . positively dislikes comedy'.

(2)

There is no need to continue with Meredith, for he does not, indeed, take us far. Though he refers to Aristophanes and Meander, and provides examples from Molière and Congreve (not from Ben Jonson), and while the entire essay is excellent reading as far as it goes, he does not consider the reason for the small number of true comedies in any closer detail, neither does he investigate the lack of title of many so-called comedies to the name, nor ask why it is so difficult to write comedy, or why comedy degenerates so quickly into farce, or why the detachment so necessary to it so easily becomes disintegrated by naturalism and ends in mere story-telling.

'The life of comedy is in the idea', said Meredith, and writing of Aristophanes he said, 'Whether right or wrong in his politics and his criticisms, and bearing in mind the instruments he played on and the audience he had to win, there is an idea in his comedies: it is the idea of good citizenship.' Thirty years later he could have written these words with immediate application to Bernard Shaw.

When I come to examine Shavian drama it will be seen that I regard the plays from the point of view of 'the idea', but not any idea, and not solely the idea of good citizenship, though that idea is implied in it; for I am concerned with the 'dramatic' idea. It is my point that the requirements of drama go far beyond what Meredith laid down – perception, tolerance, wit, gaiety, and characterization; they include in the very first place the conception of dramatic action. A stage comedy is a particular form of writing employing not simply characters and dialogue and theatrical situations but an absurd or ludicrous situation or predicament into which the leading character is placed, from the unpleasant or dangerous consequences of which he or she is delivered. The presentation of the problem and its resolution constitutes the dramatic action. It is because so few writers percieve the nature of dramatic action that we have so few genuine comedies.

(3)

Comic genius in drama is the power to perceive the general predicament of mankind, or the particular predicament of an individual, as absurd and laughter-making. It arises from the vision of the folly, the lack of understanding or the sheer stupidity in society or in a particular man. It is the recognition of imperfections in human nature as the subject matter of mirth. The mirth may be cynical, or ironic, or unsympathetic, depending upon the outlook and state of mind of the artist; but in the true artist what he perceives is matter for contemplation and the outcome is increase of happiness. The true comedian does not set out to cause men to forget who they are or to cover up their failures, but, by arousing laughter, to heighten their sensibilities and

83

enlarge their equipment for life. The attack may be sharp and stinging, there may be bruises and shocks, but the aim is transformation. Shaw was a comic genius in this sense.

(4)

With the exception of two plays, and disregarding the short pieces, Shaw's plays are in the sphere of comedy as I have just defined it, and I propose in the immediately following chapters to discuss briefly the themes, construction and characters of the plays. But before I do so I have some further observations to offer. Shaw's fame does not rest as does Ben Jonson's upon less than a dozen plays, or as does Goldsmith's upon one, or as Sheridan's or Wilde's upon three or four, but upon more than fifty plays of which thirty are major works. The extent is astonishing when we consider that he was approaching forty years of age before he started; and though quantity is not a sole criterion of greatness, it must be treated with respect as possibly indicating it. Furthermore, the vitality of his plays is indicated by the fact that even the first imperfect ones have gained in the course of time larger audiences than ever.

We receive today with a composure absent from the minds of their original audiences the comedies of Aristophanes, as well as those of Molière, to say nothing of Shakespeare, even those of the Restoration writers, because the cutting edge is off their wit. The barbs of Shaw's comic intention still assault readers and audiences, and in discomfort fault is sometimes found with the work, and there is often a pretence that he has not hit the mark, but the pain the plays once caused is no longer so acute.

Yet never, even when most aroused, was Shaw malicious. He was a true comic dramatist in Meredith's sense, and, except in the three unpleasant plays, not even a satirist, nor an ironist, and he was never superior. His wit was inherent in the presentation of characters and theme; it was not an ornament of language or a savage reaction. It sprang out of his sympathetic appreciation and love of people and insight into their problems. He saw with dazzling clarity, even if he did not always see the whole, and took immense pains to make clear to others what he saw. In him, wit was the clear-sighted mind playing upon and brooding over the confused and contradictory world, an astringent element blowing the mind bright. He had no animus against even his bitterest enemies, and never showed spleen. He was never cruel or spiteful. Furthermore, he went into the market place and spoke to all, and because he was concerned with the state of mankind he was mistakenly looked upon as a proletarian writer who fell astray when he belaboured the Labour politicians and their supporters who were his friends. In truth he was essentially an aristocratic writer, though he laid about the aristocracy with the utmost vigour. Thus he was an enigma to those who would not accept him on his own terms, which were those of a craftsman who used his skill for a purpose not his own. He filled with despair those who could not detach themselves from the immediacy of their problems so as to view themselves and their world without attachment and thus were unable to laugh.

(5)

His was the pure comic spirit, which is joyous. He did not start from the conviction of the irremediable evil of man, but from belief in equality – that is, goodness – a belief more profound than any rationalistic notion. He would never have anything to do with the anaemic rationalism of some of his friends, or with any soured outlook upon human affairs. Invariably impatient with what men do, and scorning their stupidity, he was essentially tolerant, for he believed in the ultimate saving virtue of the specific human quality – the intellect. This attitude of mind prevented any bitterness in his comedy, without making it less keenly pointed. He could afford to say the worst because he believed in the best. This causes his work to possess a benevolence not always recognized, but invariably present, which makes him as a comedy writer unique, except for Shakespeare. His comic genius was honest – 'spiritually conscientious', in Nietzsche's sense – liberal, courageous, and gay.

(6)

Shaw's mind was not speculative as, for example, was that of his contemporary W. B. Yeats, but concrete and practical, though no less imaginative. He brought his imagination to bear upon such practical matters as the responsibility of people for social conditions, and in politics upon such fundamental matters as the reconstitution of Parliament. In economics he put forward with powerful arguments the idea of equality of incomes. But imagination in practical politics no less than in theoretical economics is regarded as a form of madness. In Shaw, however, a practical mind was shown in the extraordinary ability with which he ran his own trade of authorship, and his great fortune was largely the outcome of an acute business sense.

Always, however, in whatever he did, the comic spirit prevailed. No doubt he wrote too much and on too many subjects, for he could not stop writing, but the comic spirit never deserted him. This not only made him disagreeable to those who thought that serious subjects should never be treated other than seriously, it also prevented him from being more than an incipient poet. When the comic spirit remains uppermost it is too strongly astringent for poetry. If I may be forgiven the commonplace, the comic spirit springs from the activity of the intellect, poetry from the activity of the heart. Shaw was genuinely poetic, in the sense of Plato's remark that 'all arts are kinds of poetry and their craftsmen are all poets', and he wrote out of direct poetic apprehension, but his drama is not poetry. There is, indeed, a conflict between drama and poetry, which explains why there are few poets who can write poetic drama, for, unless the opposites are reconciled in the imagination, drama does not come into being. The sphere of comedy is thought, reason its weapon, and its equipment is warlike. Indeed, the comic dramatist uses Satanic means, and not for nothing had Shaw a Mephistophelian image. Because he attacked the minds and consciences of his audiences, Shaw aroused much hatred, as Molière did in his day when in formal verse he assaulted the vices of the French bourgeoisie.

(7)

Shaw had much in common with what he called 'the comic foe of the gods', Punch, always turning up unexpectedly, dealing devastating blows upon the heads of his conventional, respectable, satisfied, heartless neighbours. He was condemned and execrated by the virtuous as loving mischief for mischief's sake, which was only as it seemed. Shaw was a foe of the mammon of unrighteousness dressed up in the garments of virtue. He was against all deception, except his own pretended irresponsibility – a comic genius who was the most responsible dramatist who ever lived.

Yet, as did Shakespeare, Shaw at times descends to idle laughter, never, however, accidentally or from failure in skill, but deliberately, to provide relief from the mental efforts to which he invited his audience. Apart from two or three small pieces his work was never frivolous, though it had its frivolous moments. He disdained no trick of the low comedian to raise a laugh for the sake of providing a rest from the labours of thought. 'Tomfoolery is as classic as tragedy', he said, justifying himself, and at another time he referred to his use of 'plenty of laughing gas'. The rough and tumble in *Misalliance* and *The Apple Cart*, and the low comedy in *Heartbreak House*, were devised to give relief from the serious elements in the plays. Like Shakespeare, too, Shaw was in love with words, as are all comic writers. The comic genius revels in the sound of words, as well as in their form and content, and finds the comic idea in speech itself.

What Meredith could have said in Shaw's hearing, and what he certainly uttered prophetically in the famous lecture was this:

> . . . if the comic idea prevailed with us, and we had an Aristophanes to barb and wing it, we should be breathing air of Athens. Prosers now pouring forth on us like public fountains would be cut short in the street and left blinking, dumb as pillar-posts, with letters thrust into their mouths. We should throw off incubus, our dreadful familiar – by some called boredom – whom it is our present humiliation to be just alive enough to loathe, never quick enough to foil. There would be a bright and positive, clear Hellenic perception of facts. The vapours of unreason and sentimentalism would be blown away before they were productive.

Shaw's comic genius was of such an order. Serving his time through that genius there are few in the world at any time or place who can be compared with him. Though only tragic poetry is sublime, the laughter in his plays raises the heart to the contemplation of tragedy, and without that laughter the cleansing is incomplete.

II. Better than Shakespeare?

We allow ourselves to be brought to the heart of the matter by
considering the question Shaw himself mischievously posited in
one of his earliest prefaces, two years after he had ceased to be a
dramatic critic trouncing the London stage on which Shakespeare was 'butchered to make a Cockney's holiday' – the question
of Shakespeare. He answered the question immediately by
saying, 'I do not profess to write better plays', and later said with
asperity that 'Anyone is a fool who thinks that I or anyone else
wrote better plays than Shakespear'.[1] Shaw was not challenging
the supremacy of Shakespeare, 'the king of dramatists', as he said,
only the nonsense written and talked about him, attacking the
murderous productions by Henry Irving and others, and the
atmosphere of bardolatry in which Shakespeare was 'ranked as
a giant among psychologists and philosophers'. He was assaulting
a false idol, and desired the true figure of the man and his works
to be seen, with the plays performed as the dramatist had
written them. He was indeed, altogether on the side of Shakespeare.

Shaw's self-imposed task of false idol-smashing must be remembered when in his theatrical criticisms he found in the Shakespeare
plays 'not good sense – not even good grammar', and drew
attention to Shakespeare's indifference to social conditions, and
thought the title of *As You Like It* to indicate contempt for the
audience, and particularly when he asserted the superiority of
Bunyan over Shakespeare. In that task, Shaw laid about him with

[1] Shaw spelled the name without the final 'e'.

verbal violence, delighted at the shocked faces as he pointed out the shortcomings, or what could be made to appear to be shortcomings, in the idol. Yet although he seemed to be writing recklessly it was not done with his tongue in his cheek. His attack upon the Shakespeareans was serious, though it was with pain that he said at the end of his critical labours, 'His worshippers overwhelm my name with insult'.

Tolstoy's condemnation of Shakespeare could have been made equally of Shaw and for the same reasons:

It is at once evident that he [Shakespeare] does not believe in what he is saying . . . and so we do not believe either in the events or the actions, or in the sufferings of his characters.

What Tolstoy objected to was Shakespeare's detachment, his moral neutrality, as he called it, and his lack of sincerity. Shaw had such detachment, which is not to be confused with indifference, much less with insincerity or lack of moral judgment. Shakespeare's profound comprehension of humanity, his catholicity and compassion were what endeared him to Shaw.

Thus the importance of Shakespeare to Shaw cannot easily be exaggerated. 'When I was twenty', he said, 'I knew everybody in Shakespear, from Hamlet to Abhorson, much more intimately than I knew my living contemporaries.' Furthermore, Shakespeare provided him with the dramatic method he adopted, for he grasped that the significance of Shakespearean drama lay not in verse, characters, or plot, but in dramatic action. Shaw had his own dramatic outlook, Shakespeare, however, was his model. Four years before he died he wrote an indignant protest to *The Observer* against the statement by an eminent theatrical historian who 'describes my return to sixteenth century practice . . . as a development of the practices of Scribe'.

(2)

Yet it was William Archer and his versions of Ibsen's plays and his enthusiasms for the Norwegian dramatist that turned Shaw's mind to playwriting, though Archer did not encourage him. Ibsen was attacked so violently and with so little comprehension of the meaning of his plays that Shaw was driven to become his expositor, and from expositor a fellow dramatist. Thus he was looked upon as an Ibsenite dramatist, which he was not, though he said 'Nobody who does not remember the impact of Ibsen in 1889 can understand how devastatingly he knocked out his predecessors', by whom Shaw meant in particular the English and French dramatists of the Victorian period. Praise of Ibsen did not mean that Shaw put Shakespeare as a dramatist in any but the supreme place, though he said that 'Shakespeare survives by what he has in common with Ibsen, not by what he has in common with Webster and the rest'. For Shaw was no more favourable to Elizabethan dramatists in general, nor to those of the Restoration, than he was to nineteenth century playwrights, all because of their moral irrelevance. It was not only Ibsen's attitude to the social and personal problems of the time, but Shaw's knowledge of Shakespeare that enabled him to appreciate Ibsen.

(3)

Shaw recognized that what was important in Ibsen and Shakespeare was not simply that they both approached drama as poets but that both understood the significance and place of the leading character. Each of their plays contains a central character in a comic or tragic situation: Shakespeare's are concerned with Romeo, Brutus, Rosalind, Viola, Hamlet, Macbeth, Othello, Lear and others; Ibsen's with Peer Gynt, Nora, Mrs Aveing, Dr Stockmann, Hedda Gabler, and the rest. Attention is focused by each dramatist upon the central character, and while other characters make their contribution, the dramatic action is concerned with what happens to him or her.

I return to this subject later. What I intend at the moment is to indicate the particular indebtedness of Shaw to Shakespeare and Ibsen. Shakespeare is the greatest of dramatists because, with the most extended fecundity of imagination and the greatest poetic gifts, he perfectly presented in dramatic action a central character with his or her problem and its resolution. His character-drawing, invention, humanity, even his verse, also his theatrical skill, were the means whereby he effected this, but they did not, singly or together, make him what he is. The same can be said of Ibsen, and, I suggest, of Shaw, his being an achievement in a different category of drama at least equivalent to Ibsen's. Shaw was essentially a comic dramatist, while Ibsen was tragic or tragi-comic. Shakespeare was essentially a tragedian, and while he wrote many comedies, all had tragic undertones. Shaw, the comedian, wrote two tragedies in which the undertones of comedy are strongly heard. Above all it should be recognized that Shaw, like Shakespeare, knew what a play was. Certainly, he did not define that knowledge, and what he said so copiously and well about playwriting was no more than discussion of the incidentals of the craft, which can also be said of Ibsen. Shakespeare had said nothing, apart from the famous speech about holding the mirror up to Nature. The secret was unfolded by none of them, but is to be discovered in their works.

(4)

Though Shaw was not a poet, his early ambition was to write poetry, as his boyhood friend, Edward McNulty, relates, and he was not without facility in verse making, as he showed from time to time – a facility often displayed by comic writers – but he seems deliberately to have avoided its development, considering prose dialogue to suit best what he wanted to say and the audience for which he was writing. The fact that Ibsen gave up verse writing may have had some influence upon him. He professed to think that blank verse was easy to write; but when he attempted it in *The Admirable Bashville*, it was as a joke, and his variation on Shakespeare's ending of *Cymbeline* proved (what he already knew) that it was nothing of the sort.

Those who find no emotion in Shaw must, it seems to me, be devoid of sensibility. In his very last completed work, at the age of ninety-two, he has a character who says 'I stop short of your eating and drinking and so forth, and of your reproductive methods. They revolt me.' And a girl asks the question 'No passions, then?' To which the reply is made 'On the contrary: intellectual passion, mathematical passion, passion for discovery and exploration: the mightiest of the passions.' And it is true that these passions are in his plays, but so indeed is simple human love. Who can fail to find it in *Pygmalion*? Yet the emotional motive is presented in terms of thought, the senses are pleased but the appeal is to the mind, not to them.

(5)

When Shaw agreed that Ibsen's plays had an immoral tendency he meant that they presented conduct that did not conform to current ideals. 'All religions begin with a revolt against morality', he said. 'Bunyan places the town of Morality, with its respected leading citizens, Mr Legality and Mr Civility, close to the City of Destruction.' Shaw was defining his own point of view. In that sense Shakespeare was not an immoralist, for he represented the religion and thought of his time. Shaw's plays were products of a more complex civilization, and contradicted the prevailing philosophy, which was rationalistic and materialistic and denied purpose to the life of man. In Shaw as in Shakespeare, however,

93

the conflict is between divine will or creative purpose and egotistic passion; it is between spiritual order and moral anarchy.

The intensity of concentration characteristic of Shakespeare's plays is also characteristic of Shaw's. The plays of each dramatist transcend merely personal issues; their characters are set in a world context, and present situations that belong to human nature. What Shaw said of Ibsen may also be said of his own writing:

> There is not one of Ibsen's characters who is not, in the old phrase, the temple of the Holy Ghost, and who does not move you at moments by the sense of that mystery.

When Shaw's plays were first performed they aroused excitement and surprise, often acute displeasure, but always there was to be felt the white heat of mental energy, the flame of moral purpose, and the force of imagination. In the place of the superficial smoothness of familiar theatricality there was gusto of life and audacity of thought.

(6)

The dramatist whose work comes most forcibly to mind in relation to Shaw's is Molière. Both placed emphasis upon the central character, both presented characters in the everyday language and situations of their time, both were concerned with ideas and were criticised for the lack of action in their plays, both cared little for plot, and both were attacked as enemies of religion. In a comparison of the two dramatists Rémy de Gourmont said with Shaw's early plays before him:

> Molière has never drawn a doctor more comically 'the doctor' than Paramore, nor more characteristic figures of women than those in the same play, *The Philanderer*. The character drawing is admirable.

94

The quotation is taken from the excellent study of Shaw by his first French translator, Augustin F. Hamon, contained in *The Twentieth Century Molière*, published in Paris in 1912, and in London in 1915. The humanity and humour that make Molière's plays supreme in their kind are found in Shaw no less, and both have in common the frank criticism of society and morals. Both take an extended view of human behaviour and cover a wide range of human emotion. While Shaw never was an actor as was Molière all his life, he was a stage producer who knew what he wanted no less than did Molière. I recommend to the reader a study of this book.

(7)

At this point something should be said about what Shaw had in common with Anton Chekhov, a dramatist who was born, worked, and died in the course of Shaw's life. The two dramatists lived far apart, without contact, and their influence upon each other was small, though Shaw once said that after seeing a play by Chekhov he wanted to tear up his own. They were both comic geniuses, their outlook upon life was not dissimilar, both admired Ibsen, both were concerned with their contemporaries. Chekhov worked on a smaller scale than Shaw, choosing a canvas with more detailed physiological and psychological examination of his subjects. He was a doctor, while Shaw was a politician.

Both were dissatisfied with the stage of their time, Shaw with its unreality, Chekhov with its naturalism. What Chekhov said of the stage, 'those scaffolds where they execute playwrights', was also said by Shaw in almost identical words. When Chekhov wrote to a friend after a production of *The Cherry Orchard*, 'My play was performed yesterday and therefore I am not in a particularly bright mood today', he was saying what Shaw often said. Chekhov's advice to a playwright, 'do not be afraid to be silly', might have been offered by Shaw, and his remark about sex as a theme, 'it is not everywhere that it is of decisive importance', expressed exactly Shaw's view.

Shaw's particular likeness to Chekhov is thought to be in *Heartbreak House*, but had he not entitled his play 'a fantasia in the Russian manner', and referred to Chekhov in the preface, the likeness might not have been perceived. Shaw says his play is about 'cultured, leisured Europe before the war', as Chekhov might have said about *The Cherry Orchard*. Shaw wrote comedy as Chekhov did, and his theme was as serious as Chekhov's; and his play ends inconclusively and with an explosion, as Chekhov was apt to end his plays. But this kind of dramatic ending was already present in Ibsen and there was no need to go to Chekhov for it. Much nearer the truth would it be to point to the difference between them, that Chekhov was essentially a story-teller in his plays, while Shaw was not. Chekhov was much more realistic (as a story writer has to be) than Shaw, who was hardly ever realistic. Chekhov's dialogue is direct, austere, and economical while Shaw's is rhetorical and abundant. Both were poetical, without writing verse. Yet the dramatic effects aimed at by the two dramatists are radically different: Chekhov seeks to establish an atmosphere of intimate personal confusion, while Shaw is concerned with the idea. Shaw is no less interested in persons than Chekhov, but in a different way: personal clashes do not concern him but the clash of people's ideas.

The fact that Chekhov wrote only five major plays and died comparatively young, while Shaw wrote very many and died old, conveys a major difference between them. Yet because of the intensity of their comic vision, their extraordinarily good writing, and their seriousness, the plays of the two writers deserve to be mentioned together. What Chekhov wrote was what Shaw himself was ever saying:

He who is sincerely convinced that higher aims are as unnecessary to man as they are to a cow and that 'our whole misfortune' lies in having those aims, has nothing left but to eat, drink and sleep, and when he gets sick of all that, to take a good run and smash his head on the sharp edge of a trunk. . . .[1]

(8)

The relation between Shavian and Shakespearean drama deserves a volume to itself, and what I have to say in this brief introduction is that Shaw was what he was because he learned from Shakespeare, as Shakespeare learned from Marlowe. What Shaw wrote in an early essay can be said of the work of both dramatists, that dramatic art was 'a discovery of reality under the insane chaos of daily phenomena, an attempt to make experience intelligible'. In the programme note for the original production of *The Dark Lady of the Sonnets* in 1910 what he made Shakespeare say reads rather like a self-confession:

I was really a gentle creature. It was so awful to be born about ten times as clever as anyone else – to like people and yet to have to despise their vanities and illusions. People are such fools, even the most likeable ones, as far as brains go. I wasn't cruel enough to enjoy my superiority.

Indeed, in that play his Shakespeare is a comical self-portrait. For the present we can leave it at that.

[1]*Chekhov the Dramatist* by D. Margarshack (London, 1952), pp. 43-4.

III. Themes

Why Bernard Shaw wrote plays he explained himself in words that deserve to be recalled:

> I am not an ordinary playwright in general practice. I am a specialist in immoral and heretical plays. My reputation has been gained by my persistent struggle to force the public to reconsider its morals. In particular, I regard much current morality as to economic and sexual relations as disastrously wrong; and I regard certain doctrines of the Christian religion as understood in England today with abhorrence. I write plays with the deliberate object of converting the nation to my opinions in these matters.

This explanation is significant because he made it at the opening of his statement before the Parliamentary Committee on the Censorship in 1909, a statement the committee refused to consider. Although he intended to be provocative, it was with the object of making plain the particular qualities of Shavian drama. He was not merely provocative, but anxious that it should be understood that he wrote plays because he must do so. As he afterwards made Fanny O'Dowda say in the prologue to *Fanny's First Play*:

> I had to write it or I should have burst. I couldn't help it.

It was his themes that made Shaw a dramatist: an immoralist in the sense of opposing current morals and manners, and a heretic in challenging beliefs he wished to transform. In that sense only was he a propagandist. It would not be possible to tell from his plays that Shaw was a socialist, or (in the popular sense) an atheist, or vegetarian, or teetotaller, because he wrote as an artist and a free man. Shaw's socialism was the outcome of his passion for order. His constant charge against the existing social order was that it was inefficient, wasteful, cruel, stupid, and shameful. Highly individualistic as he was, he was opposed to any form of anarchy, which he considered the existing order to be. His opposition to the censorship of plays was largely due to his 'abhorrence of anarchism', as he explained at length. He argued that the censorship was anarchical because it applied not law but opinion. Why should a dramatist's work be subject to the likes or dislikes, beliefs or disbeliefs, whims or fancies of another man? Shaw challenged social ideas and stage conventions, yet only once did he challenge the censor on his own account. Possibly he expected the censor to fall foul of his early *Mrs Warren's Profession*: certainly he never disputed the censor's action. He did, however, oppose him with all his might when his play on religious conviction, *The Shewing-up of Blanco Posnet*, was banned. When his little political piece *Press Cuttings* was refused, he laughed. No other play of his came under the censor's disfavour, though there was some discussion over scenes in *Back to Methuselah*.

(2)

Shaw's themes were the relations between men and women, husbands and wives, and parents and children; the problems of conscience, character and disposition; the problems of the individual and society; and the conception of life as creative energy. Hence he presents the classic themes of drama, the clash within the individual mind, the clash between individual characters, and between the individual and the customs, manners, religion, and policies of his time.

A 'clash' belongs to the nature of drama, which is action. The action is contained in the clash of the protagonist with those who are opposing him in the situations in which he is placed. Shaw declared (in *The Quintessence of Ibsenism*) that drama was in the discussion, which is a clash of minds. He found what he called 'the technical novelty in Ibsen's plays' in exposition, situation, and discussion, replacing exposition, situation, and unravelling, which constituted the plays of the Victorian stage. Thus, he claimed, in the 1913 edition of this book, that Ibsen founded 'a new school of dramatic art'. Shaw certainly adopted the method of discussion, carrying it much further than Ibsen, but, all the same, discussion is only a form of unravelling. For that reason if for no other he was justified in declaring 'I am not an Ibsenist even at second hand'.

(3)

Indeed, drama is neither in the clash, nor the discussion, any more than in the exposition, it is in the resolution of the problem in or over which the clash arises. Unless there is a resolution, a solution, there is no drama, for the action is not complete; in drama, action is always completed, comically or tragically.

This will be seen as we come to examine Shaw's plays. At the moment let us think of the early *Widowers' Houses* and *Mrs Warren's Profession* where the theme is conscience, the same theme as that of *Major Barbara*. In the first play the clash is between Trench's conventionally held principles and the facts of ordinary life; in *Mrs Warren's Profession* it is between Vivie's honesty of purpose and her dependence upon her mother's ill-gotten income; in *Major Barbara* it is caused by Barbara's scruples against accepting what she regards as tainted money for her Salvation Army work. There is no doubt that the last is the better play, being written with more competence, with perfected characterization, and the dialogue richer in content. But what gives the play its superiority is that the protagonist is presented more fully, the problem is more developed and its resolution more certain. Trench in *Widowers' Houses* merely collapses, his problem is solved by his surrender. Vivie does not surrender; she arrives at a solution of her problem by claiming independence and rejecting the money, but experiences no sense of victory. Barbara, on the other hand, sees that on the level on which the Army works her father millionaire's money can be accepted, but she gives up the work, and adopts a new kind of life that she is convinced will make such work and the gifts it is dependent upon unnecessary. What more essentially Christian conclusion could any play possess?

In all the plays of his best period the problem, the clash, and the resolution are worked out. In *Arms and the Man* there is romance exposed to the onslaught of common sense and comically defeated; in *Candida* the poet is in conflict with the world but is undefeated; in *You Never Can Tell* the irrational lover overcomes the reasonable objections to him; in *Man and Superman* the life force is triumphant; in *The Doctor's Dilemma* the doctor defeats himself; and in *Saint Joan* the martyred country girl is recognized as a saint.

(4)

To attempt to classify the themes of any dramatist is a task proper to an academic study, which this does not pretend to be, but I think it may be interesting to make a classification of Shaw's dramatic themes from the point of view from which I am now writing. I indicate below what seems to me the predominant theme of each play (neglecting the minor works), though the fact is not to be ignored that there are secondary themes in each of the plays, sometimes strongly developed.

CONSCIENCE: *Widowers' Houses, Mrs Warren's Profession, Major Barbara.*

LOVE: *The Philanderer, You Never Can Tell, The Doctor's Dilemma, Pygmalion, Heartbreak House, Buoyant Billions.*

MARRIAGE: *Getting Married.*

PARENTS AND CHILDREN: *Misalliance, Fanny's First Play.*

ROMANCE: *Arms and the Man, The Devil's Disciple, John Bull's Other Island.*

HIGH POLITICS: *The Apple Cart, Too True to be Good, On the Rocks, The Millionairess, Geneva, In Good King Charles's Golden Days.*

RELIGION: *The Shewing-up of Blanco Posnet, Androcles and the Lion, Saint Joan.*

GREATIVE EVOLUTION: *Man and Superman, Back to Methuselah, The Simpleton of the Unexpected Isles.*

Two early plays, apart from the small pieces, are omitted: *Caesar and Cleopatra* which Shaw called 'a history', written for J. Forbes-Robertson, 'to pay an instalment of the debt that all dramatists owe to the art of heroic acting', and *Captain Brassbound's Conversion*, written a little later for Ellen Terry. These two plays go beyond their particular purpose, but they are essentially actor's plays, other considerations being subordinated to the object of providing characters in which two actors admired by Shaw could display themselves.

(5)

What I am insinuating is that what determines the dramatic theme is the standpoint of the leading character or protagonist. That is to say it is in the problem or dilemma facing him or her. As Shaw's plays are comedies it is not always easy to decide who is the protagonist, i.e. the character from whose point of view the dramatic action takes place. In tragedy there is never any doubt; but in comedy the action is so interlocked with two or more characters, and its direction is (usually deliberately) made so uncertain, that it is often difficult to decide what the action is. It is a question, however, not to be ignored because of its difficulty.

The answer can be found by looking closely at the play. The protagonist is always the one who has the central place in the action, and around whom, for that reason, the movement of the play revolves: it is his (or her) position that is expounded, his situation that is established, and his problem that is resolved.

When the protagonist is recognized the theme appears. There is never any final doubt in Shaw's plays (or Shakespeare's) although on the way to the conclusion there is often scope for debate. As an example of the difficulty take one of Shaw's important plays, *The Doctor's Dilemma*. From the title of the play we should decide at once that the doctor, Sir Colenso Ridgeon, is the protagonist, but Shaw calls the play a tragedy. Sir Colenso, however, despite the ambiguity of his action, has, at first sight, no tragedy. So we have to consider Jennifer, the artist's wife, who is so striking a character and has so desperate a problem that she seems to be pointed to as the leading character. Yet when we compare the two characters we find that Jennifer, delightful as she is, is not fully presented, and as a character has only secondary significance, for her devotion to her husband and belief in him are no more than asserted, supported only by superficial evidence, and her personality is seen as through coloured glasses, made glamorous, but never clearly defined, as a protagonist's must be. Moreover, the loss of her gifted husband, painful as it was, is hardly in itself a tragedy. Except for the value of his painting, he was a worthless man, and it is not Shaw's suggestion that his life, good painter as he is represented to be, should be preserved at all costs. That was Jennifer's idea, held by no one else. Were Jennifer the protagonist, and the play really her tragedy, it would be a poor work.

On the other hand the doctor is carefully and fully drawn. He is, in fact, the one fully self-conscious character in the play: this was my situation, he says, as he observes himself, ruefully, in the retrospective contemplation that is the essence of drama. He has to make a decision, and his judgment is confused because the artist's wife fascinates him and he is emotionally drawn to her. He does not believe in her love for her husband, nor in the value of the husband, so prefers that the artist should die, choosing to treat the other man, whose life as Shaw makes clear deserves to be saved. But the doctor's judgment, clouded by his personal feelings, puts him into an absurd situation. He is the tragic protagonist, and the play is his, but his tragedy is presided over by the comic spirit. On that level the play is a masterpiece.

The theme of this play offers an example of Shaw's presentation of love. The honest and level-headed Sir Colenso is made ridiculous by allowing self-interest to influence him because of his infatuation for the wife. She, however, does not deserve him, being so unintelligent that on her artist husband's death she makes a fool of herself by dressing up – to please the dead man, she says!

(6)

Shaw never makes adultery or the eternal triangle a theme. In one of his earliest prefaces, after he had been attacked for his levity about love in *The Philanderer*, he wrote:

> I have a technical objection to making sexual infatuation a tragic theme. Experience proves that it is only effective in the comic spirit. . . . Let realism have its demonstration, comedy its criticism, or even bawdy its horse-laugh at the expense of sexual infatuation, if it must; but to ask us to subject our souls

to its ruinous glamour, to worship it, deify it, as if it alone makes our life worth living, is nothing but folly gone mad critically. . . .

His plays and indeed his other writings show that he was interested in sexuality in its intellectual and comic aspects, for his work never indicates a simple sexual attitude, and there is never anything approaching sensuality. Yet no dramatist was ever more reproached for shameless sensuality as well as heartlessness, which certainly go together.

Shaw's lovers never behave conventionally, but always reveal the peculiarly dangerous relations in which they find themselves. The love that is the play between the sexes is unaccountable, mysterious, irrational in the extreme, offering no basis in its natural aspects for practical life, so that he never glamorizes romantic love. He does not ignore it but is deliberately anti-romantic, laughing at its illusions. He shows the helplessness of those who are possessed by the brevity of passion. He is so candid in his love scenes that it is supposed by superficial readers that he was cold hearted; but examination of these scenes proves him to have been a man not only of exceptional insight but of the deepest feelings. He treats love with the respect of one who realizes its importance, but without false sentiment, or exaggeration, or triviality. He is concerned above all with conscious love. Apart from Shakespeare, there are no love scenes the equivalent of his in the entire range of English drama.

His early comedy *You Never Can Tell* contains what is perhaps Shaw's most characteristic love episode. The impecunious Valentine has fallen hopelessly in love with the lovely Gloria at first sight, and has to tell her so, hating himself for his helplessness:

GLORIA: I wonder what is the scientific explanation of those fancies that cross us occasionally!

VALENTINE: Ah, I wonder! It's a curiously helpless sensation, isn't it?

GLORIA: Helpless?

VALENTINE: Yes, helpless. As if Nature, after letting us belong to ourselves and do what we judged right and reasonable for all these years, were suddenly lifting her great hand to take us – her two little children – by the scruffs of our little necks, and use us, in spite of ourselves, for her own purposes, in her own way.

GLORIA: Isn't that rather fanciful?

VALENTINE: I don't know. I don't care. Oh, Miss Clandon, Miss Clandon: how *could* you?

GLORIA: What have I done?

VALENTINE: Thrown this enchantment on me. I'm honestly trying to be sensible and scientific and everything that you wish me to be. But – but – oh, don't you see what you have set to work in my imagination?

GLORIA: I hope you are not going to be so foolish – so vulgar – as to say love.

VALENTINE: No, no, no, no, no. Not love: we know better than that. Let's call it chemistry. You can't deny that there is such a thing as chemical action, chemical affinity, chemical combination: the most irresistible of all natural forces. Well, you're attracting me irresistibly. Chemically.

GLORIA: [*contemptuously*] Nonsense!

VALENTINE: Of course its nonsense, you stupid girl. Yes, stupid girl: that's a scientific fact, anyhow. You're a prig: a feminine prig: that's what you are. [*Rising*] Now I suppose you've done with me for ever.

So it goes on until:

VALENTINE: Ah, it's come at last: my moment of courage. [*He seizes her hands: she looks at him in terror.*] Our moment of

106

courage! [*He draws her to him; kisses her with impetuous strength; and laughs boyishly.*] Now you've done it, Gloria. It's all over: we're in love with one another.

To suppose from this that Shaw regarded love as mere chemical attraction is, of course, utter nonsense. A one-time not over-enthusiastic admirer of Shaw, A. R. Orage, in an essay 'On Love', first published in 1932, wrote 'Instinctive love has chemistry as its base', no doubt echoing Shaw, but misjudging him. Orage distinguished between instinctive, emotional, and conscious love, pointing out, however, that there are other kinds of love. Shaw's emotional love in this play appears to be instinctive because the hero does not dare to put it on too high a level; as the play proceeds he is shown to be a man of imagination in whom love becomes lyrical ecstasy, and within the limits of his comic situation he attempts to bring it on to the level of conscious love, without, however, fully succeeding. To play the scene from which I have quoted as burlesque, or farcical comedy, is completely to misinterpret it, for Valentine is not laughing at himself but vainly trying to be rational in an irrational situation: a sinking man struggling to save himself. For the actor to laugh at the character is to destroy Shaw's intention, though it is now often done.

Another characteristic love scene is that between Hypatia and Percival in *Misalliance*, with a desperate and excited girl taking the initiative. Tired of good manners, the girl invites the young man, whom she has only just met, to play with her. She makes him realize that he cannot help himself; she will fight like the devil to stop him kissing her, but kiss her he shall. 'Nothing', she says, 'is worth doing unless the consequences may be serious', and she slaps the reluctant man in the face. She is tempting him to be free, and he bolts, she after him. This again is not farcical comedy: it is an operatic duet.

There are in these plays the themes of the relations of husbands and wives, parents and children, and the rapidity with which advanced ideas become out-of-date, these themes being interwoven within the main theme of love. They are both highly skilful pieces of comedy writing.

(7)

In an earlier play, *Arms and the Man*, romantic love and its pretences were contrasted with the practical love of a man of sense, the honours going to the latter. To display idealized love at odds with the love of convenience is a familiar stage theme, but Shaw offers nothing so commonplace. He shows the prettiness but also the hollowness of romance, topples hero and heroine off their pedestals, and replaces self-deception by the genuine thing.

A somewhat similar handling of romance appears in *John Bull's Other Island* where the clever sentimental Irishman is defeated by the cleverer but highly absurd Englishman.

In a later play, *Heartbreak House*, he shows the attainment of conscious love in a girl who passes through emotional love and the love of convenience to spiritual union. This remarkable play, which is rarely produced with its love theme in mind, is one of Shaw's most distinguished works. It offers a number of varieties of love as well as that with which it ends when the heroine finds her 'spiritual husband and second father'. This is not mere comic nonsense but a light if comic touch upon a deep theme.

The play that preceded it, *Pygmalion*, is the second in what may be regarded as a triology of plays upon love. There the hero creates an image that against his will falls in love with him: an artist concentrates upon his task with scientific concentration, and as he thinks complete detachment, to find that the human heart is not only incalculable but has powers beyond his control. The theme is that to leave the human heart out of account is to ruin the worthiest enterprise. This is a comic but touching play in which the pure sentiment is not disguised by the wit.

The plays in which there are variations on the theme of love, with particular applications, are, in addition to *Misalliance*, *Getting Married*, *Fanny's First Play* and *Too True to be Good*.

In one form or another love is present, however, in all the plays, even when not the main theme, and provides evidence of the heart Shaw is said not to possess.

(8)

The six plays on 'high politics' have relation to the three on 'religion' and the three on 'creative evolution'. To Shaw, as to William Blake, religion and politics were one. Creative evolution is concerned with the meaning of life from which the two other themes cannot be disassociated. Shaw's aim as a dramatist from the beginning was to concern himself with contemporary life, its people, its problems and situations, and the condition of mankind. Although he was active in party politics, his interest went far beyond it into politics as relations between people and societies, and in the problems of government in a fundamental sense. He touches upon particular political issues only lightly and devotes himself to what he calls 'navigation', the guidance of the nation, the choosing of rulers, and to the attainment of consciousness to replace the blind and instinctive processes of life. His political plays express in various forms of extravagance the need for political philosophy. *The Apple Cart* is concerned with the absence of political education, *Too True to be Good* with the uselessness of political institutions without purpose, *On the Rocks* with lack of leadership, *The Millionairess* with how to choose leaders, *Geneva* with the challenge of false leadership, and *Good King Charles's Golden Days* with how to decide upon who are fit to choose leaders. Virtually, the single theme is leadership, and the elimination of natural ignorance. Without a captain the ship will go on the rocks (*Heartbreak House*). Shaw's answer is the Platonic one of the education of men capable of self-leadership:

> Until there is an England in which every man is a Cromwell, a Rome in which every man is a Caesar, a Germany in which every man is a Luther plus a Goethe, the world will no be more improved by its heroes than a Brixton villa is improved by the pyramid of Cheops. The predication of such a nation is the only real change possible to us.

He was no more in favour of dictators than of romantic heroes, and his praise of Fascist and Soviet leaders was the outcome of exasperated impatience with our pretended democracy: he would have neither the dictatorship of the proletariat nor that of the trade unions in a general strike. His political doctrine was 'the sacred mystery of equality', which he applied in the proposal for equality of incomes; but he derided the idea that every man's vote was of equal value.

Essentially, Shaw was no politician, however, for politics are the short view, while Shaw's was a long view. For that reason, his frequent excursions into practical politics were usually unhappy for those concerned. These plays all treat of the condition of civilization as a philosopher and artist must see it. To Shaw, politics were a means of furthering a new culture for human evolution.

(9)

This brings us to the three religious plays, and the three on creative evolution. We cannot expect to find Shaw a systematic philosopher, though the fact seems to surprise some critics who forget that the functions of artist and academic philosopher are not identical. He had philosophical ideas, but was a comic genius, and to expect to find a worked out philosophical system in the plays of comic genius is folly. It can be argued that philosophically he was Platonic in his insistence on the art of navigation, in particular in his pre-occupation with the question of how rulers should be chosen, and in emphasis upon the importance of education, to which he gave a wide interpretation, not finding much value in schools and schoolmasters, but agreeing with Plato that the mind must be taught 'to look straight at reality'. Shaw's philosophical ideas were essentially religious, that is to say they were given practical (and dramatic) expression in conscience and individual life.

The Shewing-up of Blanco Posnet (1909) shows how the sudden idea of a purpose beyond oneself interferes with a worthless man's life: a man who has 'gone west' in both the literal and the moral sense discovers his real self to his own astonishment. *Androcles and the Lion* (1911–12) is a picture of Christians thrown to the lions by the Romans for the sake of their faith, and how simple faith saves them. The theme of *Saint Joan* (1923) is 'it was never "I say so"; but "God says so".'

These are emotionally moving plays, easy to quarrel with, but each a dramatic masterpiece in its own right. But a religious content is found throughout his work from the gentle mysticism of Keegan in *John Bull's Other Island* to the remarkable affirmations of Isaac Newton in *In Good King Charles's Golden Days*. The latter play contains the most deeply religious declaration of Shaw's long career. Newton is talking with the artist Kneller who says with contempt that to the scientist 'the universe is merely but a clock'. Newton's reply is:

Shall I tell you a secret, Mr Beautymonger? The clock does not keep time. If it did there would be no further need for the Clockmaker. He is wiser than to leave us to our foolish selves in that fashion. When He made a confusion of languages to prevent the Tower of Babel from reaching to heaven He also contrived a confusion of time to prevent us from wholly doing without Him. The sidereal clock, the clock of the universe, goes wrong. . . . But I do not know what is amiss with it. Not until the world finds this out can it do without the Clockmaker in the heavens who can set the hands back or forward, and move the stars with a touch of His almighty finger, as He watches over us in the heavens.

The rhythm of the dialogue and its emotional content lifts this play into the realm of poetry. The 'almighty finger' which will not leave us alone is the profoundest of religious conceptions. Here Shaw declares himself not only on the side of the artists, 'You and God are both artists', but on the side of those whose understanding of life is spiritual.

Shaw discussed Christianity in many plays, and asked 'Why not give Christianity a trial?' In the preface to *On the Rocks* there is a remarkable dialogue between Jesus Christ and Pilate, which is a plea for tolerance, another aspect of Shaw's belief in equality: tolerance being liberty in practice, respecting truth in others, having the courage of the truth one sees oneself.

(10)

But as religion always means a particular religion, and as the particular religion for Shaw as contained in the Christian Church had too many features that offended him, he attached himself to the doctrine of Creative Evolution, which he called a religion, though it had no Church. With that subject two of his longest works are concerned, *Man and Superman*, in which the Nietzschean idea of the Superman becomes the eternal purpose to which man must give himself, and *Back to Methuselah*, a herculean work of five plays in one, in which he attempts to consider human life as the expression of the will to create, through which man could make himself anew. Finally, a shortish piece *The Simpleton of the Unexpected Isles*, a difficult play to which little justice has hitherto been done, suggests that the reasonable life for man is to live in the world as on an unexpected isle, ready for anything, treating every day as a judgment day.

He called *Man and Superman* 'a comedy and a philosophy'. The entire work is an exposition of the idea of the Life Force, expressed in the comedy in the eternal chase of man by woman to create a better mankind, and more profoundly in the 'Don Juan' episode in Hell, which is a plea for the extension of consciousness in men so that we may choose to do 'the world's will, not our own'. Shaw's Life Force, or world will, is the creativeness of life in the Bergsonian sense: spiritual energy – moral passion, Shaw called it. It is the idea of God depending on man to get his work done, which gives human life meaning. It is expressed in noble words in the play. When the Devil sneers at Don Juan's notion of purpose, the latter exclaims:

Were I not possessed with a purpose beyond my own I had better be a ploughman than a philosopher; for the ploughman lives as long as the philosopher; eats more, sleeps better, and rejoices in the wife of his bosom with less misgiving. This is because the philosopher is in the grip of the Life Force. This Life Force says to him 'I have done a thousand wonderful things unconsciously by merely willing to live and following the line of least resistance; now I want to know myself and my destination, and choose my path; so I have made a special brain – a philosopher's brain – to grasp this knowledge for me as the husbandman's hand grasps the plough for me. And this', says the Life Force to the philosopher, 'must thou strive to do for me until thou diest, when I will make another brain and another philosopher to carry on the work.'

'What is the use of knowing?' asks the Devil, to which Don Juan replies:

> Why, to be able to choose the line of greatest advantage instead of yielding in the direction of the least resistance. Does a ship sail to its destination no better than a log drifts nowhither? The philosopher is Nature's pilot. And there you have our difference: to be in hell is to drift: to be in heaven is to steer.

Shaw complained later on that 'nobody noticed the new religion in the centre of the intellectual whirlpool' of this play. But the special characteristic of Shaw's comedy has always been ignored, that it is the point of view of one who deplores the misuse men and women make of their possibilities in personal and social relations and their lack of conscience. To listen to Shaw is not merely to be amused, but to realize that we neglect at our peril the demands made by Creative Evolution, which he calls Nature in this play, but has no objection to others calling God.

In the long preface to *Back to Methuselah* Shaw says that his natural function as an artist was as 'an iconographer of the religion of my time'. He went on:

> I had always known that Civilization needs a religion as a matter of life and death; and as the conception of Creative Evolution developed I saw that we were at last within reach of a faith which complied with the first condition of all religions that have ever taken hold of humanity: namely, that it must be, first and fundamentally, a science of metabiology.

This 'masterpiece', as Shaw called it himself, is one of the few that needs the reading of the preface fully to appreciate it. Although, of his plays in general, I sometimes think it would have been better for their reception as dramatic works had he not written the prefaces, I take the contrary view of this play, for here play and preface are one. Not only the original preface should be read but the Postscript to the 1944 edition of the play included in the Worlds Classics edition. He wrote that postscript as 'in the vein of apology and explanation rather than a fanfare of brazen exultation'. It is one of the most touching things that ever came from him, because despite what he had put into the play he was unsure of it. He was right to be unsure, for, masterpiece as it truly is, it exhibits his weaknesses, his verbosity, his mischievousness, his deliberate banality, and, what was new, his disregard of form. Indeed, the play's fundamental weakness is that it has no protagonist.

He said that in writing it 'I threw over all economic considerations', which applies not only to its inordinate length, but to the practical problems of production, for the play cannot be divided into convenient lengths. All the same it is an astonishing work in conception, and it is possible that the nineteen-twenties could not provide the ideal audience for it; perhaps a later time will be able to interpret the play in its own intellectual terms more fully. I think that the play will increase rather than decline in meaning and that what now seems trivial and merely journalistic will show a different aspect to our grandchildren.

That a man should consciously live as an 'instrument of a Will or Life Force that uses him for purposes wider than his own' (*Major Barbara*, 1905), is, as I say, always his leading idea. The 'Life Force (often called the Will of God)' (*Misalliance*, 1910), 'the Life Force (or whatever you choose to call it) cannot be finally beaten by any failure, and it will even supersede humanity by evolving a higher species if we cannot master the problems raised by the multiplication of our own numbers' (*Androcles and the*

Lion, 1916). He was against natural selection as a basis for social and political action, the doctrine our 'anarchist Liberal' teachers seek to impose. Shaw was, of course, by no means against science as a habit of mind, a method, whose aim is truth, but he opposed the assumption that mechanistic determination was the law of life for man. He said:

> Impostor for impostor, I prefer the mystic to the scientist – the man who at least has the decency to call his nonsense a mystery, to him who pretends that it is ascertained, weighed, measured, analysed fact.

Yet Shaw did not penetrate to the mystery of perfection in union with God. Man had, he said, to create God, which perhaps meant to create God in himself, to bring the unconscious life force in himself to consciousness. Shaw, however, would not contemplate a perfect Creator as responsible for imperfect man, and his enthusiasm was for the human creative effort towards perfection. Such was his sense of the great value in human life. It caused him to support the artist and his creative work against all dogmas, whether those of scientists, religionist, or rationalist. He believed in free inquiry, and in the possibilities of conscious design, and urged that men should take responsibility for their own future. For 'human perfection', he declared through Don Juan, 'men will die', or, to go back to one of his earliest works, though not a play, he said, in *The Sanity of Art* (1895), that men must be got 'to look life straight in the face, and see in it, not the fulfilment of a moral law or of the deductions of reason, but the satisfaction of a passion in us of which we can give no rational account whatever'.

These ideas were not original and to take them as seriously as they deserve does not depend upon thinking that they were. He found some part of the confirmation of them, if not their inspiration, in the fundamental ideas of the German natural philosopher Lorenz Oken, to whom he refers in the preface to *Back to Methuselah*. Shaw appears to have learnt of Oken through the reference to him in August Weismann's *History of Evolution*, which had been translated by J. Arthur Thomson in 1909. Weismann was a thorough-going Darwinian, and Shaw was arguing against him. Oken, born in Baden in 1779, was a remarkable man, a scientist who found in the human skull the forms of the human body. Weismann dismisses him, with some uneasiness, for 'want of moderation'. Oken defined natural science as 'the science of the everlasting transmutations of God (the Spirit) in the world'. This quotation fired the imagination of Shaw though not, apparently, to the extent of his getting further acquainted with Oken's work, which would have corrected his errors; but only one volume of Oken, entitled *Elements of Physiophilosophy*, has been translated into English (in 1847). In that book Oken declared that 'the whole animal Kingdom is none other than the representation of the several activities or organs of Man; naught else than Man disintegrated . . . . Man is the entire image or likeness of the world. His language is the spirit of the world. All the functions of animals have attained unto unity, unto self-consciousness in Man.' Whether Shaw had read those words or not, I do not know; but they might serve as a text for what he wrote himself.

(11)

Because their themes are of eternal interest his plays go beyond the merely comic. They do not end in a joke but in a vision of life, so that we do more than smile when we see them. 'Though my trade is that of a playwright, my vocation is that of a prophet', he said in 1932. Because he is a prophet he is the dramatist of the future. What we see in his plays is a mind at work, a mind that

117

grasped what it set out to do, and had the lucidity and discipline, the generative power and technical skill, to accomplish it. What T. S. Eliot put forward as characteristic of Shakespeare, that his work was '*one* poem', is true also of Shaw, his plays as a whole are one play; and what Mr Eliot formulates as the condition of Shakespeare's greatness, that we feel his work 'to be united by one significant, consistent, and developing personality',[1] may equally be said of Shaw. 'I believe in the life to come!' says Anna in *Man and Superman*. Shaw announced the future which is a reason to suppose that his plays will endure; for by the words of the prophets men live! He spoke for those yet unborn in whom the new man and the new society will be affirmed as he affirmed it. 'Is *No* enough?' he asks in his play of prophecy, *Too True to be Good*. The answer is 'For a boy, yes; for a man, never'.

[1] *Selected Essays* (1932), p. 203.

IV. The Characters

When critics have said of the characters in Shaw's plays that they are versions of himself they have been paying him unconscious tribute, for they show perception of the unity of his work. Without the unity produced by an artist's energy and vision his work is partial and elementary, and however large in quantity falls short of greatness. Unity, however, is not sameness; and to say that Shaw's characters lack diversity, which is what the critics referred to mean, or to say that he repeats the same character over and over again, is untrue, while to accept Archibald Henderson's remark that Shaw in his character drawing was 'playing ventriloquist' is to be blind and deaf at once. He ridiculed this idea when he made Vaughan the critic say in the Prologue to *Fanny's First Play*:

> Well, at all events, you can't deny that the characters in this play are quite distinguishable from one another. That proves it's not by Shaw, because all Shaw's characters are himself: mere puppets stuck up to spout Shaw. It's only the actors that make them seem different.

The puppet Shaw stuck up for public entertainment was the G.B.S. he manipulated to draw attention to his work and to other matters in which he was interested. But as he never mistook this character to be himself, so he never introduced it as a character into any of his plays. Of course, every artist puts himself into his work, every painter and sculptor, as well as every playwright, but Shaw was an exceptionally conscious man: in his life he was wholly himself, and the characters he created were equally wholly themselves.

An outstanding characteristic is, as Desmond MacCarthy said, 'the exceptional variety and vividness of his characters'. Shaw had the insight to enter into the minds of people, to grasp their points of view, and to objectify them in the expression of their personalities, which accounts for the wide range of his characters. He declared, himself, over and over again, that he always started with people. Yet he did not take actual people as models, any more than he took the situations of actual life, but conceived original characters who created their own situations. As Coleridge said of Shakespeare, Shaw drew his characters from observation but they were the fruits of 'meditation'. He was not concerned to put upon the stage men and women in their lives of weakness, confusion and commonness, or natural life in its monotony, but living people in their hidden selves, displayed in the bright hues of their masked absurdities. He was deeply interested in people for their own sakes, and intended that his characters should speak for themselves. That explains why it is often possible to hear a character present an argument against what is assumed to be Shaw's own point of view with utterly unprejudiced freedom.

That is why, too, Shaw's themes are always inseparable from his characters. To quote Coleridge once again, one of the characteristics of Shakespeare as dramatist was that 'interest in the plot is always in fact on account of the characters', which can be said with equal truth of Shaw. His plots are no more than scaffolding from which the characters, no less than the themes, become independent in the completed work.

In the variety of his characters, MacCarthy likened Shaw to Charles Dickens, and what is true of Dickens, that his characters are his own, such as no other novelist could create, can also be said of Shaw. Not one of his characters could be in any other play than his. Furthermore, each character belongs to the play in which he or she appears. There are likenesses, as between Broadbent, Undershaft and Tarleton, each being given to talking at length, yet not one of these three could be mistaken for the other, or could appear in any play but that to which he belongs. The same is true of Shaw's clergymen, Morell, Anderson and the Bishop of Chelsea; also of his artists, Marchbanks, Cusins, and Dubedat; even of his low comedy characters, Burgess, Doolittle, and the Burglar. His women, too, are equally well individualized: Mrs Warren, Candida, Lady Cicely, Ann, Major Barbara, Eliza, Hesione Hushaby and Epifania Fitzfassenden, to name but a few, could never be mistaken for one another.

(2)

The above characters are chosen at random, but a dramatist stands or falls by his central characters or protagonists, while not all the names I have given come within that category. It is noteworthy that in praising Shaw's characters Desmond MacCarthy refers to Prossy, Broadbent, Straker, Ann, and B B, not one of whom is the central character in the play in which he or she appears. Each of these characters deserves praise, for Shaw could create admirable secondary characters, as can all good dramatists, but genius resides in the leading characters. Shaw lives by virtue of Bluntschli, Marchbanks, Valentine, Larry, Jack Tanner, Major Barbara, and Saint Joan, as Shakespeare lives by Petruchio, Proteus, Berowne, Rosalind, Viola, Helena and Leontes, to mention only the comedies.

It is true that in every play the central or leading character must have one other character, even more than one, who can meet him, or her, as an equal, a person with whom there must be the clash that creates drama. It is also true that sometimes this other character may be so sympathetic to the dramatist, or so interesting in himself, that he may be drawn larger than the protagonist, as in Shakespeare's *Merchant of Venice*, where Shylock became a more fascinating figure than the Merchant, and in the *Henry IV* plays where Falstaff is the favourite; so in Shaw's *John Bull's Other Island*, the Irish Larry is overshadowed by Broadbent, and in *Heartbreak House* the young Ellie appears insignificant beside Hesione Hushaby, to say nothing of the overpowering Shotover. It none the less remains true that without a sufficiently strong, interesting, and well presented protagonist, a play contains elements of confusion and loses its full effect. That is to be said of the plays mentioned, high as they stand in the catalogue of both dramatists' works.

(3)

The leading characters in the plays of every dramatist are necessarily of great interest to himself, being concerned with a situation that he finds significant, and to that extent are in a fundamental sense versions of himself. That can be said of Brutus, Hamlet, Lear, Macbeth and Coriolanus, and also of Marchbanks, Larry, Valentine, Tanner, and Higgins. As Shakespeare's leading characters were aspects of himself as he appeared to himself, so were Shaw's.

That is not to say that the dramatist is involved in his characters, as the critic I referred to at the opening of this chapter wrongly supposed. Shakespeare's and Shaw's characters are not to be identified with the dramatists; for both dramatists detached themselves from their characters. Shakespeare set his characters free; and although it is right to acknowledge the presence of Hamlet or Macbeth in Shakespeare, to create an image of Shakespeare out of Hamlet or Macbeth is impossible, for once these characters exist in imaginary being the creator is no longer involved. He gets rid of the problems of Hamlet or Macbeth in himself in the creation of the character and the resolution of his problem, in exactly the same way as may the audience when participating in the performance of the play. Shakespeare did not suffer with his tragic heroes, for he was not attached to them. Neither did Shaw, having projected the comic situation of his heroes, suffer the comic consequences of their follies. In this respect Dickens identified himself with his creations and suffered accordingly. That perhaps explains why Dickens was never able to write a satisfactory play.

Thus we can accept each protagonist, with the characters who appear with him, as the presentation under the discipline of dramatic action of a problem of conscience, or personal relations, or social difficulty, set in a situation of emotional tension. The drama is in the spiritual conflict as the protagonist not only experiences but perceives it. A protagonist who is not aware of his situation is no protagonist at all, but the helpless instrument of story telling. As Shaw's plays are comedies, the situation is reflected upon by the Comic Muse in the person of the protagonist, and the conflict is perceived by an eye that pierces into, and a mind that interprets, as well as by a heart that feels, the comic element. The first quality of the comic spirit is perception, not merely the clarity of vision upon which Shaw prided himself, but perception by all the senses of the body and all the powers of mind and heart.

Because of the nature of drama, we should note that no character appears in the play as he (or she) is in himself, only as the protagonist presents him (or her). Even the protagonist is presented as he appears to himself, not as he really is, or as he is seen by others. To recognize this is of the utmost importance in considering Shaw's characters, or, indeed, the characters in any drama. Therefore, to discuss the characters without regard to the concentration with which they are presented, under the limitations in which they exist, is to be in danger of misunderstanding them.

The dramatic art is not the representation of actuality (or the thing in its natural self), but the representation of images in a vision (or, as Shakespeare said, in a mirror), the vision being the dramatist's in the first place, projected in the light of the play through the eye of the protagonist.

To compare one character with another (a favourite occupation of critics), as, for instance, to compare Marchbanks in *Candida* with Octavius in *Man and Superman*, and to draw the conclusion that the one character is a version of the other is to be absurd. Marchbanks exists in relation to his own situation, and is seen through his own eyes, while Octavius exists in his relation to Tanner, and exists through Tanner's eyes. Even though two characters may have been supposed to have had the same model, they are necessarily different beings in different plays. What I am trying to make clear is my view that the characters in Shavian drama are drawn by the dramatist in relation to the theme of a particular play and to the protagonist in that play. They do not stand on their own feet as beings in the round (as it is said), and while the dramatist gives them verisimilitude, in which he is aided by the actor, their visionary nature is their true nature. This applies as much to Shakespeare's characters as to Shaw's. I have something to say about each of the characters of the plays in Part Three of this book, and I wish now to consider further certain of their general characteristics.

(4)

The world of Bernard Shaw has a large place for women. He honoured women, showing in his plays that they were not only to be loved, but respected, even feared. Life with women was as large a subject to him as religion. Though his love scenes burst with emotion he tended always to intellectualize sexual relations, and approached emotion as though it needed to be intellectually experienced. By that I do not mean that he rationalized sex. On the contrary, he emphasized its irrationality. Sex as a natural force is capable of rational explanation, but, as Shaw well knew, its expression in experience is beyond rational control. Therefore it has to be approached with respect. That is why sex is never given frivolous treatment in his plays. It is a natural force of such power, so fundamental to the life of man, that while leading men into comic situations and having its comic aspects, it needs to be illuminated for man's salvation with the light of intelligence. A programme note upon the Don Juan in Hell episode when it was first performed at the Court Theatre in 1907 is worth recalling in this connection:

Dona Anna, being a woman, is incapable both of the Devil's utter damnation and of Don Juan's complete supersensuality. As the mother of many children she has shared in the dawn travail, and with care and labour and suffering renewed the harvest of external life; but the honour and divinity of her works have been jealously hid from her by Man, who, dreading her domination, has offered her for reward only the satisfaction of her services and affections. She cannot, like the male Devil, use love as mere sentiment and pleasure; nor can she, like the male saint, put love aside when it has once done its work as a developing and enlightening experience. Love is neither her pleasure nor her study; it is her business. So she, in the end, neither goes with Don Juan to heaven nor with the Devil and her father to the palace of pleasure, but declares that her work is not yet finished. For though by her death she is done with the bearing of men to mortal fathers, she may yet, as Woman Immortal, bear the Superman to the Eternal Father.

Shaw put the women in his plays on a pedestal with full consciousness that he was doing so, and why. They had to be adored for the sake of the race, and love too must be lifted on to the plane of consciousness for the sake of the future. There is a significant speech in *Heartbreak House*, when Ellie's father says, 'You see, I have been in love really; the sort of love that only happens once. That's why Ellie is such a lovely girl.' In his love scenes, notably in *You Never Can Tell*, *Man and Superman*, and *The Apple Cart*, Shaw says what no other dramatist has said, displaying the anatomy of love. Instead of supposing that he lacked a human heart, it would be nearer the truth to say that he had excess of it. That, indeed, was one of his weaknesses, for he dared not trust his heart. He intellectualized passion so as to bring it into the light of intellect. Higgins in *Pygmalion* represents at least one aspect of Shaw's attitude to emotion, which was to appear oblivious of its existence for the sake of self-protection.

(5)

A further aspect of this attitude to women is that few of Shaw's plays are based upon or take their themes from family life and the home. *The Devil's Disciple* shows a son's revolt against a disagreeable home; in *Too True to be Good* a daughter escapes from a domineering mother in a dream-delirium; in *Candida* the young children are left by their mother at the seaside; and in *Heartbreak House* there is no sign of Hesione's young children. Only in *Candida*, *Misalliance*, *Fanny's First Play* and *Buoyant Billions* is the action set firmly in a home provided by a woman. Candida's home, however, the poet abhors; *Misalliance* is preceded by a long Treatise on Parents and Children; and the Tarleton's is the comfortable home of a rich man, with a daughter looking for adventure, which she has no hope of finding there: it is a picture of a commonplace domesticity tolerable to the outsider. *Fanny's First Play* is essentially a domestic piece, with two ordinary tradesmen's homes, but, again, there is a son in revolt in one and a daughter in the other. The very late *Buoyant Billions* presents two wealthy homes, one with a 'post-Atomist' son bent on world betterment, discarding his father and home; the other with a daughter, who escapes to the jungle, but returns to get married and to be a 'working bee'. Neither of these homes contains a mother, and it seems that Shaw's attitude to the home is equivocal and uneasy.

His most interesting reference to the family is contained in *The Simpleton of the Unexpected Isles* where a young clergyman sets up a household with two sisters, themselves the products of a group marriage, which brings upon the island a United Nations' attack to reform his morals. The theme of group marriage is not made explicit, though it is unmistakably there. Shaw makes the Day of Judgment itself the prominent theme, the end of the world's childhood, and the beginning of its responsible maturity, so that 'We shall have to justify our existence or perish', but the group marriage, treated only symbolically, is introduced for more than a comic complication of the situation. In the 'eugenic experiment', as Shaw called it, he was implicitly forecasting something beyond our present form of marriage.

(6)

It is noteworthy that it is the women who usually take the initiative in Shavian drama, not only in love but in everything else. They are the driving force. The most remarkable in this respect is Epifania Fitzfassenden, the millionairess trained as a boxer, for she is always ready to take chances and to venture, which Shaw regards as one of the greatest of human qualities. It is this apparently mannish but essentially feminine woman, who speaks of 'the infinitely dangerous heart tearing everchanging life of adventure that we call marriage'. This woman, 'ensnaring the mate chosen for her by Allah', is the type of all Shaw's women from Blanche to Clementine Buoyant. In that sense all his women are one woman.

Yet only in that sense; for the variety of Shaw's women characters is astonishing, all impelled by passion of one kind or another: from Blanche in *Widowers' Houses*, and Julia in *The Philanderer*, to Orinthia in *The Apple Cart* – there are abundant examples of the passion of love, but as different from each other as women could be. Vivie in *Mrs Warren's Profession*, Major Barbara, Lina in *Misalliance*, Lavinia in *Androcles and the Lion*, and Saint Joan, represent another kind of passion, the passion for conscience, for work, for a cause, for God. There are, however, other women such as Mrs Warren, Lady Cecily, Mrs Clandon, Lady Britomart, Mrs Tarleton, Lady Utterword, and Queen Catherine of Braganza who belong to the world, and Candida who belongs to herself. Such a gallery of remarkable women does not exist in the works of any other modern dramatist.

(7)

Without attempting even to look at, far less to examine, all the various types of characters in the plays, reference must be made to Shaw's clergymen, priests, and religious men, for there are many of them, mostly members of the Church of England, though there are Catholic priests, other orders of priests, and a sky-pilot. With one exception, all are treated with respect and allowed their say. The exception is the Rev Samuel Gardner in the early *Mrs Warren's Profession*, who is a thoroughly objectionable clergyman. When Shaw next drew a clergyman it was the Rev James Morell, in *Candida*, with his young curate, Rev Lexy Mill, both presented sympathetically, with humour and made ridiculous, but there is no malice. In *John Bull's Other Island* the mystical ex-priest Peter Keegan is one of his best characters, so is the Bishop of Chelsea in *Getting Married*; and Father Anthony in the same play is allowed to expound the Church's doctrine of holy matrimony. The Anglican Bishop in *Geneva* is made a comic official figure, but in one of the last plays, *In Good King Charles's Golden Days*, there is the unforgettable George Fox.

It is of course in *Saint Joan* that a very full gallery of ecclesiastical characters appears, in which Shaw attempts to do justice to points of view that conflict, harmonize, and together maintain a pattern of discussion upon the highest level. He had models in the documents for these characters, but he brought them to life and made them real men.

Elder Daniels in *The Shewing-up of Blanco Posnet* and the Elder and sky-pilot in *Too True to be Good* are three religious men of another sort. There are many others, enough to show that Shaw did not ignore those whose office it is to instruct and enlighten other men; his treatment of them proves the wideness of his interests, to say nothing of what he considered to come within the comic sphere. In every instance he allows them to express themselves in the intonations and accents proper to them, each is drawn in utter conscientiousness, and each contributes to the beauty of the drama, a beauty that arises out of lightness and clear vision.

(8)

Here we may raise specifically the question of the extent to which Shaw modelled his characters on particular persons, or repeated in an episode in a play something that occurred in actual life. As I have said, all such questions should be regarded as irrelevant. Shaw may have said that he based Blanche in *Widowers' Houses* upon Florence Farr, or that he took an episode in *The Philanderer* from a personal experience, or the character Cusins in *Major Barbara* from Dr Gilbert Murray, or Dubedat in *The Doctor's Dilemma* from Edward Aveling, or one of the doctors in that play from a distinguished physician, but all such likenesses are misleading. He certainly must have allowed a hint from an experience of certain characteristics in a person to influence him, but no more. To suppose that he repeated in *The Apple Cart* an episode from his love affair with Mrs Patrick Campbell is nonsense. A play cannot repeat life. If it pretends to do so it is false. Art is not life, but an image of what is in the artist's mind as he contemplates life. The truth in art is in fidelity to the image. Shaw often spoke about vision, and claimed that he had normal sight, that is to say that he saw with clarity. What he put into his plays, however, was not what his clear natural eyes saw, but the image as it appeared to his inner eye. There are analogies between Shaw as a man, the characters he created, and the plays he wrote, as there were, too, between Ibsen's life and plays, but to attempt to understand or interpret the plays of either dramatist by searching for incidents in the life of the man is fruitless. Greatness in a dramatist as in every artist depends upon non-identification with his work and experiences. I think Shaw's plays, and in particular the characters in his plays, show that he possessed that quality of greatness. His characters were not himself nor actual people as he or anyone saw them, but creatures of the imagination.

No doubt some day in the future a research scholar will identify many if not all of the characters in the plays with friends and acquaintances of Shaw and other people of his time. It will be a very large field of study, but the results will have no more significance for students of the plays than the similar studies that have been made of Shakespeare. The same may be said of the study of allegorical meanings and parallels in classical myths in the names of characters. That Shaw was interested in names there can be no doubt, for he was interested in words as such, and he has many comical names of characters. He even once referred to himself as 'Shoddy' when there is talk in *Back to Methuselah* of 'an ancient writer whose name has come down to us in several forms as Shakespear, Shelley, Sheridan, and Shoddy'.

(9)

A similar comment must be made upon the plays Shaw is said to have written for particular players. A dramatist may have a player in mind for a character as he is writing a play, but that is not the same as drawing a character for the player, as Shaw said he wrote Napoleon in *The Man of Destiny* for Henry Irving, or the Lady in that play for Ellen Terry. Indeed, he said many times that when he thought of characters and started them in a play he did not know what was going to happen. What Shaw said about a character was usually intended to flatter the player, and when others say he wrote for one or another actor the statement should be taken with a pinch of salt. Twice he did, undoubtedly, write for an actor as *Caesar and Cleopatra* for Forbes-Robertson, and *Captain Brassbound's Conversion* for Ellen Terry, but it was at the expense of his gifts as a dramatist, for the plays were obviously weakened by it. Shaw was always much concerned about the relations between dramatists and actors, and wrote well upon the subject in the chapter he contributed to the memoirs of Herbert Beerbohm Tree (reprinted in *Pen Portraits and Reviews*). The dramatist must, he said, 'assume an executant who can perform and sustain certain physical feats of deportment, and build up vocal climaxes with his voice through a long crescendo of rhetoric. Further, he assumes the possession of an English voice and an English feeling for splendour of language and rhythm of verse.'

(10)

These words indicate how he looked upon his dialogue, and how he intended the actor to treat it. A play depends upon the manner in which the characters are enabled by the actors to express their individuality in the relation each has to the dramatic action. They have to appear to be freed, but are not, for each is held very firmly: I mean both characters and actors. No dramatist, except Shakespeare, ever held his characters more firmly in hand than Shaw. A play is dialogue, and the actor is held by means of the word. Shaw's dialogue is allusive, jesting, generalizing yet visual, with rhythms akin to verse rather than to prose; it often has long periods, and always a sense of climax. His models were the James I Bible and John Bunyan. His dialogue is rhetorical because rhetoric is the art of speech, and Shaw wrote words to be spoken. He always had the actor in mind, heard the words spoken and saw the actor as he wrote. The object of rhetoric is to give form to speech, also to give it energy, to enable the speaker to make his speech shapely and to achieve its end. 'Energy', said William Blake, one of Shaw's admired poets, 'is Eternal Delight': this delight gives the tune to Shaw's words.

Shakespeare wrote in the manner of his time with metaphor and ornament, with images and phantasy, with quibbles and puns; his blank verse contained the action of the play, and his prose had poetic rhythms. Shaw's dialogue was that of common speech, selected, heightened, never naturalistic, always given the form and individual qualities of his genius. He employed a wide range of analogies and illustrations from history, literature, music, painting and daily life. It does exactly what he set out to do.

(11)

Yet there never was a dramatist who allowed his characters more freedom. They so take charge of the situation that his manipulation does not appear. When he professed to be indifferent to plot, and to start with the characters, that is to say what I am saying, that the plot did not determine the characters' behaviour or take away the freedom of their actions, any more than Darwin's natural selection reduces human freedom in general. The shape of the play came from the human personalities in it. For this reason

Shaw's characters are of the essence of his plays, and to study the characters, and the direction of their thoughts and actions, is to arrive at the dramatic action. We cannot fail to notice, as a matter of detail, their demeanour, which is always well-mannered.

Because it involves paying attention to the characters, comedy is much harder upon the audience than tragedy, unless made very light, or given the mechanical form of farce. Farce is all plot. The light comedy of our time is easy enough, for it depends mainly on plot, and keeps only on the skirts of true comedy. The naturalistic story-telling, which now occupies much of our stage, is another matter; often called comedy, it is nothing of the kind. Shaw made his comedy as easy for the audience as possible by using the tricks of low comedy to a surprising degree.

What he once said of Ibsen (not thinking of comedy when he said it) can be applied to his own plays, that their enjoyment 'is a question of strength of mind'. Unless the spectator comes to Shaw's plays with his mind, he will not enjoy them in the way Shaw intended. As an old man he warned his readers:

> Please do not think you can take in the work of my long life-time at one reading. You must make it your practice to read all my works at least twice over every year for ten years or so.

(12)

Shaw is a dangerous dramatist to imitate, as many young playwrights have discovered; as dangerous as Shakespeare. To follow his paradoxical treatment of situation, his lightness and inconsequence, his rhetorical style, even his verbosity, without the essential form and substance, and without observing the fundamental dramatic principle, is to court disaster. To build up their own characters on his characters as some playwrights have attempted is to reduce their work to nothing.

V. The Prefaces

As the published versions of Shaw's plays contain prefaces whose popularity is only less than the plays themselves, and as there are people who say that the prefaces are to be preferred to the plays, a short note upon them is required. In the collected *Prefaces by Bernard Shaw* published in 1938, Shaw explained clearly in an Introduction why they were written:

> I hope it is not necessary for me to remind critics unversed in literary tradition that the prefaces to my plays have nothing to do with the theatre. Most of them were written long after the plays to which they are attached had been repeatedly performed. The practice of weighting volumes of plays with political and philosophical disquisitions dates back to Dryden; and I have kept it up in a simple desire to give my customers good value for their money by eking out a pennorth of play with a pound of preface.

He published his plays in the first instance because the theatre would not have them and made them tolerable for reading by lengthy and highly interesting descriptions of the stage settings and the characters; the prefaces were added for the sake of the reader. These were, he said, 'a series of pamphlets and essays on current political and social problems'. He said explicitly that they 'have nothing to do with the theatre', and it is true that if one looks at a preface with the object of getting an introduction to the play one is generally disappointed.

There are a few exceptions. The preface to *Widowers' Houses*, written after the play had been performed in 1893, contains an explanation of how the play came to be written, with an Appendix addressed to the dramatic critics who had attacked the play and the author, and another containing references to correspondence about the play. Also in 1898 when he came to publish *Plays Unpleasant* and *Plays Pleasant* he attached prefaces to the two volumes presenting the plays to the reader in more or less the conventional manner. When, however, two years later, he published *Three Plays for Puritans*, the first of the polemical essays appeared of a kind that was afterwards attached to most of the plays. These prefaces were on politics, doctors, parents and children, religion, marriage, science, the censorship and other subjects. The longest is the preface to *Androcles and the Lion*, which takes ninety-nine pages, the subject being Christianity, the next longest is the preface to *The Doctor's Dilemma*, which has seventy-seven pages 'On Doctors'. Although these prefaces, and many others, have some relation to the plays, they are independent of them. *Man and Superman* has a thirty-page epistle dedicatory, and, following the play, *The Revolutionist's Handbook*, a treatise of fifty-six pages referred to as the work of the leading character. His last volume contains his last long preface of thirty-six pages to the thirty-page piece, *Far Fetched Fables*, written at the age of ninety-two. All this was done in each instance for the sake of making a saleable book, and in this Shaw was undoubtedly successful, for it made the volumes admirable reading. No other dramatist has ever equalled him in this respect.

I do not propose to discuss the prefaces, for those that deal with plays are self-explanatory, and the others would lead us away from the subject of this book. Yet no view of Shaw's work as a whole can be taken without reference to them, for they are among his most important writings, and can be read with almost as much enjoyment today as when they were first written.

In their own kind, nobody has done better polemical writing, neither Swift, nor Defoe, nor Cobbett. Indeed, mention of Defoe leads one to say that, leaving the plays out of account, Shaw is possibly the nearest approach in English literature to Daniel Defoe. In inventiveness of mind, the variety and vitality of his writing, in journalistic skill, and in his challenging outlook on affairs, Shaw is very close indeed to Defoe in at least some respects. Both had a Protestant upbringing, which they never forgot, and both owed much to the Bible. Both had immense intelligence and outspokenness, and wrote with gusto. Both wrote into his old age. Defoe, too, could write excellent dialogue, though he was no dramatist.

To say, however, that the prefaces are superior to the plays is to take an untenable position. Some people might argue that Defoe, or Swift, or Cobbett wrote better than Shaw in his prefaces. It can hardly, however, be argued that anyone, apart from Shakespeare, was a better dramatist in the English language than Shaw.

A Note on Printing the Plays

The first of Bernard Shaw's plays to be printed was his first, *Widowers' Houses*, published the year after its first performance, in 1893, by Henry & Co, otherwise J. T. Grein, who had been responsible for its production. There was no further printing of the plays until Grant Richards published *Plays Pleasant and Unpleasant* in two volumes in 1898. These two volumes had taken a long time to prepare, for, under the typographical influence of William Morris and Emery Walker, Shaw had developed very definite ideas about how he wanted his plays printed. He had been recommended by Sidney Webb to entrust the work to R. & R. Clark Ltd of Edinburgh, and Grant Richards, anxious to have Shaw in his first list of authors, went to them; Shaw insisting, however, upon a fair wages clause in the printing contract. He had the books set by hand in Caslon, long primer, solid; italics in the dialogue were replaced by spacing the letters, and there were other perculiarities in setting, the omission of apostrophes, for instance, which became standardized in the printed plays. The title pages were set in 24 point Caslon, upper and lower case, starting at the top of the page, not centred. To show the meticulous attention Shaw gave to the printing, the following letter to his publisher on 26 August 1897 deserves quotation:

> . . . it has cost me endless letters and revises to get the page right, to teach him, the printer, how to space the letters for emphasis, and how to realize that I mean my punctuation to be followed. I had no idea of the magnitude of the job.[1]

[1] *Author Hunting* by Grant Richards (Hamish Hamilton, 1934), p. 129 from which the following letter is also taken (p. 120).

Another letter followed the next day:

> If we could get all six into one volume, I should have the unpleasant ones printed on light brown paper (Egyptian mummy colour) in an ugly style of printing, and the pleasant ones on white paper (machine-hand made) in the best Kelmscott style. No one has ever done a piebald volume before; and the thing would make a sensation.

The style of printing then established was maintained by Shaw throughout his life, with certain modifications in the Collected and Standard editions. The binding of these first two books was in dark green cloth, with pale green dust jackets, which Shaw kept for many years, to be discarded, however, in the Collected and Standard Editions as it had been found that the colour faded badly. The delay in bringing out the volumes was caused not only by Shaw's great care over their printing but by his insistence upon simultaneous American publication.

After the Pleasant and Unpleasant Plays the next volume to appear was *Three Plays for Puritans*, issued by the same publisher in 1901 as a companion to the earlier volumes. A stage edition of *Mrs Warren's Profession*, with photographs of the players, was published in 1903, after the play's private performance. Separate editions of the other plays in green paper covers and green cloth were also issued.

Shaw had offered to pay for the publication of *Three Plays for Puritans*, an offer the publisher refused. When Richards had become bankrupt and a proposal to John Murray to publish *Man and Superman* was declined, Shaw decided to have his plays published on commission and arranged for this to be done by Constable & Co. Thereafter he dealt directly with printer and binder, paying them himself, and bought his own paper. A very full account of his relations with his printer was given in an article by

James Shand in the final issue of the typographical quarterly *Alphabet and Image* (No. 8, December 1948), to which I am partly indebted for what I have written here. Writing to William Maxwell, head of R. & R. Clark Ltd, on the occasion of the firm's centenary in 1946, Shaw said: 'ever since it printed my first plays . . . in 1898, it has been as natural a part of my workshop as the pen in my hand'.

Shaw made extensive alterations in proofs, and was a meticulous proof reader. When making corrections on page proofs, he always gave the printer the exact number of words required, to prevent over-running. Mr Shand says of his work, 'Here is sense and sensibility in book-making, well ahead of its typographical time'. We can suppose that Shaw's great care over the printing of his plays had some relation to his desire to avoid the fate of the text of Shakespeare's plays, some published in his lifetime without the playwright showing any interest in them, the complete plays after his death by other hands.

The plays were extensively pirated in the United States of America. In the authorized editions an attempt was made to follow the R. & R. Clark typography, line for line; but there was more than one publisher using a variety of types and styles, and Shaw had to give up his strict control.

Great attention was paid to the issue of the limited Collected Edition started in 1931, when the plays were reset for a larger page. Shaw at first insisted on the text being set again by hand, not by machine, but Mr Shand relates that when specimen pages were submitted to him, one hand set, the other machine set, without telling him which was which, Shaw chose the machine setting. The same year the cheaper unlimited Standard Edition was started, in which the plays were also reset. There was some revision of the text in these editions. All the plays are available not only in the limited Collected but in the Standard Edition;

both editions include Shaw's other works.

It was Shaw's custom to have fifty copies of each play printed for rehearsal purposes, the authorship being 'By a Fellow of the Royal Society of Literature'. Sometimes further rehearsal copies were required when his name was given.

The Complete Plays of Bernard Shaw in one volume was published by Constable & Co in 1931 and re-issued by Odhams Press Limited in 1934, 1938 and 1950; the last volume contained all the plays. The complete prefaces were published in a single volume by Constable & Co in 1938, and have not been reprinted. To celebrate the dramatist's ninetieth birthday in 1946, nine volumes of plays and one other volume were issued in the Penguin Library; some other volumes have followed. There have been separate illustrated editions of *Geneva*, *In Good King Charles's Golden Days*, and *Buoyant Billions*. All these volumes were printed by R. & R. Clark Ltd.

There are German, French, Spanish, Italian, Russian and other editions of the plays, and translations have been made in Swedish, Norwegian, Danish, Finnish, Dutch, Polish, Hungarian, Czech, Japanese and other languages. And there is an edition of *Arms and the Man* in Basic English by L. W. Lockhart, published in 1939.

PART THREE

The Plays

The Plays

(1)
Widowers' Houses

A PLAY
(1885–92)

The importance of Bernard Shaw's first play is that it proved to himself that he was a playwright; all the rest followed. It had been started when he was twenty-eight, but put aside as hopeless for five years, then picked up again two years later, quickly completed and given two performances at the Royalty Theatre in December 1892. The thirty-six year old man found that the drama was a medium of expression in which he could achieve mastery. All the same, he afterwards wrote on a copy of the first edition 'My first and worst play'.

As a first effort, however, *Widowers' Houses* has remarkable qualities. Its dialogue is original, its construction thoroughly workmanlike, and, though by no means a masterpiece, it still holds the stage. Shaw's retort to those of his critics who said he was imitating Ibsen was that when he had written the first two acts he knew nothing of Ibsen; so that while the play was finished and produced under the influence of the Ibsen movement in London, we must agree that the slightness of its form supports Shaw's claim. Indeed, he protested that it 'could only have been written by a Socialist economist'.

The theme is a problem of conscience in a society that does not allow for conscience. Characteristically, the play is an attack upon society, not upon individuals, and Shaw's slum-landlord is permitted to justify himself. Shaw is by no means kind to him, for he hated the type, but he is just, and lets him say:

> No gentlemen: when people are very poor you *cannot* help them, no matter how much you may sympathize with them.

It was always Shaw's way to let a character speak for himself. Only when Sartorius turns from honest rogue into a conspirator intending to swindle the public does Shaw's irony become infused with scorn.

The story is that a young doctor, Harry Trench, and his companion, William de Burgh Cockane, are on tour up the Rhine in the eighteen-eighties, when they meet a wealthy English gentleman, Sartorius, with his daughter, Blanche. Trench and Blanche fall in love, countenanced by her father when he learns that Trench belongs to a titled family. The second Act is in the Sartorius' villa at Surbiton, the titled family having approved of Blanche, and everything promises to go smoothly. There Trench encounters by accident a man named Lickcheese, who has just been dismissed by Sartorius from his employment. From this man Trench learns that Sartorius's wealth comes from the ownership of slums, and that Lickcheese's dismissal was due to his having spent twenty-four shillings on what his employer regarded as unnecessary repairs. Trench thereupon tells Blanche that when they marry she must take nothing from her father but live on his own £700 a year; for he could never consent to his wife living on tainted money. Neither Blanche nor her father will agree to this, and Sartorius has the pleasure of telling Trench that a mortgage of £10,000 on the same slum property provides the latter's own unearned income. Thus is Trench confounded, and, simple fellow, feels he can do nothing but accept the situation. Blanche, however, will not accept it and refuses to have anything more to do with Trench.

Four months later, Lickcheese, now a prosperous speculator in real property, calls upon Sartorius with a proposal to improve his slum so that he can get increased compensation when the land is required for a public improvement scheme of which he has secretly gained information. Sartorius agrees, but the consent of the mortgagee has to be obtained, so Trench is once more brought upon the scene. Simple as he is, he sums up the position: 'So we're to give up dirt and go in for decency.' He agrees. And while the bargain is being made, Trench, left alone for a little while, is pounced upon by Blanche and they make it up.

Shaw the idealist had no intention of making a hero of his Dr Trench. The problem of conscience is without glamour, for knowledge of the facts makes the unheroic hero 'coarsened and sullen'. Only when the situation is put right (in a kind of way) for him is he reconciled to it.

The play is farcical in conception, but comedy in execution, presenting a problem in actual life. It is uncomfortable, and rightly called 'unpleasant', because none of the characters is in the least admirable. Its weakness is partly in plot but chiefly in the leading character, for Trench arouses no sympathy and we do not in the least care what happens to him.

Characters

DR HARRY TRENCH is an exaggerated version of Shaw himself, so exaggerated as to become rather a boor, about twenty-four, dark, well-built, 'thick in the neck, close-cropped . . . undignified medical student manners, frank, hasty, rather boyish'. Being divested of personal qualities, which is where Shaw separates himself from the character, he is negative while the other characters are positive. The raw youthfulness of the character is important.

SARTORIUS is fifty, tall, of upright carriage, with a domineering and imposing manner, a self-made man, sometimes not quite sure of himself: the impersonation of middle class respectability.

BLANCHE is 'well-dressed, well-fed, good looking, strong-minded', with a violent temper, about twenty-four or less, not presented as a wholly pleasant creature, being seen through a candid lover's eyes, but Shaw did not intend her to be disagreeable. In his reply to the critics, who did not like the girl at all, he said 'the author confesses to having jilted *the* ideal lady for *a* real one'. Her 'animal excitement' aspects should not be over-emphasized, but they must be present. She is said to have been modelled on Shaw's intimate friend at the time, Florence Farr.

COCKANE, travelling companion of the hero, is over forty, 'an ill-nourished, scanty-haired gentleman', affected, and not at all agreeable.

LICKCHEESE, the rent collector, is shabby, dirty, going bald, 'a nervous, wiry, pertinacious sort of human terrier'. He has a Cockney accent, and in the last act is dressed as a prosperous man. Shaw knew the type intimately and his intense dislike did not intefere with delight in the character's humorous aspects.

There is a German WAITER who tries to speak English in the first act, a PORTER, and a Cockney MAID in the Surbiton house.

Production

Called by Shaw 'a play', the piece did not commit him to any category of drama. In fact it is farcical-comedy. Attention must therefore be given to situation throughout, though the marked comedy features are to be respected. It needs to be played quickly, with not too much deliberation, not naturalistically but with exaggeration; though not, of course, burlesqued in the slightest degree. The two love scenes are to be specially noted, for they show the woman taking the initiative. The climax is in Act II when Trench asks Blanche 'Are you fond of money?' The anti-climax occurs in the same act, when Sartorius says to Trench 'Yes: a mortgage on *my* property', and the play continues on that anti-climax.

The play depends on the setting and dressing of the eighteen-eighties. The first act is in the garden restaurant of a Rhine hotel, with the riverside as background. The second and third acts are in the library of a handsomely appointed villa in the London suburb of Surbiton, excessively substantial in the Victorian manner.

A Note on Productions

When first performed on 9 December 1892 the part of Blanche was played by Florence Farr, who had plenty of humour; Lickcheese played by James Welsh; the play produced by H. de Lange. It was not performed again in England until Miss Horniman's company gave it at the Midland Theatre, Manchester, on 7 October 1907, when it was produced by B. Iden Payne. Two years later the same company included it in its season at the Coronet Theatre, London, when Mona Limerick played Blanche, her exotic personality suiting the part well; Lewis Casson was Trench. The first American production was at the Herald Square Theatre, New York, on 7 March 1907. The play acts well, though somewhat oddly, and has been revived with success.

(2)
The Philanderer

A TOPICAL COMEDY
(1893)

'May I ask, Mr Charteris, is this the New Humour?' remarks one of the characters in *The Philanderer* to the hero. The play was, indeed, an example of the new humour that had come into the theatre – Shavian humour – the nature of which was to be disconcerting, exasperating, and too true to be good for everyone. It is not a deliberately hurtful humour, for there is no malice, but at times the humorist is brought dangerously near to indifference to personal feelings. Written at the height of the Ibsen controversy, by one of the provokers of the controversy and Ibsen's champion, this play made fun of the intelligentsia, which is shown in anything but a favourable light. The second of the unpleasant plays, its theme is love and marriage, treated as a game between the sexes, within a highly unpleasant fantasia upon Victorian standards; for beneath its playfulness sex is given the serious treatment that did not become popular for another thirty years.

Charteris, the leading character, is Shaw, and the woman with whom Charteris had got entangled, Julia, as Shaw made out twenty years afterwards, was based upon Mrs Jenny Patterson, 'the enterprising widow, one of my mother's pupils (who) appealed successfully to my curiosity'. All the same to suppose that it is less than an invention is to do the play injustice. 'I am of the true Shakespearean type', he wrote to Frank Harris, about the play. 'I understand everyone and everything, and am nobody and nothing.'

The play opens with Charteris in the arms of Grace Tranfield, a pretty young widow, living in a flat in Ashley Gardens. Charteris wants to marry her, but she will not have him, for she dislikes his philandering and won't take him away from her friend Julia. He wants to be rescued, however, and does not hide from Grace that to be saved from Julia is his reason for wanting to marry her. While they are discussing this problem, Julia bursts into the room in a jealous rage, attempts to assault Grace, slaps Charteris's face, and when Grace goes out has a great scene with her lover, showing herself to be a fully developed instinctive woman. Then Grace's father, Joseph Cuthbertson, and Julia's father, Colonel Craven, interrupt the quarrel. The two men realize that something is up, but cannot find out what, until, at the end of the act, Charteris tells them, 'I am the matter'. In the second Act, which is at the Ibsen Club, Charteris explains to the two fathers that Grace, whom he wants to marry, won't have him, and Julia whom he doesn't want to marry, won't give him up. Julia comes in, but Charteris dodges her, and Sylvia, who is Julia's sister, suggests to Charteris that Dr Paramore, a member of the Club, is in love with Julia. Charteris sees a loophole of deliverance. Then, when the others have gone to lunch, Grace appears, in a more melting mood, and tells Charteris that she loves him, but says they must part, for as a New Woman she will never marry a man she loves too much: 'It would give him a terrible advantage over me.'

In the third act, still at the Ibsen Club, Paramore learns from the *British Medical Journal* that a report from the continent proves that the liver disease, on which his life's work is based (and for which, incidentally, he had been treating Colonel Craven), does not exist. Here is Shaw's first gleeful attack upon the medical profession. Paramore finds consolation in the friendly interest of Grace, and Charteris suggests to Julia that her young man (Paramore) is being carried off by Grace, so Julia falls into the trap, interrupts the conversation, and because she cannot resist the man-hunt begins to chase Paramore, who is delighted.

The fourth act finds us the same afternoon in Paramore's sitting room in Savile Row, with the doctor and Julia having tea. Paramore proposes to Julia because 'it is your heart, your sincerity, your startling reality' that appeals to him. Charteris and Craven come to join them, and Julia being left alone with him tells Charteris that she is engaged to Paramore. The relieved Charteris declares, 'My beautiful Julia', kissing her hands. Julia is furious at his undisguised pleasure, and when Paramore and Craven come back, they find her shaking Charteris and 'growling over him like a tigress over her cub'. Charteris gets her out of the difficulty by declaring that he had insulted her; he admits that he is in love with Julia, but that she utterly despises him, and always did. The play, however, ends on a note of tension, relieved by Grace's comment – for she and her father have appeared by now – 'Never make a hero of a philanderer.'

The true Shavian qualities appear in dialogue, characters, and situation, the play's construction being strictly of the period. There is a considerable advance on the first play. Shaw's friends did not like it – Janet Achurch and William Archer being the most vehement, for they considered it vulgar, dull and worthless; and he was not altogether pleased with it himself, as his corre-spondence with Ellen Terry in 1896 shows. Writing to her, he called it 'a combination of mechanical farce with realistic filth which quite disgusted me'. His enemies could not have said worse. Ellen Terry replied saying 'It's perfectly wonderful with a swing in it from beginning to end.' To which the delighted Shaw answered, 'If it is good enough for you it is good enough for the rest of the world.' The judgment is a right one, and Shaw did not go back on it, constantly urging its merits.

Characters

LEONARD CHARTERIS is not described beyond the statement that he is a few years older than Grace and is unconventionally but smartly dressed. The character is an undisguised and unin-hibited amorist, yet always acceptable, and the play depends upon the realization that the entire action is from his point of view; he sees or imagines all that takes place throughout.

GRACE TRANFIELD is about thirty-two, 'slight of build, delicate of feature, and sensitive in expression', intelligent and smartly dressed, an appealing character.

JULIA CRAVEN is 'beautiful, dark, tragic-looking', passionate, unscrupulous, and as Charteris sees her highly dangerous to him.

COLONEL CRAVEN is a simple veteran, a fine upright figure, good-natured, matter-of-fact, impulsive, credulous.

JOSEPH CUTHBERTSON is a complete contrast to the colonel, being fervently idealistic, perpetually outraged by the facts of life, therefore in an habitual state of indignation. The character was a caricature of the dramatic critic Clement Scott, who had said of Ibsen's plays that they are 'nasty, dirty, impure, clever if you like, but foul to the last degree'.

DR PARAMORE is barely forty, the conventional doctor, with a cultivated 'bedside' manner, and highly self-satisfied.

SYLVIA CRAVEN is eighteen, small and trim.

There is a PAGE BOY.

Production

The play is satirical comedy, not to be treated naturalistically or burlesqued. It needs spirit, energy, and pointed speech in the players, and depends largely on creating the atmosphere of the period, the early nineties. Balance has to be established between Charteris and the two women. The climax of the first act is when Julia enters, and the anti-climax when Charteris leaves the room, the rest of the play develops from that.

There are three interiors, the lady's drawing room in Ashley Gardens, the Library at the Ibsen Club, with the bust of Ibsen, and the doctor's sitting room; they are all described. The dressing must be of the period.

A Note on Productions

The author would not allow the play to be performed until he found a satisfactory Julia, a charmer of men, which shows how much importance Shaw gave to casting, for she is not the leading part. He found the player he wanted at the Vedrenne-Barker season at the Court, when Lillah McCarthy was made to take it, but at the last moment was unable to play. Thus, notwithstanding an excellent cast including Edith Wynne Matthison as Grace and Ben Webster as Charteris, the production failed. The play even more depends upon Charteris, a character too candid to be merely agreeable, and Ben Webster was too dignified, even moralistic, though with much of the necessary lightness. When Shaw wrote the play for the Independent Theatre, J. T. Grein could not cast it, for as Shaw gleefully admits 'I had written a part which nobody but Charles Wyndham could act'. The part requires sure comedy handling, for Charteris is never unpleasant, closely as he sometimes approaches it. The play has been revived a number of times with popular success. Desmond MacCarthy said 'It "dates" only super-ficially' and 'beneath . . . lies a formidable sincerity, immensely and lastingly refreshing'. The German version was performed at Warsaw in 1907, and a Bohemian version at the National Theatre, Prague, in June 1909. The first American production was by Winthrop Ames at the Little Theatre, New York, on 27 December 1913.

(3)
Mrs Warren's Profession

A PLAY
(1893)

This is a play for women. The first unpleasant play was about slums, the second about women and marriage, and this, the third, about prostitution. It is the best of the three, showing its author to be increasing his powers. The play was written, he says:

... to draw attention to the truth that prostitution is caused, not by female depravity and male licentiousness, but simply by underpaying, undervaluing, and maltreating women so shamefully that the poorer of them are forced to resort to prostitution to keep body and soul together. . . . Society, and not any individual, is the villain of the piece.

Shaw always thought well of the play, and rightly. 'Ah,' wrote Shaw to Ellen Terry, 'when I wrote that, I had *some* nerve.' Although it is about prostitution, as *Hamlet* is about the murder of a king, its theme is that of conscience, as was the theme of the first play.

Indeed he had nerve; for he knew that in dealing seriously with prostitution he was not only flying in the face of convention but in the face of the censor. When a licence was refused the otherwise enterprising Grein refused to produce it privately, and it remained for Shaw to publish the play five years later in 1898. Not for twenty-one years was it permitted to be performed publicly in England. It was, however, publicly performed by Arnold Daly in New York in 1902, when owing no doubt to its announcement as a banned play the police took action and hauled the actor and his company off to gaol; but the magistrate refused to convict, and on appeal by the police the judge decided that the play was not immoral.

It could hardly have been thought immoral by reason of its dialogue, which though outspoken is delicacy itself. The trouble was not so much the attack upon prostitution, but because the play was a vehement attack on social conditions which made prostitution possible and upheld it. Thus its indictment was of every man as a citizen, not of those engaged in the trade. It was too revolutionary for the time.

Mrs Warren is the prosperous head of a syndicate that organizes international brothels under the description of hotels. She herself had taken to the prostitute's career because there was no other escape from a life of grinding poverty. Having a head for business and a sister who had a head for business, too, she capitalized her good looks, and was so successful that she got financial support to operate on a large scale. She has a daughter, Vivie, who had been brought up without knowledge of her mother's business, and as the play opens has just come down from Newnham, where she had tied with the third Wrangler. She is awaiting a visit from her mother at a cottage at Haslemere, Surrey, where she is having a holiday before starting her professional career as an actuary in London. Mrs Warren arrives, and with her Sir George Crofts, who helps to finance her business; she has also invited an old friend, Praed, to come to be introduced to her daughter. Vivie is already friendly with Frank Gardner, son of the local rector. When his father, the Rev Samuel Gardner, turns up Mrs Warren recognizes him as an old acquaintance; so to his consternation does he, for she was the barmaid at Redhill to whom years ago he had once offered £50 for some letters he had written her – a story he had already told his son Frank as a warning to him.

The situation is established in the first act; in the second, that night, Mrs Warren warns both Frank and Sir George Crofts against entertaining any serious intentions regarding Vivie, and Vivie left alone with her mother learns the secret of her life. The next morning Crofts makes love to Vivie, and when she refuses to have anything to do with the horrid old man he makes her realize that she is sharing with him the profits of her mother's business. Finally he tells her that the Rev Samuel Gardner is her father.

This is all too much for Vivie and she goes off to London to start work at once, for she will take no more money from her mother; in the fourth act we find her at her friend's office in Chancery Lane. Frank arrives to tell her that his father had denied

Croft's statement and Vivie declares that she had never believed it; but she has finished with love's young dream. Mrs Warren also comes to get a reconciliation, but Vivie declares: 'I don't want a mother; and I don't want a husband', and sends her mother about her business. 'From this time forth,' says Mrs Warren, 'so help me Heaven in my last hour, I'll do wrong and nothing but wrong. And I'll prosper on it.'

It is a hard play without sentiment, because conscience is hard, and Vivie's conscience is what the dramatic action is concerned with. Max Beerbohm wrote of its first private production: '*Mrs Warren* is a powerful and stimulating, even an enobling piece of work.' There is a resemblance to *Widowers' Houses*, but the writing is more developed, and the drama has become personal, as all drama must be. The personal problem is Vivie's, with the background of the effects of capitalism, the position of women, morals, and social conscience. Having written it, Shaw was done with unpleasant plays for ever.

Characters

VIVIE is twenty-two, 'strong, confident, self-possessed', an attractive, highly educated young middle-class women. The action is as she sees it, for the problem is hers. Her outlook is unsentimental; she says good-bye to false happiness, for she is wholly competent and has a planned life.

MRS WARREN is intended to be likeable, though in the eyes of her disillusioned daughter she is monstrous. Ellen Terry preferred the character to Candida, which is understandable. She is much the largest character in the play, and the best drawn, good-looking, showily dressed, between forty and fifty years of age. 'Rather spoiled and domineering . . . but, on the whole, a genial and fairly presentable old blackguard of a woman,' is Shaw's amiable description.

PRAED is hardly past middle-age, well-dressed, able, amiable and considerate, the only quite pleasant character.

SIR GEORGE CROFTS is tall, powerfully built, about fifty, very disagreeably described: 'nasal voice . . . bull-dog jaws, large flat ears, and thick neck, gentlemanly combination of the most brutal types of city man, sporty man, and man about town.' In fact he is meant to be loathed.

FRANK GARDNER is not long turned twenty, pleasant, smartly dressed, entirely good for nothing. Agreeable and tolerable at first, but in the end not admirable, for he is as Vivie sees him.

THE REVEREND SAMUEL GARDNER is over fifty, and over-bearing, self-satisfied and noisy. Vivie did not like him, but he should not be made grotesquely unpleasant.

Production

The play is satirical comedy, with the satire uppermost. It should be kept out of the realm of naturalism, though it enters that of realism, should be done sharply, quickly, and with as much brilliance as the characters permit, and without any apparent self-consciousness. The turning point is in Act III when Vivie discovers where the money spent upon her comes from: the climax immediately follows when Crofts informs her that Frank is her half-brother. The rest of the play is anti-climax, but the interest is maintained. The theme of the play is not out of date.

The staging needs bright treatment, smart, in the mid-nineties style. The first act is in the garden at Haslemere; the second act in the living-room of the cottage; the third act in the Rectory garden; the fourth act in an office in New Stone Buildings, Chancery Lane. The settings are fully described. The dressing must be of the period.

A Note on Productions

The first Mrs Warren at the private performance by the Stage Society on 5 January 1902 was Fanny Brough, a comedy actress of much personality, whose acting Shaw admired. She made a great success in the part. The first Vivie was Madge McIntosh, the first Frank, Harley Granville Barker. The play was first publicly performed by Arnold Daly on 27 October 1905 at New Haven, Connecticut, and three days later at the Garrick Theatre, New York. The first public performance in England was by the Macdona Players at the Prince of Wales Theatre, Birmingham, on 27 July 1925 and in London at the Regent Theatre, on 28 September that year. It has been revived a number of times and justifies the dramatist's high opinion of it.

A Bohemian version was performed at the National Theatre, Prague, in December 1907. A French version, performed at the Théâtre des Arts in 1912, did nothing like credit to the play. When the Comédie Française proposed to produce a new French version in March 1955, the selection committee arrived at the remarkable decision to reject it as unsuitable for presentation at the French national theatre.

(4)
Arms and the Man

AN ANTI-ROMANTIC COMEDY
(1894)

Written as a deliberately pleasant play, this is an 'onslaught on idealism . . . which is only a flattering name for romance in politics and morals' and the cause of national and personal 'moral chaos and anarchy'. Shaw was then under the influence of his own writings upon Ibsen. He presents in this play an anti-hero as protagonist, the hero being secondary. In that sense the play was revolutionary.

A prosaic professional soldier is introduced into a situation between a typical romantic hero and a typical romantic heroine, with disastrous consequences to both. On a lower level there is a romantic serving girl in conflict with an ordinary matter-of-fact manservant. Shaw's aim is to destroy illusions, and to compel his audience to face realities. 'To me,' he says, 'the tragedy and comedy of life lie in the consequences, sometimes terrible, some-times ludicrous, of our persistent attempts to found our institu-tions on the ideals suggested to our imaginations by our half-satisfied passions, instead of on a genuinely scientific natural history.' Give up party and political romance and get down to biological facts is what he means. He does not disguise his mean-ing; but because he cannot help being entertaining, and because also, as always, he avoided naturalism and appeared to satirise Bulgarians, not Englishmen, this play was popular from the start, despite the shock it gave on first hearing. It is not only a pleasant play but an easy one for readers and audiences, though not for actors.

Bulgaria and Serbia are at war in the year 1885. The Serbian Army is in flight, and a fugitive officer, Captain Bluntschli, takes refuge in a Bulgarian house. It is night, and he climbs up the front of the house, entering a bedroom on the first floor. In this room lies the heroine, Raina Petkoff, dreaming of her lover, who had led a recent victorious charge of the Bulgarian cavalry. The fugitive forces her to light a candle, threatens her with his revolver, takes her cloak, and when the pursuing Bulgarian troops enter the house and demand to search the room, he throws the cloak back to her and prepares for a struggle; on impulse she hides him.

When the search is over she in 'her most genteel society manner' sits down and talks to him, and as he is starving offers him the only food she has, chocolate creams: he says that he prefers them to cartridges. He goes on to describe the magnificent cavalry charge and how the officer at the head of it was carried away by his horse. Thus Bluntschli attacks, unconsciously but devastatingly, the heroine's cherished ideals. Outraged, she would turn him out of her room were it not for the Bulgarian soldiers in the street below. He admits that he is a Swiss professional soldier who joined the Serbian Army because it came first on the road from Switzerland; he has no illusions whatever about war. She feels herself immeasurably superior to him in her belief in glory and heroism; so superior, that she will be chivalrous and persuade her mother to let him stay until the search is over. The first act ends with the soldier asleep with exhaustion on the girl's bed; it is easy to see what a conquest he has made.

In the second act, four months later, the war is over. It is a fine spring morning in the garden of Major Petkoff's house. The major returns with the hero of Slivnitza, his daughter's lover. They tell the story of how a Swiss officer had taken part in an exchange of prisoners and had impressed the two men by his commercial-mindedness; he had also told them a funny tale about his life having been saved by two Bulgarian women. Raina and her mother rebuke the two men, 'I did not know you would tell such a story before me', says Raina on her high horse. Then Raina and Sergius give an exhibition of the 'higher-love', followed immediately by an exhibition of ordinary love by Sergius and the serving girl, Louka. Before the morning is over Bluntschli unexpectedly turns up to return a coat lent him by the women. He is greeted heartily by the men, with blank looks by the women, pretending not to know him, and forced to stay to lunch.

The third act opens with the professional soldier helping the amateurs over the foraging arrangements for some cavalry regiments. They are working in the Petkoff's library. Bluntschli, being left alone with Raina, who cannot let him be, is as prosaic as she is romantic, and ends by toppling her off her pedestal by his imperturbability. 'How did you find me out?' she asks when she is defeated. 'Instinct, dear young lady', he promptly replies, 'Instinct and experience of the world.' Sergius finding himself in company with Louka for the second time that day is also thrown off his heroic pedestal by her, and told the true story of Raina and the Swiss. Sergius thereupon challenges Bluntschli, and charges Raina with having allowed Bluntschli to make love to her. The major finds a portrait of Raina in a pocket of his old coat with the inscription 'To my chocolate cream soldier'. He asks for an explanation. He gets it. There is high tension. Bluntschli, always the practical man, cuts the knot by promptly asking for Raina's hand. Sergius finds himself committed to Louka. Bluntschli has to go off to look after his father's affairs. 'What a man!'

Characters

BLUNTSCHLI, the leading character, the anti-hero, sees everyone including himself with Shaw's normal vision enlarged by his admiration for Raina. He is 'of middling stature and undistinguished appearance, with strong neck and shoulders, roundish obstinate-looking head covered with short crisp bronze curls, clear quick eyes, and good brows and mouth', trim, soldier-like, energetic, and with all his wits about him. Bluntschli suggested Sidney Webb, in his extreme efficiency and absence of pretence, a fact that should be remembered, but it must also be remembered that the actor needs a pleasing personality.

RAINA is not described by the author; she must be tall and dark, highly romantic, completely attractive, a woman in a thousand, for she captivates Bluntschli as he defeats her.

SERGIUS, a Byronic hero, is tall, romantically handsome, with the physical hardihood, the high spirit and the susceptible imagination of an untamed mountaineer chieftain, civilized.

CATHERINE PETKOFF is over forty, imperious, energetic, 'a splendid specimen of the wife of a mountain farmer' who is 'determined to be a Viennese lady'. It is an advantage for her to be shorter than Raina.

MAJOR PETKOFF is cheerful, excitable, insignificant, about fifty. He is smaller than Bluntschli.

LOUKA is 'a handsome proud girl', insolent to Raina, but afraid of Catherine. She should be shorter than Raina.

NICOLA, the man servant, middle-aged, cool, smooth, described as having his head 'shaped up to the crown, giving him a high Japanese forehead'. He should not be taller than Louka.

RUSSIAN OFFICER in Bulgarian uniform, impatient but polite.

Production

The play is romance, through which moves the anti-romantic leading character. The romance must be genuinely there so as to be upset. The tendency to burlesque must be resisted. When the play opens, and Raina is standing at the window gazing at the snowy Balkans, her reverie is concentrated upon her hero, which means that her pose as she stands and her first speech when she answers her mother must be on the fervent romantic level, not that of comedy, certainly not of naturalism. The opening sets the tone of the play. Raina does not drop her romantic pose, except for a few moments in the third act when Bluntschli causes it to collapse. Then she changes her manner, as the author says, 'from the heroic to a babyish familiarity'; but she is back on the pedestal by the time she leaves the room after speaking to Louka. Sergius also is romantic throughout, though in the third act he is in difficulties. Bluntschli must have a quiet, smooth, and quick manner; the part can be underplayed, but it is fatal to overplay it. The climax of the first act is when Raina shows Bluntschli the photograph; in the second act, the scene between Raina and Sergius, the turning point when Bluntschli is announced; in the third act the climax is when Raina collapses, and the anti-climax when she says to him: 'Next time, I hope you will know the difference between a school girl of seventeen and a woman of twenty-three'.

The first act is a bedroom, with a double window opening on to a balcony at the back: the window opens inwards, and there are shutters which open outwards. There is a door, opening inwards, on the right, below the bed; there must be a practicable lock with a key. The garden in Act 2 shows the Bulgarian mountains in the distance with the little town in the valley. On the right is the door to the house reached by a flight of steps. On the left, the stable-yard, with a gateway behind to enable Sergius and Louka to hide from the house. At the back, between the house and the stable-yard there is a paling with a gate at the right. The library in Act 3 contains one shelf of nineteenth century paper-covered novels, and a couple of small hanging shelves with gift books. Three large windows at the back open on to the mountain view. In the left upper corner, standing out in the room, a square earthen-ware stove. Lower down a door opening inwards. An electric bell-push is in the right wall. There is a table, couch, and chairs.

The first act is lit by a single candle: when the window is open, light comes from there; it is a bright moonlit night. In the other acts there is bright daylight.

The period is 1885–6 and the costumes of the time are required. Raina wears in the first act a long mantle of furs, which well covers her; it is not a light cloak. Catherine wears a fashionable Viennese tea gown, throughout. Petkoff's coat in Act 3 is important: it should be an old one.

The properties are described in the text. The bed should not be so high that Bluntschli cannot easily sit on it; he should not have to climb upon it.

A Note on Productions

The first production at the Avenue Theatre, Northumberland Avenue, London, on 21 April 1894, was Shaw's introduction as a dramatist to the London theatre-going public. Florence Farr who played Louka was responsible, and the cast included Yorke Stephens as Bluntschli, James Welch, A. E. W. Mason, and Bernard Partridge. It was the first play by the author to be seen in America, where it was produced in New York on 17 September the same year by Richard Mansfield; though not a success, Mansfield frequently appeared in it afterwards, as did Arnold Daly, the latter playing it also in London. Trebitsch's German version was first performed by the Freie Volksbühne in Berlin in 1903, and in Vienna and Cracow next year. Altogether it has proved to be one of the most popular of Shaw's plays everywhere, but the tendency to treat it as self-conscious burlesque, evident in late revivals, instead of full-toned romantic comedy, does it no justice. An operatic version, the libretto by Leopold Jacobson and Rudolf Bernauer, *Der Tapfere Soldat*, with music by Oscar Strauss, was produced in Berlin in 1909 with success, but without the author's consent; he returned a cheque sent to him, but finally withdrew opposition on condition that the opera was described as a burlesque of the play, and he always refused to receive any fees. The year after, on 10 September, it was performed in London as *The Chocolate Soldier*. An attempt to film this version in America in 1927 was successfully prevented. A film version, of the original play with no addition to the dialogue but some cuts, was directed by Cecil Lewis in 1932, and commercially exhibited that year as a straightforward version of the play; it had little interest, however, except to show that plays could not successfully be filmed.

(5)
Candida

A MYSTERY

(1894)

This is Shaw's best constructed play, classic in its economy and observance of time and place, and in some ways probably his most important play, highly interesting from a technical point of view as a play of anti-climax. In it, too, he disclosed himself as he seldom did before or after, displaying the naked conflict between the poet and commonsense.

The story is that the Reverend James Mavor Morell, a Christian Socialist clergyman of the Church of England, finds a young man sleeping on the Thames embankment. He takes him home and discovers that he is a poet, nephew of a peer, who does not understand the everyday affairs of life. Young Marchbanks, the poet, becomes a visitor to the house and devoted to Candida, Morell's wife and mother of two children. She mothers the poet. One day Marchbanks tells Morell that he is in love with Candida, that he, the poet, understands her and that Morell, the husband, does not, and demands that Morell give up his wife to him. Morell treats the matter lightly, but becomes angry when he discovers that Marchbanks is serious, and is moved to shake the silly boy, to Marchbanks' terror. When she comes in he tells his wife what has happened, for he too becomes serious, and learns not only that the news does not surprise her, but that she knows his, Morell's, weaknesses so well that he cannot believe that none the less she still loves him. In his masculine obtuseness he demands that Candida should choose between him, the honest, popular, industrious husband, and the weak, disliked and misunderstood poet. She replies, having already said to her husband that he should put his trust in her love for him, that she will give herself to the weaker of the two. Marchbanks knows that he has lost and goes away with a secret in his heart. In Frank Harris's biography we may get near to Shaw's conception of the play when Harris (or Shaw) says of Morell that he 'hasn't the least inkling that Candida possesses a soul. . . . So little conception, indeed, has her husband of his wife's mind and heart, that he closes his offer by saying, self-confident in his manly philistinism: "That is all it becomes a man to offer a woman".' This relates the play to *A Doll's House*, in which Ibsen's theme is the same, that Helmar has no notion that Nora has a soul of her own. In Ibsen's play the wife leaves her husband when she makes the discovery; in Shaw's she holds to him, for Candida has more wisdom than Nora, having known the truth all along. What is Marchbanks' secret? Part of the play's attractiveness lies in the mystery. Shaw, himself, gave several different answers to the question, not, of course, that he did not know the true one, which is that the poet has discovered that there is another love than the love of women. When Candida puts to Eugene the commonsense fact of the difference between their ages, he finds that he has awakened, grown up, finding himself as old as the world, no longer identified with woman, or love, or himself as lover: he is a free man.

Characters

EUGENE MARCHBANKS, shy, eighteen, slight, aristocratic, with a delicate voice, dreamy, 'almost unearthly'. The part has to be played by a youth, though it demands considerable technique. It should not be played for sympathy, for there is hardness and inhumanity in the unawakened Eugene until he awakens in the play. He has to display ecstasy, and it must be remembered that the entire dramatic action is as he sees it as the protagonist.

CANDIDA is thirty-three, 'now quite at her best with the double charm of youth and motherhood'. An ordinary woman, however, not intellectually remarkable, nor with artistic tastes; with nothing remarkable about her, indeed, for her good looks she shares with other women, except that she possesses largeness of mind and dignity of character. Also the insight of love, which enables her to know her husband and still to love him, and to know the poet and not to allow his love to unbalance her. She should be of medium height, either dark or fair, it does not matter. She is Shaw's ideal woman. 'Candida', wrote Shaw to Ellen Terry, 'is the Virgin Mother, and none else.' To try to imagine her as the daughter of Burgess is not necessary: Marchbanks did not so see her, and she exists only in his imagination. When we see Candida presented by Marchbanks as protagonist we accept her as the marvellous creature he sees her to be; but if she be treated as the protagonist, presenting herself, the character becomes an intolerable prig and bore. Much of the distaste sometimes expressed for what is essentially an exquisite play is due to this error.

MORELL is 'a vigorous, genial, popular man of forty, robust and good-looking, full of energy, with pleasant, hearty, considerate manners, and a sound unaffected voice, which he uses with the clean athletic articulation of a practised orator'. Thus Shaw describes a first rate Christian Socialist clergyman, by no means devoid of masculine understanding, sympathetic and with plenty of feeling; but a typical male, as the candid eyes of Marchbanks see him.

PROSERPINE GARNETT, Morell's secretary, is about thirty, pert and quick of speech, not very civil, but sensitive and affectionate, and of course devoted to Morell.

ALEXANDER MILL is the well-intentioned, enthusiastic, immature curate, with an Oxford accent.

MR BURGESS, Candida's father, is sixty, 'a vulgar, ignorant, guzzling man, . . . a dust coloured beard, . . . small watery blue eyes with a plaintively sentimental expression'. A first rate character part, which must not be overdone, though as Marchbanks sees him he is utterly objectionable.

Production

The play is poetic comedy, on the emotional rather than the rational level; therefore needs to be given more than the surface brilliance of comedy, and, while the setting is realistic, there must be nothing naturalistic, no burlesque with the curate, no very low comedy with Burgess. It is written with economy; the plot is well defined and fully worked out. There are no loose ends.

Marchbanks, the central character, is highly difficult because of the boy's complete unselfconsciousness. Unless the part is played with instinctively controlled ecstasy the play fails. There is contrast between Morell and Marchbanks, but the conflict is between Candida and Marchbanks: between commonsense and poetry.

The point of the play is in the anti-climax. The climax of the first \\ act is when Marchbanks says: 'I love your wife'; it is maintained until he goes; in the second act the climax is when Candida mentions Eugene; in the third act when Candida asks the two men to make their bids for her. The anti-climax of the first and second acts is in the last line, which means that the curtains are specially important, and in the third act it is in Marchbanks' last speech to Candida about the secret in his heart, a very short episode, difficult to do. //

'I purposely contrived the play in such a way as to make the expenses of production insignificant', says the author, which is true enough; the difficulty is in casting. The action takes place during a morning, afternoon and evening in the year 1894, in the drawing room of St Dominic's Parsonage, in the East End Borough of Hackney, the room used by the parson to work in.

The window at the back looks over the park, on the left wall is the door leading out on to the hall, and on the right wall the fireplace. In Act 3 the stage is lit by a reading lamp on the mantle-shelf and by another lamp on the table. The fire is alight throughout the play.

The date should be observed: the setting and costumes are described to some extent in the text. The properties are all fully described; they should create the sense of the room being well lived in.

A Note on Productions

When the play was licensed the censor drew attention to the opening of the third act, and requested that the words be strictly adhered to, which puzzled everyone at the time. The play was performed in the English provincial cities by Janet Achurch from 1897 onwards, but Shaw would not allow her to bring it to London. She had already been to New York to play it with Richard Mansfield, but Mansfield, who had reluctantly accepted it, abandoned the play in rehearsal as 'impossible'. It was left to Arnold Daly to acquire the American rights and give it a trial matinee at the Princes Theatre, New York, on 8 December 1903, which was so successful that it was put on at another theatre and became the event of the season. It was not done publicly in London until 26 April 1904 under the Vedrenne-Barker management, when an admirable cast gave an ideal performance: Granville Barker played Eugene, Kate Rorke, Candida, and Norman McKinnel, Morell. This production and its subsequent revivals at the Court Theatre have never been equalled. Superficially it is an easy play; actually it demands first rate comedy playing by Candida and Morell, and romantic comedy playing by Eugene. The difficulty in casting Eugene I have never seen overcome, except in Granville Barker. Desmond MacCarthy considered that Stephen Haggard's performance at the Globe Theatre in February 1937 excelled Barker's, but Haggard did not approach the elevation and complete conviction of Barker's performance. The play is the second most often revived work by Shaw. It has been broadcast and televised, and both media have shown that without satisfactory casting and direction equal to the understanding of the play it can fail.

A German version was successfully produced at Cracow in 1907. A French version performed on 7 May 1908 at the Théâtre des Arts aroused much controversy, being considered a badly constructed play, as it was by current French theatrical standards; it had earlier been performed at Brussels on 7 February 1907.

(6)
The Man of Destiny

A FICTITIOUS PARAGRAPH OF HISTORY
(1895)

The play shows Napoleon when twenty-seven years of age, two days after his victory at Lodi in 1796. He is at an inn at Tavazzano, on the road from Lodi to Milan, waiting for his dispatches. When the young officer bearing the dispatches arrives he confesses that he had been duped by a youth he had met on the road, who had stolen them. The officer is put under arrest. A woman arrives and the officer recognizes her voice as that of the man who had robbed him. She declares that the man was her brother. Napoleon is not duped and demands the dispatches. She does her best to beguile him, but he makes her give them up, being quite unscrupulous in his methods. She asks him not to read a private letter contained in the packet, which, she says, was not intended for him. 'I am not in the habit of reading other people's letters', he replies.

But he goes into the garden, taking the packet with him, and when he returns admits that he has read its contents. 'I adore a man who is not afraid to be mean and selfish', says the lady. He gives the letter to her and she burns it. The point of the play is the battle of wits between Napoleon and the lady.

Characters

THE LADY is tall and graceful, a delicately intelligent, apprehensive, questioning face', with character in the chin, 'keen, refined and original'. Very feminine, but by no means weak. Note what pleasure Shaw shows in the play's writing, for the famous man is seen through her eyes.

NAPOLEON is the genius of twenty-seven, the figure of tradition. Shaw does not describe him, though he says of him as the play opens with Napoleon sitting at the table that he shows no revolutionary untidiness about dress or person, though his long hair trails into the risotto when he forgets it. Study the many portraits of Napoleon for the man, but his youth must be remembered.

GUISEPPE is 'a swarthy, vivacious, shrewdly cheerful, black-curled, bullet-headed, grinning little innkeeper of forty'.

THE SUB-LIEUTENANT is tall, twenty four, with a loud confident voice. Shaw despises him.

There is a SENTINEL in the garden, and a young GIRL looks in at the window when the play starts.

Production

The play is comedy not farce, though the situation in its comic aspects is stressed. Napoleon the soldier, a man all over, has pitted against him a lady, woman all over. Her only weapons are her woman's charm – her sex appeal. She wins in the conflict; but

Napoleon, being as unscrupulous as she, does not permit her victory to be complete. Let this be brought out and the little play is done. The climax is when Napoleon, returning from the garden, tells the lady that he has read the letters. This is carefully worked up to. The playing must be hard and bright: it requires, as Shaw says, 'virtuosity'.

The scene is the principal room at the inn, opening on to a vineyard. The open doors at the back are wide. There is a door on the right which leads to the street entry and a fireplace and another door on the left. The room is excessively bright. The period is 1796 and the costumes are described in the text.

The properties are fully described. The packet of dispatches is the most important one: it should not be too bulky; but remember it contains dispatches, and that the lady has opened and read them.

A Note on Productions

The part of Napoleon was written for Richard Mansfield who had made a personal triumph in a play called *Napoleon* by Lorimer Stoddard. Mansfield refused the play, though Shaw told him that 'Napoleon is nobody else but Richard Mansfield himself'. At the time of writing it Shaw was corresponding with Ellen Terry and told her that he had her in mind for the lady. It was first produced by Murray Carson at the Grand Theatre, Croydon, on 1 July 1897: Shaw, who saw it, said the performance was appalling; afterwards it was done at the Comedy Theatre, on 29 March 1901, when Granville Barker played Napoleon; then at the close of the Vedrenne-Barker season at the Court Theatre on 4 June 1907 when Barker did not. Arnold Daly first produced it in America at the Vaudeville Theatre, New York, on 11 February 1904. Earlier than this the German version was produced at Frankfurt on 21 April 1903, and in Berlin the following 10 February. The play has often been revived. It can easily be made not very interesting, and deserves players who do not treat it as a trifle.

(7)
You Never Can Tell

A COMEDY
(1895–7)

This is Bernard Shaw's most popular play, and perhaps the easiest, for it was written with consideration for the requirements of managers in search of fashionable comedies for West End theatres. He wanted to attract an audience of 'perfectly commonplace people'.

Though the play has the ordinary practical comedy form, from which Shaw did not for some years attempt to get away, it is by no means conventional in treatment. On the contrary, it is a topsy-turvy comedy, every character being different from what he or she appears to be, and every situation having an unexpected development. The theme is love, and it deals with the relations of husband and wife, parents and children, and lovers, treated in comic manner.

The story is that an 'emancipated' woman long separated from her husband, having lived for eighteen years in Madeira, comes with her three children to a fashionable watering place on the coast of Torbay in Devon. The play opens with the younger daughter paying a visit to the local dentist, a likeable young man, whom, when her brother calls for her, she invites to luncheon. When he discovers that they do not know who their father is, the young dentist, a stickler for respectability, declines the invitation until he is informed that they know their grandfather to be a Canon of Lincoln, when his objections vanish. The mother arrives with her elder daughter, at the sight of whom the dentist is overcome. The invitation to luncheon is confirmed, and extended to the dentist's landlord, when it is learnt that the latter expects the dentist to lunch with him.

At the luncheon party in the second act the woman's solicitor is present, she having previously sent for him to discuss how she should tell the children about their father; before the dentist turns up with his landlord, the unfortunate woman discovers from the lawyer that the second guest is her not-forgotten and still-loathed husband, the father of the children. What a situation! However, when the unsuspecting men arrive they make the best of it. The luncheon proceeds, its uneasiness partly smoothed by a silky mannered waiter. A conference to discuss the family's affairs is arranged for the evening. The dentist and the elder girl being left alone he makes a declaration of love. Husband and wife remain unrelenting, but in the third and fourth acts the audacity of the twins, aided by the pertinacity of the dentist-lover, pursuing his own aims, overcomes their animosity, and a happy conclusion is finally effected by the blunt common sense of a barrister who is on the spot. The barrister happens to be the waiter's son – 'You never can tell, sir!' Upon this thin domestic plot is woven the love episode of the dentist and the elder girl, the treatment of which is the novel feature of the play.

Shaw sets himself to tear down the veils of illusion and to present a naked picture of love. He makes us understand that it is true love, however, therefore irrational; and he dissects it as an unsentimental artist. Here, he says, is love in its biological and essential truth, and having looked at it in the vein of high comedy, he shows that it is to be valued none the less, and that no less lyrical ecstasy is in it when it becomes conscious love than when kept shrouded in pretence.

In construction, the play is flimsily well made: its excellence lies in the treatment of its theme, the wit and light-heartedness of its dialogue, making it one of the gayest pieces of domestic comedy in the language. The title *You Never Can Tell* is echoed from Shakespeare's *As You Like It*, and to say that Shaw was inspired by Shakespeare is to place his play on a level it deserves.

Characters

VALENTINE, the hero, whose problem is to break down the sentimentalized objection, her own and her mother's, to his natural love for Gloria, is a young man of thirty; his professional manner does not hide the 'thoughtless pleasantry' of a man still in search of adventures, as he first appears, nor the awakened man that he becomes. Highly attractive, very noticeable, keen witted, poetical, he falls head over heels in love against his will: a high comedy character throughout. He is the alert man who discovers himself to be blind.

WILLIAM, the waiter, who has nothing to do with the plot, is the most famous of the characters in the play and perhaps the leading favourite among Shaw's creations. It is he who sums up the play's philosophy, 'It is the unexpected that always happens, isn't it? You never can tell, sir, you never can tell.' As head waiter of the hotel at which the Clandons are staying he is devoted to them: the perfect waiter, never at a loss, always ready at the right moment, never in the way. He knows that it is his duty as a waiter to please and to serve, and makes the most of his 'quiet voice with a gentle melody in it'. He exists as Valentine, for whom he does such admirable service, sees him, so that he is speckless in appearance with not the slightest touch of vulgarity.

GLORIA CLANDON 'is hardly past twenty . . . the incarnation of haughty highmindedness', because she is unaware of herself, inexperienced, and protecting herself by 'a freezing coldness of

manner'. A highly attractive young woman. Unexpected love
causes her to become the victim of her own sincere nature.
Shaw describes her lovingly, for she is the type of woman he
admires, and of whom he is afraid, for he adds, 'A dangerous
girl'. She must pair with Valentine in appearance and acting
skill.

DOLLY CLANDON is 'a very pretty woman in miniature', hardly
eighteen, and may look even younger, gay, irresponsible. Her
twin brother PHILIP is 'a handsome man in miniature', elegant,
muscular, decisive, unexpectedly deep-toned, 'with perfect
manners and a finished personal style'. They play together
throughout.

MRS CLANDON, their mother, is between forty and fifty, a slight
tendency to fat and a fair amount of good looks. She carries
herself well, but somewhat old-fashioned for her age in dress
and manners. Her voice and ways are kindly, for she is a good
mother. She is a survival from the Dialectical Society of Shaw's
youth.

FERGUS CRAMPTON is about sixty, tall, hard and stringy, shrewd,
obstinate, ill-tempered, with 'a querulously dogmatic voice'.
Crampton must have weight, for all his sensitiveness, but he
must not be made over-grotesque, for he is tolerated by
Valentine.

FINCH MCCOMAS is 'about fifty, clean-shaven and close-cropped,
with the corners of his mouth turned down purposely', a fully
crusted-over solicitor. He too must have weight.

MR BOHUN, QC, is a stout, impressive man between forty and
fifty, 'with a midnight oil pallor emphasized by stiff black
hair, cropped short and oiled, and eyebrows like early Victorian
horsehaired upholstery . . . when he speaks, his powerful men-
acing voice, impressively articulated speech, strong inexorable
manner, and a terrifying power of intensely critical listening,

raise the impression produced by him to absolute tremendousness.' Thus we know what Shaw thinks of lawyers, but there is no burlesque, and sharp competent handling of the situation is required.

There is a PARLOUR-MAID for the dentist; and one or two ASSISTANT WAITERS for the luncheon party.

Production

The play is high comedy and requires to be kept on that level. It never becomes farce, and to treat it as such is to lose its charm. It must have sharpness, liveliness and quickness, the pointed dialogue well spoken, the characters well defined. This play will not stand naturalistic treatment, though the luncheon must be realistically carried out and carefully timed; it need not be rushed, for it is part of the action and can be made of interest to the audience. Particular attention should be paid to the love scene between Valentine and Gloria and to its repercussions in the remaining two acts: it is ecstatic love divested of sentimentality; there is feeling in it, with no self-consciousness except on Gloria's part. Without ecstasy, well sustained in Valentine, the character becomes nothing and the play fails, for this scene is the play's central feature.

The first act is a sitting room in a seaside apartment-house converted into a dentist's operating room. The second act is on the terrace at the Marine Hotel with a parapet at the back and a view of Torbay; the entrance to the hotel is on the right, with a servants' entrance behind it, and there is a door to the beach on the left. The third act is a private sitting room at the hotel, an expensive apartment on the ground floor, with a french window leading to the gardens. The fourth act is the same room.

The lighting is bright and gay. In the fourth act it is night, but the gardens outside are gaily lit.

The play belongs to the period 1896. The costumes and properties are described in the text.

A Note on Productions

The first public production in London was at the Strand Theatre on 2 May 1900, when Yorke Stephens played Valentine and James Welsh the Waiter, virtually the same cast as had played in it at the private performance by the Stage Society on the previous 26 November. Shaw would allow only six matinees as 'the rehearsals lacerated my very soul'. I think there is no doubt that the high comedy playing of the original Court Theatre production on 2 May 1905 has never since been equalled, for it is only too easy to take the play on a lower level. Shaw did not spare himself in rehearsal on that occasion and regarded the play as a success. He went to the length of getting a luncheon brought in from the Queen's Restaurant nearby the theatre and served in the second act: though it is not necessary to give the players a real meal, what is suggested by this fact should be noted. Granville Barker as Valentine displayed lyrical intelligence. Louis Calvert's playing of William had melody of speech and his sure timing made the part outstanding. There appears to be a steady degeneration in the quality of the acting this play receives. Although each character is closely observed in its writing the play's success depends largely on Valentine and Gloria, and to treat these characters in any other manner than that of high comedy is to throw their quality away, while self-conscious burlesque at any moment and by any character is fatal. Nearly sixty years after it was written the play is as vital as ever – not so devastatingly comic as at first, but a fine comedy still.

The play was first produced professionally in America on 9 January 1905 by Arnold Daly at the Garrick Theatre, New York.

The German version was produced in Cracow in 1906. A French translation, under the title of *On ne peut jamais dire*, was produced in 1913 at the Théâtre des Arts.

(8)
The Devil's Disciple

A MELODRAMA
(1896–7)

This 'story drama' is melodrama; but its spirit is romance or anti-romance, for Shaw once again takes the romantic hero and turns him inside out. He uses the conventional paraphernalia of melodrama: soldiers, clergyman, heroine, hero, deserted orphan, comic man, villain, sacrifice, trial and execution, with, of course, a happy ending: all the stage tricks are here, but he could not leave them just as they were, so that his hero is also the villain – the devil's disciple. Shaw does not allow him a romantic or even a moral motive: for the play is 'an exercise in Diabolonian ethics'. The hero risks his life on behalf of the heroine's clergyman husband, and makes it clear that he cares nothing for either of them. He says:

> I had no motive and no interest: all I can tell you is that when it came to the point whether I would take my neck out of the noose and put another man's into it, I could not do it. I don't know why not: I see myself as a fool for my pains; but I could not and I cannot. I have been brought up standing by the law of my own nature; and I may not go against it, gallows or no gallows.

The last sentence expresses Shaw's fundamental philosophy that there is something in the nature of every man, which, when put to the test, responds to the highest demands made upon it. It is not a matter of reason, or morality, or self-interest, but of human nature: the philosophical basis of his doctrine of equality.

Shaw chose for this play the period of the American War of Independence, in 1777. From the little town of Westerbridge in New Hampshire, a man has gone to Springtown where his brother was to be hanged by the British soldiers as an example to the rebellious inhabitants. On his way home after the execution the man dies. The news is brought to his wife, Mrs Dudgeon, sitting at home awaiting his return, and at the same time she is told that he had made a new will. The family gathers together to hear the will (we have to ignore the fact that they had hardly had time to hear the news) and with them comes the eldest son Richard Dudgeon, who has not been home for many years; he is a reprobate and of the worst reputation. The will, made on the dying man's deathbed, shows that he left everything to his son Richard, the main conditions being that 'he shall not let my brother Peter's natural child starve or be driven by want to an evil life'. This child, Essie, lives with Richard's mother and is as cruelly treated as the woman had treated her own children. Richard gladly accepts the charge, and, before his mother, the minister and his pious relations, declares himself to be the Devil's Disciple – for 'he comforted me and saved me from having my spirit broken in this house of children's tears'. He goes on: 'From this day this house is his home; and no child shall cry in it: this hearth is his altar; and no soul shall ever cower over it in the dark evenings and be afraid.' Then, before they have recovered from the shock, Richard tells them that the British soldiers are on their way to the town looking for another man to hang. So they all go hurriedly off.

In the second act, the minister Anthony Anderson and his wife Judith are at home. Anderson has sent for Richard to warn him that he is in danger; for who is more likely to be hanged than this reprobate? Then the minister is sent for to visit Mrs Dudgeon who is ill, and Richard and Judith are left alone. The soldiers appear, and arrest Richard as the minister: he does not undeceive them. When the minister returns he finds his wife on the floor unconscious. Gradually he gets the truth from her, and learns, what she did not wish him to know, that Richard has been arrested in mistake for him. This arouses the minister to action, he sends his wife for a horse and gets ready for immediate departure. Judith thinks he has gone to save himself.

In the third act, Richard is being tried by court martial. Before the trial, Judith comes to tell him about her husband's dastardly conduct and to thank him for his heroism. There is a curious one-sided love scene. During the trial, it is proved that Richard is not the minister; but that makes no difference: he is to be hanged. We are introduced to General John Burgoyne, the famous soldier-politician, who is drawn with elegance and humour as an example of the intelligent English aristocracy. He and Richard pit their wits against each other. In a second scene, Richard has the rope around his neck ready to be hanged. In the original version his last words were 'Long live the devil, and damn King George'; but when the play came to be published they had been altered to 'Amen. My life for the world's future!' The punctilious Burgoyne will not let the execution take place until the exact stroke of the hour, and as they are waiting in the market-place the minister dashes in with a safe conduct, empowered on behalf of the American militia to make terms for the evacuation of the town by the British, and Richard is saved. The minister forces home the moral in the true spirit of melodrama:

Sir: It is in the hour of trial that a man finds his true profession. This foolish young man boasted himself the Devil's Disciple; but when the hour of trial came to him, he found that it was his destiny to suffer and be faithful to the death. I thought myself a decent minister of the gospel of peace; but when the hour of trial came to me, I found that it was my duty to be a man of action, and that my place was amid the thunder of the captains and the shouting.

Actuality is thrown to the winds throughout the play so far as the situations are concerned, though the dialogue is actual enough. The plot is mere theatre and stands no examination, but it is an effective stage piece and proved to be Shaw's first box-office success. He made so much money out of the American production that he gave up his post as dramatic critic of *The Saturday Review*.

Characters

RICHARD DUDGEON, reckless, sardonic, defiant, high-spirited – the typical, handsome hero of romance, who has not only to look well but to speak well, for he carries off the play.

MRS DUDGEON, old, disagreeable, an example of cruelty and bigotry, the one utterly objectionable and unsympathetic character the author ever created; in her Shaw attacks 'religion . . . an excuse for (the) . . . master-passion of hatred in all its phases of cruelty and envy'.

ESSIE the orphan is about sixteen, mild, timid, and pretty, young for her age.

CHRISTY, the second son, is a round-faced, stupid, loutish fellow.

THE REV ANTHONY ANDERSON, about fifty, a genial, shrewd Presbyterian, a strong healthy man, full of vitality.

JUDITH, his second wife, not more than thirty, pretty, proper, and ladylike: she is the sentimental heroine.

LAWYER HAWKINS, a brisk middle-aged man.

WILLIAM DUDGEON, large, shapeless, bottle-nosed, not prosperous.

MRS WILLIAM DUDGEON, an anxious little woman who says nothing.

TITUS DUDGEON, a wiry little terrier of a man and well off.

MRS TITUS DUDGEON, large and prosperous, and says nothing.

THE SERGEANT, the bluff, instinctively-respectful-to-his-betters, typical British soldier.

MAJOR SWINDON, conscientious, fair-minded, about forty-five, a true soldier.

GENERAL BURGOYNE, fifty-five, a man of fashion, aristocratic, witty, intelligent, altogether a highly distinguished person, a character in whom the playwright delighted and to whom he devoted some of his best lines.

MR BRUDENELL is the military chaplain at the execution.

There are BRITISH AND GERMAN OFFICERS comprising the Court Martial. There are many SOLDIERS and a CROWD in the market-place at the end, together with a TOWN BEADLE.

Production

This melodrama with the atmosphere of romance should contain no burlesque. The weakness of all melodrama, which is that the protagonist, if there is one, cannot function well, is present here. Richard is the protagonist, of course, and the piece takes its wilful, light, irresponsible note from him; but there is confusion of motives, characteristic of such plays. The production needs to be straightforward, however, though, as always with Shaw, full blooded. The tension intended to be created by the crowd at the end depends largely upon this, it also requires sufficient people – not too many children and girls, but men. The court martial must give a sufficient setting to the polished Burgoyne. In the first act the action works up to the entrance of Richard; the climax is when Richard says 'which of you good men will take this child and rescue her from the house of the devil'. The climax of the second act is when Richard is arrested; the anti-climax when Judith says 'He took your place'. The climax of the third act, second scene, is when Judith says 'That man is not my husband'; and the climax of the third scene, and of the play, when the minister enters.

There are four settings, which are described in the text together with the properties. The period is 1777 in New England, and the costumes must have attention, particularly the soldiers' uniforms.

A Note on Productions

The play was first performed in America by Richard Mansfield on 1 October 1897, at Albany; three days later, on 4 October, at the Fifth Avenue Theatre, New York. It was a very great success, though Shaw wrote to Mrs Mansfield to say that from what he had heard from eye-witnesses he would cross the Atlantic one day and play the executioner 'and on that occasion Anderson will arrive too late'. Its first production in England was by Murray Carson at the Kennington Theatre two years later on 4 October 1899. Shaw was abroad when the production took place and lamented that he 'had not even a chance of publicly forgiving' the actors. It was afterwards successfully performed in the English provinces by Harold V. Neilson, before J. Forbes-Robertson brought it to London on 7 September 1900, at the Coronet Theatre, Notting Hill. Shaw conducted these latter rehearsals. Dick Dudgeon has also been played by Matheson Lang, Granville Barker (on tour), Claude Rains, Martin Harvey, Robert Donat, Tyrone Power, and others, and Basil Sydney and Maurice Evans in New York. The many character parts make it a play requiring a large and competent company. Its revivals have always been successful. The German version was first produced in Vienna on 25 February 1903 and at Lwow on 27 October the same year.

A Hollywood film version was made in 1959 from a script in

which the play was re-written, with additional scenes, providing star parts for Burt Lancaster, Kirk Douglas and Laurence Olivier. It possessed little Shavian quality.

(9)
Caesar and Cleopatra

A HISTORY
(1898)

In this play Shaw wrote history in the idiom of contemporary life. His aim was to attempt to deal with a great classic theme for 'the classic actor of our day', as he said; though this was possibly an afterthought. He declared that he had in mind that Shakespeare had not been equal to Caesar, he 'never knew human strength of the Caesarian type'. This was a curious criticism, for while Shaw's Caesar is a genuinely original man he is displayed (except in the fourth act) not in moments of greatness but doing what he naturally wants to do. Though this Caesar speaks as an ordinary man, however, Shaw's aim was not to diminish his greatness, and in fact the man is great. As for Cleopatra, she was, he wrote to Ellen Terry, 'an animal, a bad lot'.

The play is written in the classic manner, in five acts, and opens with a short scene, which introduces the names of the conquering Caesar and the (at the moment) lost Cleopatra. Shaw replaced it by a long speech as a Prologue, spoken by the God Ra, in which the 'quaint little islanders . . . ye compulsorily educated ones' are told what Shaw thinks of them as they sit awaiting his play. The first act is in the shadow of the Sphinx. Julius Caesar appears, and, being alone as he thinks, hails the Sphinx, which awakens Cleopatra who has been sleeping between the great paws. 'A child at its breast, a divine child', says Caesar as he sees her, and Cleopatra bids the (to her) 'old gentleman' come up to her, which he does and they talk, she, not knowing who he is, telling him her fears of the barbarian Caesar and his soldiers. He says he will teach her a way to prevent Caesar from eating her, and hearing the sound of the approaching army the terrified queen brings him to the palace. Afterwards Caesar takes charge and shows Cleopatra how a queen should behave, and she discovers who he is. It is important to note that Caesar is the protagonist – the play is his – and it is of equal importance that he is not old.

In the second act at the Palace in Alexandria, the boy king, Ptolemy, and his sister meet and quarrel; Caesar makes them behave. The precariousness of Caesar's position is discussed, and news comes of the burning of the library of Alexandria, Caesar unperturbed at the news. 'What is burning there is the memory of mankind', he is told. 'A shameful memory, let it burn', he answers. 'Will you destroy the past?' 'Ay, and build the future with its ruins.'

The third act is in two scenes and opens with Cleopatra on the edge of the quay trying to get across to Pharos island across the harbour, where Caesar is. She is not permitted to go, but is allowed to send a carpet as a present to Caesar. Caesar receives the carpet, and as it is unrolled Cleopatra comes out. Then the Egyptians attack the island, and Caesar, his way of escape cut off, jumps into the sea and Cleopatra is thrown in after him.

In the fourth act, six months later, Cleopatra in her palace at Alexandria is invited to plot against the victorious Caesar, which she refuses to do. When Caesar hears of it he spares the plotter, but Cleopatra gets her nurse to murder the man. The angry Caesar threatens to leave Cleopatra, and his captain kills the nurse. This act is very well constructed and contains the climax, for Caesar knows what he has to do. His self-confessions are operatic airs, and give the play distinction. Otherwise, the play as a whole is thinly written.

In the last act Caesar is about to leave for Rome, he has forgotten Cleopatra, but she appears, in mourning for her nurse; Caesar tells her that the captain is to be governor in Caesar's name. Cleopatra will not bid him farewell. He tells her he will send her a man 'Roman from head to heel and Roman of the noblest . . . Mark Anthony', and she throws herself into his arms. 'He will return some day', she is told as Caesar's ship moves off. 'I hope not', she replies.

Characters

JULIUS CAESAR is the classic Roman figure, bald but dignified, a kingly man of original power, not at all conventional, having 'virtue he has no need of goodness'. The part dominates the play without obviously appearing to do so, which means that the actor must have marked personality.

CLEOPATRA is a child queen, a ripe sixteen, spoiled, ignorant, not in the guise of a great lady, but of a plaything, though she is imperious enough when she gets the chance.

PTOLEMY XIV is six years younger than his sister.

BELZANOR, the captain of Cleopatra's guard, is a warrior of fifty.

BEL AFFRIS is a fair-haired dandy, novice in the guard of the temple of Ra.

FTATATEETA, the queen's nurse, is a huge fat woman, powerful, a person of consequence, intended to be a good character part.

POTHINUS, the guardian of Ptolemy is fifty, a eunuch, passionate, of common mind, uncontrollable.

THEODOTUS, the tutor of Ptolemy, is a little old wizened man.

ACHILLAS, guard of Ptolemy's troops, is a handsome dignified man of thirty-five with a large black beard.

RUFIO is a burly Roman officer, middle-aged, rough, made governor by Caesar.

BRITANNUS, Caesar's secretary, is forty, tall, serious, and expresses British sentiments.

LUCIUS SEPTIMUS is a Roman officer, tall, thin, athletic, resolute.

CHARMIAN, thin and dark.

IRAS, plump and red.

APOLLADORUS is a young Sicilian of twenty-four.

PERSIAN GUARDSMAN, ARABIAN SENTINEL, WOUNDED SOLDIER, PROFESSOR OF MUSIC, CENTURION, SOLDIERS, SLAVES, LADIES attendant on Cleopatra, etc.

Production

The period is the end of the XXXIII Dynasty, from October 48 B.C. to March 47 B.C., the scene Egypt, opening on the Syrian border, the remaining scenes in Alexandria. The play is historical anti-romance; it needs to be handled with spirit and staged with magnificence. If the Prologue is used the God Ra needs a Hawk's mask: the original scene can, in fact, also be played. The play depends upon the leading character, who must convey the impression of the Caesar of tradition. The necessary settings, properties, lighting, are described. The play can successfully receive Shakespearean treatment.

A Note on Productions

The play was first publicly produced in German by Max Reinhardt at the Neues Theater, Berlin, on 31 March 1906; first production in America with Forbes-Robertson as Caesar on 30 October that year; and first produced in England by Forbes-Robertson at Leeds on 16 September 1907, coming to London at the Savoy on the following 25 November. The part suited the distinguished actor, for it requires classic comedy playing. It has been played by Cedric Hardwicke, Malcolm Keen, and Laurence Olivier. Though nothing like so important, the part of Cleopatra has been played by Gertrude Elliott, Gwen Ffrangcon-Davies, Peggy Ashcroft and Vivien Leigh. The play was filmed by Gabriel Pascal in England and Egypt in 1945, a highly extravagant pictorial version, in which the acting had a minor place, and the dramatic action became lost.

(10)
Captain Brassbound's Conversion

AN ADVENTURE
(1899)

As this play was written for Ellen Terry, Shaw, for the one time in his dramatic career, seems to have cared very little for the other characters. When she saw the play she did not like it, much to Shaw's chagrin. 'More fitted for the closet than the stage', she said; and her judgment implies that the play is not one of Shaw's most inspired efforts. It is thin and inconclusive, for form and thought are not fused. In fact, Shaw lost his hold upon his dramatic method.

The setting in Morocco was, says Shaw, stolen from Cunninghame Graham; he got his plot from fact. In this play Shaw gives evidence of his interest in dialect, which makes for rather hard reading as he spells Cockney, Scots and American as he considered them to be spoken.

At the house of a Presbyterian missionary in Mogador, Morocco, Sir Howard Hallam and Lady Cicily Waynflete come to stay, because there is no hotel. Lady Cicily wants to take a trip into the interior, and, though she is told it is not safe, insists on going. Captain Brassbound, who has not an altogether good reputation, is engaged to escort her. He warns Sir Howard, who is a judge, that he may meet justice in the hills.

In the second act, in a Moorish castle, Brassbound informs Sir Howard that he is a prisoner; for he, Brassbound, is the nephew of Sir Howard who he declares was responsible for the death of his mother, who was a native of Brazil, and responsible, too, for the theft of his own inheritance there. He proposes to hand Sir Howard over to the fanatical Moors. Lady Cicily sets about Brassbound's conversion. She tells him he is very like his uncle, and artfully gets round him so that his confidence goes. Brassbound attempts to make terms with the Sheikh to whom he was proposing to hand over Sir Howard, as he has now changed his mind; and while they are bargaining the Cadi appears with orders from the captain of a US cruiser to rescue the travellers, so Sir Howard is doubly saved and Brassbound taken prisoner.

The third act is back in the missionary's house, the naval captain holding a court of inquiry into the affair. Sir Howard is prepared to let justice take its course on his nephew, but Lady Cicily gives her version of the affair, with the result that Brassbound and his men are set free. Then Brassbound tells Lady Cicily that he wants a commander, for left to himself he has become half a brigand, so he orders her to marry him. As she is about to yield the guns of a British ship are heard, thus she is saved from folly, and, he declares, as he escapes, that he has got his life's purpose restored.

The play's weakness is that it has no protagonist, for it is no more than a set of characters put into a contrived situation. Attention is absorbed by Lady Cicily, but she is presented not with dramatic point, only as a fascinating woman of great distinction and 'immense self-complacency'. This is a good example of how not to write a dramatic work. All the same it contains considerable Shavian quality.

Characters

LADY CICILY WAYNFLETE is between thirty and forty, tall, good-looking, intelligent, tender – in fact, Ellen Terry. The play depends upon her being, as Shaw said of the character, the great English lady.

CAPTAIN BRASSBOUND is about thirty-six, handsome, joyless, grim, attractive, but not sympathetic.

SIR HOWARD HALLAM is elderly, rectangular, tight-lipped, imposing, with an air of authority.

LESLIE RANKIN, the missionary, is an elderly Scotsman, a wiry, tanned, small-knit man. He has to uphold some rather dull patches.

DRINKWATER is a weedy Cockney, under forty, product of the slums, ready and fluent.

REDBROOK a worthless young English gentleman gone to the bad.

JOHNSON, black-bearded, thick-set, middle-aged ruffian.

MARZO, another of Brassbound's ruffians.

SIDI EL ASSIF, a nobly handsome Arab Sheikh under thirty.

OSMAN is second to the Sheikh.

THE CADI, a white-bearded, vigorous Arab.

CAPTAIN HAMLIN KEARNEY, a robust Western American naval man.

AMERICAN BLUEJACKET, BRASSBOUND'S MEN, THE SHEIKH'S FOLLOWERS, THE CADI'S FOLLOWERS.

Production

The play is romantic comedy, despite its melodramatic elements, requiring much histrionic skill to be made tolerable. Indeed, virtuosity is required. The play must not be sacrificed to Lady Cicily, for, while it depends upon her, Brassbound is important, and without a strong and attractive player in the part the balance cannot be kept. There are delightful moments and theatrically effective ones, but as a whole the play is uncertain as drama, though it can be made a vehicle for the display of feminine charm, and thus become an excellent entertainment. The settings are in the garden of the missionary's house; a room in a Moorish castle; a room in the missionary's house.

A Note on Productions

The first production was by the Stage Society at the Strand Theatre on 16 December 1900, with Janet Achurch and Charles Charrington. It was toured by Harold V. Neilson and produced on 12 May 1902 at the Queen's Theatre, Manchester. Vedrenne-Barker included it on 20 March 1906, with Ellen Terry, who afterwards toured it in England and America. When she came to act in the play, Ellen Terry could not remember her lines, and, despite a charming personal appearance, the play was less like a Shaw comedy than could be believed. Shaw calls it an 'old-fashioned, orthodox, and easily understood melodramatic comedy'. It has been revived many times, usually, though not invariably, with success, for it needs experienced playing, and very sure production, simple as its seems. Lady Cicily has been played by Gertrude Kingston, Flora Robson, Ursula Jeans and others.

(11)
The Admirable Bashville

OR CONSTANCY UNREWARDED
(1901)

Shaw was told that several stage versions of *Cashel Byron's Profession* were being performed in America, and, as the law did not then prevent any person making a stage version of a novel in that country and calling it his own, when he realized the position he sat down and wrote within a week a stage version under the above title to preserve his stage copyright. He wrote the play in blank verse, because, he said, he was fond of blank verse, and because its 'rigmarole style' was easy to write, which does not make it rank with the best models of blank verse drama, as Shaw declared it did. He was interested in boxing at an early date and became a connoisseur of pugilism. His play of the prize-fighter, Cashel Byron, who falls in love with the high-born Lydia Carew, is in three acts, but too short to be theatrically useful. It is a highly entertaining farce, however, which acts extremely well, but needs another play to fill out the programme.

In a glade in Wiltstoken Park, Lydia, the heroine, declares herself to be longing for a mate who knows nothing of books and art and culture. As she weeps, Cashel Byron enters, and at once she falls in love with his strength, he with her beauty. His trainer Mellish recalls him to duty, for Cashel is a professional pugilist, and bids him think of his mother, but Cashel declares 'Two things I hate, my duty and my mother'. He will not listen to Mellish, and after a knock-out blow leaves him to find Lydia.

In a room in Lydia's London house, her cousin Lucian calls and complains that he does not like Cashel to haunt the house. Bashville, the footman, reads to them the newspaper account of a fight in which Cashel was victorious. Cashel calls, but the footman trips him at the staircase foot, and locks the door, but Lydia insists that Cashel be admitted. She then tells him that he must not come again unless:

> You can some day look in my eyes and say:
> Lydia: my occupation's gone.

He says:

> Slave to the Ring I rest until the face
> Of Paradise be changed.

By which he means that he has to meet Paradise, a boxer, in the ring. When Lydia leaves him, Bashville hits Cashel on the nose, and when she returns, Cashel admits that 'Flush on the boko napped your footman's left'. She is enraptured and when he goes off to wash his face declares:

> His nose
> Dropt lovely color: tis a perfect blood.

Then she goes off with Cashel, and the footman declares his love in a soliloquy.

A prize-fight is to take place at the Agricultural Hall, Islington, attended by the Zulu Chief, Cetewayo, and people of fashion. There in the presence of Lydia, Cashel meets Paradise, the Zulus run amok and the fight becomes a shambles; but Cashel is the equal of all.

In the last act at Wiltstoken, Lydia is at her writing table when Cashel comes to say that the law is on his track and Lydia hides him. The police come, also Cashel's mother, and then he surrenders, ready to go to prison to escape his mother. His mother declares that he was nobly born, so that the opposition to Lydia's marriage to him is removed. Lord Worthington offers his hand to Cashel's mother, and off they go 'with might and main' to St George's Church, Hanover Square.

Characters

CASHEL BYRON is the boxer hero; there is little to be said about him (or the other characters) except that they must look their parts and be able to speak Shaw's blank verse.

LYDIA is the romantic heroine.

BASHVILLE is the romantic footman, admirable because of his protection of the heroine.

MELLISH is Cashel's trainer.

LUCIAN is Lydia's cousin.

CETEWAYO is the Zulu Chief.

PARADISE is Cashel's boxing opponent.

LORD WORTHINGTON is one of the patrons of the ring.

MASTER OF THE REVELS is the Ring Master.

A POLICEMAN comes to arrest Cashel.

ADELAIDE GISBORNE is Cashel's mother.

There are ZULUS and others in the second act.

Production

The play needs treatment equivalent to the high-powered blank verse. The acting must be exaggerated but kept in balance. The play being short, all the parts need careful casting and to be played for all they are worth. There is no realism whatever, and there must be none in the staging. The settings are the park of a country house, a house in London, the ring at the Agricultural Hall, and a room at the country house. The dressing should be of the early 'eighties or earlier.

A Note on Productions

The stage history of this piece, which Shaw regarded as a 'literary joke', is that it was first given an amateur production, not a serious affair, and afterwards included by the Stage Society in its programme at the Imperial Theatre, on 7 June 1903, Shaw not taking full responsibility. He allowed Harold V. Neilson to tour with it, and it came to Beerbohm Tree's After Noon Theatre at His Majesty's Theatre on 26 January 1909, Shaw directing it. It has been revived many times, and, played as the dramatist intended, with some exaggeration, is a highly entertaining piece.

(12)
Man and Superman

A COMEDY AND A PHILOSOPHY
(1901–3)

This is an extremely ambitious work, intended to express a philosophy of life, and, incidentally, to show that it was possible to write a play about sex without evading the sexual problem. A. B. Walkley, dramatic critic of *The Times*, and one-time colleague of Shaw's, had said that he should write a play about Don Juan: meaning, no doubt, about himself, as a notorious lady killer. So Shaw wrote the play, and published it with a dedicatory epistle to Walkley in which he explained why his friend would not like the work.

Walkley could not be expected to like it because the play went beyond being a comedy upon sexual attraction and took as its theme an exposition of the idea of the Life Force. The comedy structure is conventional, except for the middle scene, in which, and indeed throughout the play, Shakespearean influence is clearly marked; for the leading character's monologues are akin to those uttered by leading characters in Shakespeare. The relations between the sexes are displayed as the 'love chase of the man by the woman'. In the central 'dream' the theme is lifted into the realm of 'Shavio-Socratic dialogue', as Shaw calls it, constituting in fact perhaps his masterpiece in rhetorical dialogue, and standing alone in English dramatic literature. This scene is a play in itself, and can be performed apart from the comedy, just as the comedy can be, and is, performed without it. But when the complete piece is given it is seen to have unity and the play then creates its greatest effect.

'Man is not victor in the duel of sex' is the idea around which the simple comedy is built: an idea of natural biology. Man is helpless in woman's hands, says Shaw, and in 1903, when the play was published, people found the idea shocking, for it wasn't nice to say that the initiative in sex was with the woman. Today, there is not the same anxiety to deny it, for women have their way. But to say that men are the prey of women is not the same as to say that women are the leaders of men, however, and Shaw does not raise that question. He does raise the question, 'How many men would face the difficulties of life did their wives not make them?' Women are men's driving force, that which gives birth, which makes men overcome their natural inertia and become creators as women naturally are.

Shaw did not, however, stop at the mere statement of women's function in relation to man. He developed the philosophy of the Life Force, the Force that relies upon men and women for achieving its ends, and upon man recognizing himself as an instrument for the creation of something greater than himself. Hence the idea of the Superman. Shaw announces the idea and the necessity for the Superman, he does not work out the idea or attempt to define what he means by Superman, except as one who consciously carries out the purposes of the Life Force. That life is for the sake of birth and that man as we know him is to be surpassed are as far as he goes.

At the end of the play there is printed 'The Revolutionists' Handbook and Pocket Companion', by John Tanner, the leading character in the play. The Handbook appears in the first act, when it is flung into a waste-paper basket; this incident no doubt induced Shaw to prove that there was such a book; it is a treatise on marriage and the perfection of man, and contains a collection of aphorisms on a variety of subjects.

The play opens in Portland Place, where an old-fashioned radical and rationalist, Roebuck Ramsden, is consoling a young man, Octavius, on the death of a friend, father of the girl the young man expects to marry. Ramsden warns him about the bad influence of his friend John Tanner. Then to Ramsden's amazement Tanner is announced to say that the girl's father has made Ramsden and himself joint guardians of the girl. Both are annoyed, Ramsden at having anything to do with Tanner, author of a licentious book, and Tanner at having any sort of responsibility for the girl, Ann. When Ann appears, however, she beguiles both into acquiescing in the responsibility (indeed, they cannot evade it without upsetting the will). Suddenly a scandal threatens to emerge concerning Octavius's sister, Violet, who has made a secret marriage and will not disclose the name of her husband.

The first act provides an admirable introduction to all the characters, save two, and to the play's theme, and consists of a series of surprises, each carefully prepared for, so that interest is continuously excited. Shaw never wrote anything better.

In the next act we are at Ann's mother's house at Richmond where Octavius tells Tanner that Ann has rejected him. Tanner cheers him up by saying that she is only playing with him, and expounds his philosophy of woman, explaining that Ann has certainly marked him down as her victim. 'I wish I could believe that, vilely as you put it', laments Octavius. Then Tanner talks to Ann who complains about her mother's interference with her, and suggests that she should break her chains and take a motor tour with him to the continent – a daring expedition! To his horror she agrees – for he had not been serious. His horror is increased when Straker, his chauffeur, tells him that he, Tanner, is Ann's 'marked-down victim . . . and no mistake'. So, without more ado, Tanner flies, alone with his chauffeur and car, into the wilds of Spain.

The third act is in the Sierra Navada, with Tanner and his servant in the hands of Brigands. There Tanner has a dream which constitutes the dialogue called 'Don Juan in Hell'. The characters in the play become the persons in the dream: Tanner is Don Juan, Ramsden Don Gonzalo, the Brigand the Devil, and Ann the Dona Anna of Mozart's Opera. The dream is a discussion upon heaven, hell, women and the philosophy of the Life Force, of which Don Juan is the exponent. He explains why love has failed to interest him permanently, and expounds his 'passion for divine contemplation and creative activity'. The long dream ends, and in the morning Ann turns up, with her mother and sister, having come after Tanner, and soldiers also arrive, so that they are all safe, even the brigands, for Tanner pretends that they are his escort.

The fourth act is in a hotel at Grenada, where the mystery of Violet's marriage is cleared up, and Ann makes her capture of Tanner complete. 'I solemnly say that I am not a happy man', says Tanner, while Ann looks happy, but is only triumphant.

Characters

JOHN TANNER, the protagonist, is Shaw himself, with a beard and a restless blue eye: an endless talker. Shaw declared, however, that the character was suggested by the Socialist Hyndman, and there must be some truth in that, for Tanner is very well dressed. The part requires an actor with an exceptional memory, but, above all, great intensity and concentration, with the gift of lightness. There is no difficulty in seeing that the entire action is from Tanner's point of view.

ANN WHITEFIELD is a woman to 'make men dream': beautiful, passionate, though self-controlled, and fashionably dressed. Shaw admits that the weaker of her sex would sometimes call her 'a cat'. He says that the character was suggested to him when watching a performance of Everyman: 'I said to myself, why not Everywoman? Ann was the result: every woman is not Ann but Ann is Everywoman.' It is not a 'sympathetic' part, but lively, intelligent and highly feminine. She is as Tanner sees her, not as she necessarily is in herself.

ROEBUCK RAMSDEN is over sixty, a Unitarian, Free Trader, and Rationalist.

OCTAVIUS ROBINSON is 'an uncommonly nice-looking young fellow'. Shaw says he took the character over unaltered from Mozart.

MRS WHITEFIELD is a little sweet-faced woman, a sympathetic character part.

MISS RAMSDEN is 'a hard-headed old maiden lady'.

VIOLET ROBINSON is 'not a siren like Ann', but a handsome self-possessed young woman.

HENRY STRAKER is a young Cockney chauffeur, product of the London Polytechnics of the first years of this century, smart, affable, competent: suggested partly by H. G. Wells's Kipps and partly by Barrie's Admirable Crichton.

HECTOR MALONE is a handsome American of twenty-four, faultlessly dressed.

MENDOZA, the head of the band of Spanish brigands, is a Jew, a tall strong man, imposing, a figure of romantic melodrama.

DON JUAN is Tanner, ANNA is Ann; THE STATUE is a majestic old statue in white marble from Mozart's opera and resembles Roebuck Ramsden. THE DEVIL is also from the opera and is the conventional figure of Satan in the Spanish dress of the fifteenth century, also like Mendoza.

MR MALONE is an Irish-American millionaire and true to stage type.

There are SPANISH SOLDIERS with an OFFICER, also a PARLOURMAID. Also about a dozen BRIGANDS of various nationalities, representing a group of socialists of the period.

Production

Shaw refers to the play as tragi-comedy; but it is true high comedy. He also called it a 'philosophical comedy'. Farcical treatment or burlesque must rigorously be avoided. Skilful, polished comedy playing is called for, and the piece has to be done with spirit and the utmost intelligence. The first interior setting is the substantial wealthy room of the period, and the other settings and the dressing give the impression of affluence. The period is 1900–1905 and the motor-car belongs to it as well as the costumes.

When the hell scene is given either alone or in the complete play it can be done in a black setting with only the figures illuminated. It should not be forgotten that it is a dream. This scene is a test of the actors' ability to listen, which, in fact, is true of the play as a whole.

A Note on Productions

The play (apart from the hell scene) was first performed under the auspices of the Stage Society at the Court Theatre on 21 May 1905. This was the Vedrenne-Barker production first seen publicly on 23 May. The first American production was at the Hudson Theatre, New York, on 5 September 1905, by Robert Loraine for a run; he afterwards toured it throughout the United States. The *Don Juan in Hell* scene was first performed by Vedrenne-Barker at the Court Theatre on 4 June 1907. The first performance of the entire play, produced by Esme Percy, was at the Lyceum Theatre, Edinburgh, on 11 June 1915; in London the first full production was at the Regent Theatre on 23 October 1925. The entire play has not yet been performed in New York but a full performance was given by the Hedgerow Theatre on 26 July 1939. The hell scene has been separately performed and given as a reading many times. Charles Laughton toured it in the United States with Charles Boyer, Cedric Hardwicke and Agnes Moorhead, calling themselves 'The Drama Quartette'. The reading was given in evening dress without scenery or costumes, the readers sitting on four stools with microphones.

The first production at the peak of the Vedrenne-Barker management was as near the ideal performance as could be imagined. While that production cannot be repeated its qualities of serious comedy are to be remembered. Robert Loraine, who was an accomplished comedy actor and a striking personality, made a great success of it in America, but there was more than a tendency towards farce in his production. That tendency persists in later revivals in this country; but farce is nowhere present in the play.

(13)
John Bull's Other Island

(1904)

In this play Shaw writes as an Irishman for an Irish audience, for the play was intended for the Irish Literary Theatre, which preceded the Abbey Theatre, Dublin; but it proved to be beyond that theatre's resources, and, instead, assured the success of the Vedrenne-Barker management at the Court Theatre. 'The Preface for Politicians', written in 1906, was one of Shaw's most provocative and downright political pamphlets. In it he declared that as an Irishman he claimed 'the extraction of most Englishmen', for he did not belong to what passes for 'aboriginal Irish'. 'I am', he says, 'a genuine typical Irishman of the Danish, Norman, Cromwellian and (of course) Scotch invasions.' His native language 'is the language of Swift'. In fact, he was more English than the English.

The play is uncompromising in its presentation of the real old

Ireland, and the age-long conflict between English and Irish is displayed between the easily prosperous, short-sighted, thick-skinned, but still admirable Englishman, and the struggling, poor, imaginative, sensitive and no less admirable Irishman. The Englishman is presented as the Irish see him, a comic figure; but Shaw is at pains to show that the loudest laugh his countrymen could raise at the expense of the absurd Englishman is not really a laugh on their side. In this detachment there is remarkable insight, a sign of the highest genius. The Englishman is simple, almost childlike in his folly, yet with a clear purpose: a joke which has to be taken seriously. Larry, the Irishman, is a grown-up man compared with his friend, but much less practical and less adaptable. This is a subtle portrait, a character of the greatest significance in Shavian drama. Larry is the protagonist; a comic figure, but one of the most sympathetic Shaw ever drew.

The political trouble with Ireland was that it was a conquered country and 'a conquered nation is like a man with a cancer: he can think of nothing else'. This was written when Ireland was still ruled by English folly instead of its own. The preface was a passionate plea for Home Rule. Shaw spoke of the 'clumsy thumb' of English rule. 'If you would be good enough, ladies and gentlemen of England, to take your thumb away and leave us free to do something else than bite it', there would be the end of discord in Ireland and between the two countries. Well, since then the Irish question has been settled, but as Shaw said, making an addition to his preface twenty-four years later (1929), 'not as civilized and reasonable men should have settled it, but as dogs settle a dispute over a bone'. The question is not in fact settled; and will not be settled until England has settled her own question.

The play shows the offices of the firm of Doyle and Broadbent, civil engineers, Great George Street, Westminster. A piece of land in Ireland has come into their hands; it happens to be Roscullen, where Larry Doyle was born and where he lived until he came to England eighteen years before. Tom Broadbent, a typical Gladstonian Liberal, sentimental about Ireland, wants to see the land. Larry has not the slightest intention of going back, if only for the reason that there is a girl waiting for him, whom he would be glad not to see again. But when he realizes that Broadbent might be romantic enough to fall in love with the girl and take her off his hands, he is only too ready to go.

They arrive at Roscullen, and, sure enough, Broadbent succumbs to his romantic illusions, and the very first evening makes love to Nora. Next day Larry is invited by his father and the neighbouring farmers to become their Parliamentary candidate. He refuses. Broadbent snaps up the invitation with joy. Larry tells Nora that she must not think of him any more. Broadbent discovering the girl in tears gets her to consent to marry him. Broadbent is a huge success, and his popularity is not a bit damaged when he makes a laughing stock of himself over one of the small farmers' pigs. He sees a great future for Roscullen when his land development syndicate gets to work. With the land, the girl, and the parliamentary candidature his, no wonder he declares, 'I feel now as I never did before that I am right in devoting my life to the cause of Ireland'.

The contrast between English and Irish makes the delicious humour of the play. The Englishman is unmistakable. The Irish types are straight from life. Peter Keegan, a one-time priest, not quite so straight from life, is the mouthpiece of Shaw's idealistic philosophy: 'When you speak to me of English and Irish you forget that I am a Catholic. My country is not Ireland or England, but the whole mighty realm of my Church. For me there are but two countries: heaven and hell; but two conditions of men: salvation and damnation.' That is Shaw speaking.

The play was a great success on the first occasion of its performance, and is so still, because it is concerned with fundamental human problems.

Characters

LARRY DOYLE is thirty-six, a fastidious, clever Irishman. He feels everything so acutely that all is made sentimental. He is a capable man, but his feelings combined with his sense of reality overcome him: a very carefully drawn part.

TOM BROADBENT is in the prime of life, a full-blooded, energetic, successful Englishman as seen through Irish eyes. H. G. Wells professed to seeing himself in the character, but physically Broadbent was the opposite of Wells, and the physique is the man.

HODSON is Broadbent's old valet, also wholly English.

TIM HAFFIGAN is a wastrel of thirty, ruined by drink.

PETER KEEGAN does not wear clerical dress, but has the face of a saint. An intense, lyrical, talkative, sympathetic character.

PATSY FARRELL is a young Irish labourer.

NORA REILLY, the heroine, a slight, frail woman, with delicacy of manner, sensibility and Irish charm.

FATHER DEMPSEY, the Parish priest, is stout and fatherly, easy-going, amiable, accustomed to authority.

CORNELIUS DOYLE is Larry's father, a man of business, genial.

AUNT JUDY is a woman of fifty, lively, busy, narrow.

MATTHEW HAFFIGAN, an oldish peasant farmer.

BARNY DORAN, stout-bodied, round-headed, on the verge of middle-age, untidy, dusty.

Production

The play is high comedy, one of the most sparkling and brilliant of Shaw's works, and calls for the utmost polish. The tendency to farce in certain episodes in the first and third acts should be resisted. The main contrasts are between Broadbent, Larry and Keegan. The first is easy in his self-satisfaction, the second is troubled and never at rest, the third has the serene confidence of faith. The Irish characters are realistic. The different love scenes between Nora and Broadbent and Nora and Larry must be well handled, for the form of the play depends upon them.

A Note on Productions

At its first production by Vedrenne-Barker on 1 November 1904, the play made a great impression because of its freshness, wit, and acute commentary upon current affairs. It continues to hold the stage because its essential theme is changeless: the conflict between practical sense and ideal sensibility. By no means easy to handle on the stage, partly because of its length, partly because of its theme, the play is admirable when well done. At the Court Theatre it was a high favourite, for it was performed to perfection, though Desmond MacCarthy did not care for Granville Barker's Keegan; but Barker had the required dignity, and remote sweetness, and his playing was an outstanding feature of the production. Louis Calvert never did anything better than the energetic and successful, though credulous and self-deceiving Broadbent. Ellen O'Malley had the soft charm of Nora, afterwards replaced by the hard romantic charm of Lillah McCarthy. Larry was pleasantly played by J. L. Shine, but he did not make the character stand out: indeed, the part is always difficult to play. The character parts were all good. Later, Nigel Playfair was an excellent Broadbent. Keegan became William Poel's favourite part.

It was revived three times at the Court Theatre and afterwards performed by the Lillah McCarthy-Granville Barker management at the Kingsway Theatre in December 1912. The Vedrenne-Barker management took it on tour and played it in Dublin. Later the Irish Players performed it at the Court Theatre in

September 1921, and another Irish company played it at the Embassy Theatre in 1947. Arnold Daly produced it at the Garrick Theatre, New York, on 10 October 1905, eleven months after its first London production, but it was not particularly liked and was taken off after a few days.

(14)
How He Lied to Her Husband

(1904)

This little play was written at the request of Arnold Daly who wanted a curtain raiser to *The Man of Destiny*. Shaw took the hackneyed theme of husband, wife and lover and got as he declared 'an original play out of them, as anybody else can if only he will look about him for his material'. Remotely, the play is a reversal of the more obvious romantic situation inspired by *Candida*. It is a smart piece of fooling.

At eight o'clock one evening at a flat in Cromwell Road a beautiful youth of eighteen appears with flowers in his hand and waits for his love, who, when she comes in, is a very ordinary married woman of about thirty-seven. She immediately tells him that something dreadful has happened. She has lost his poems, addressed to Aurora, and she is the only Aurora in London. Her husband, she is sure, has found them. The youth is radiant. The moment has come for them to go to him, hand in hand, and bid him farewell. This does not appeal to the lady. Anyhow, she says, her husband will kill the youth. But the youth is a pugilist and tells the lady not to fear. However, she does fear – for her husband. They must break it off; but first the young man must explain the poems and lie as much as is necessary, which in ironic despair he promises to do, having grown into cynical maturity in a few minutes.

The husband comes in, very cheerful, and tells the young man at once that he has something to say to him. He shows him the poems, and the youth says he wrote them years ago to the sunrise – the rosy fingered Aurora. He had showed them to the wife because her name was the same. The husband much put out declares that he doesn't believe him – they *were* written to his wife. The poet protests that he should never have dreamed of writing poems to her. This arouses the husband's fury – 'My wife's not good enough for you, isn't she?' he asks, and goes for the poet, who, preparing to defend himself, as he can do easily, falls over a stool, and bangs his head on the floor. He gets up and tells the truth: the poems were written to the wife; he adored her; he had asked her to go away with him. The husband is delighted: he wants the poems printed at his expense. What shall the volume be called: 'How He Lied to Her Husband', says the poet.

Characters

HE is a youth of eighteen, handsome, well dressed, a poet and a pugilist. There is no mistake about who is the protagonist.

SHE is a commonplace women of thirty-seven, well dressed and well got up.

HER HUSBAND is an excessively commonplace, robust, well groomed City man.

Production

The little piece is farce touched with anti-romance, and needs quick and spirited playing, no dilly-dallying. The youth must be a contrast to the man and wife, they being conscious of it, he oblivious. The period of the early nineteen hundreds should be observed. The setting is a South Kensington flat and the properties should be good of the period.

A Note on Productions

Arnold Daly was playing Eugene Marchbanks when the piece was written but Shaw was no doubt provoked to write it because of over-much sentimentality about Candida – the character rather than the play. The piece stands upon its own feet, though no more than a sketch. It was originally played at the Court Theatre on 26 September 1904 by Granville Barker, Gertrude Kingston, a first class comedy actress, and A. G. Poulton, a character actor and comedian of great ability. Miss Kingston revived the play several times with the same cast. This was the first Shaw play to be filmed, with Robert Harris, Edmund Gwenn and Vera Lennox: it was shown in London in January 1931 at the Carlton Cinema. Arnold Daly produced it in New York on the same date as the first London production. Alfred Butt had it in a variety programme at the Palace Theatre in December 1911, and it has been revived a number of times since.

(15)
Major Barbara

(1905)

This is a play of conflict between the individual and society to which there is no resolution except by social redemption. The conflict arises over money, and Shaw puts members of the Salvation Army into the dilemma of accepting for their work among the poor money from a whisky distiller, and an armament manufacturer, or letting that work cease for want of funds. Major Barbara cannot reconcile herself to taking 'tainted money'; her colleague can. The dilemma makes a true dramatic theme, a theme of conscience, which becomes more than personal. Shaw states it with definition and objectively, so that his play is first rate dramatic material; the excess of rhetorical dialectic adds to the pleasure of those who like good talk. The play illustrates Shaw's theory of drama as discussion.

In the preface Shaw says that he is concerned with 'the tragi-comic irony of the conflict between real life and the romantic imagination'. That, of course, is always his concern. There is moral judgment in his tragi-comedy, as there must be always in such plays.

The preface is a magnificent piece of polemical writing. He starts off as he often does by answering his critics: Why should they suppose that he owes his literary ancestry to foreigners? He is not an Ibsenist, neither is he 'an echo of Schopenhauer', nor does he get his inspiration from Nietzsche. His ancestry is Irish and English, not Continental, he says with emphasis.

The object of the preface, however, is to make people realize 'the silly levity with which we tolerate poverty':

> In the millionaire Undershaft I have represented a man who has become intellectually and spiritually as well as practically conscious of the irresistible natural truth which we all abhor and repudiate: to wit, that the greatest of our evils, and the worst of our crimes is poverty, and that our first duty, to which every other consideration should be sacrificed, is not to be poor.

Here Shaw shows himself to be a prophet, indeed. In 1905 when the play was written, his passionate denunciation of poverty was regarded as a Shavian paradox, for it was then fully believed that there must always be poor people, for mankind lived in a world of scarcity, and whatever the socialist levellers might say there was barely enough to go round. Today, however, it is not disputed that poverty is a social sin. 'Take your eyes from the ends of the earth and fix them on this truth just under your nose', shouted

Shaw. And he presented his millionaire as an admirable man in every respect because his religion 'recognizes in money the first need and in poverty the vilest sin of man and society'.

We must all have money, says Shaw, because we cannot exist without it, and for that reason it is easy to suppose the Salvationists' dilemma to be a false one: 'all our money is tainted . . . and there is no other money to be had'; so let us be realistic, not sentimental, and change society, to relieve money from its taint, and enable it to be distributed fairly. There is no rational difficulty about such a way out. But Shaw indicates that while individual attempts to solve the problem are likely to raise more difficulties than the individual can be aware of, Barbara's problem of conscience remains for all of us, and it is Shaw's aim to make the audience realize it. Only by grappling with the problem of poverty and solving it can tainted money be avoided, and it may be that the hard way chosen by Barbara is after all the true way. In the play, the relations between husband and wife, and parents and children, are brought up for discussion to relieve the tension. And as the play takes us into the company of the down-and-outs and the lesser criminal types, Shaw declares that punishment should be abolished, and forces us to face the issue that if we cannot put up with the vices of criminals it may be better to send them to the lethal chamber than to prison.

The story unfolded is that Lady Britomart, wife of Andrew Undershaft, the millionaire, has called her son and two daughters together to meet their father who has not seen them since childhood. Her object is to extract a larger allowance from him for her daughters, about to marry, and to force him to give up the family tradition, which is that the Undershaft business should be left not to his son but to a foundling. When Undershaft meets his family and prospective sons-in-law, he is greatly attracted by Barbara, his daughter, and her young man, the former being a major in

the Salvation Army, the latter a professor of Greek. He accepts
Barbara's invitation to see the work of the Army at West Ham,
and afterwards gets her and the others to see how his workmen
live in his model village. Thus the contrast between poverty and
sufficiency is established, and, in the argument, which is maintained throughout the play, Undershaft develops his doctrine of
work and money, and Barbara her doctrine of God and salvation.
Barbara comes off second best, for the gospel of St. Andrew
Undershaft, that 'money and gunpowder' means 'freedom and
power, command of life and command of death', is too much for
her. Undershaft will buy the Salavation Army, he says, for 'all
religious organizations exist by selling themselves to the rich'.
As the distiller, Lord Saxmundham, has offered £5,000 to the
Army on condition that another £5,000 is raised, Undershaft
finds it, and the Army accepts. The shock to Barbara's conscience
is such that she ends her connection with the Army, and goes to
live in her father's model village. 'There is no wicked side to life',
she has discovered. God's work is to be done for its own sake,
not for the sake of bribes, either the Salvationists' promise of
heaven or the employer's offer of bread.

Characters

BARBARA is lively, robust and energetic, intelligent, attractive,
thoughtful and conscientious, Shaw obviously loves her. The
action is on her shoulders; though not the largest character, she
is the protagonist.

LADY BRITOMART UNDERSHAFT is fifty or more, a 'typical
managing matron of the upper class'; she is said to have been
suggested by the late Countess of Carlisle, Gilbert Murray's
mother-in-law.

STEPHEN UNDERSHAFT is a serious young man of twenty-five.

SARAH, his sister, is tall and commonplace.

CHARLES LOMAX is a young man about town, with a sense of humour, who 'thinks it will be rather a lark' to marry Sarah.

ADOLPHUS CUSINS is a professor of Greek, intellectual, determined, intolerant, who can also be wild and apologetic, 'capable possibly of murder, but not of cruelty or coarseness'. A very good and sympathetic, though comic, portrait of Professor Gilbert Murray.

ANDREW UNDERSHAFT is over fifty, stoutish, easy going, masterful, a man who possesses formidable reserves of strength both physical and mental. He is the largest figure in the play, and the part requires great physical and mental resources.

MORRISON is Lady Britomart's butler.

SNOBBY PRICE is a young down-and-out workman.

RUMMY MITCHENS is an old bundle of poverty and worn-out humanity.

JENNY HILL is a pretty Salvationist lassie of eighteen.

PETER SHIRLEY is a starving, worn-out elderly man.

BILL WALKER is a tough customer of about twenty-five.

MRS BAINES is a Salvation Army Commissioner, about forty, earnest, appealing.

BILTON is a foreman at the ammunition works.

Production

The play calls for brilliant comedy playing, and a certain amount of character acting. Major Barbara requires personality, for the play turns upon her, the dramatic action being hers. It is a fatal mistake to make Undershaft the protagonist, for, important as he is, he has no moral problem, only the practical problem of finding a successor, and whatever happens suits him; but the part makes great demands,. or it requires mental energy and considerable resourcefulness in speech. The late Louis Calvert who created the character in London was an actor of unusual physical powers who found the part to tax him to the uttermost. Unless the actor can convey the idea of the successful, self-assured, completely competent business man who never falters, there is no play, because Barbara is without an antagonist. It will be noted that the long explanatory opening scene, brilliantly as it is written, is not easy to save from dullness; it calls for extreme vitality on the part of the actors, energy of the highest quality, intellectual alertness and the very finest speech. Underplaying will damage the piece irreparably, for it must be performed with the utmost vigour, but without the slightest touch of burlesque. The discussion at the end is difficult to manage, impossible, indeed, unless it is understood that it must be played musically as an oratorio, the various musical parts recognized with full control of volume and timing. Otherwise the play tends to lose its extraordinary quality.

There are three scenes: Lady Britomart's library, the West Ham Salvationist shelter, and the ammunition works. They must be realistically staged. The period is 1905, which must be observed in the dressing.

A Note on Productions

First produced by Vedrenne-Barker at the Court Theatre, 28 November 1905. A long but pleasing play, it made a great original impression, which is renewed whenever it is well done. 'One of the most remarkable plays put upon the English stage', was Desmond MacCarthy's opinion. It has been revived a number of times. Shaw did his utmost to secure the American actress Eleanor Robson for Barbara, but terms could not be arranged, and the part was first played by Annie Russell; it was also played at the Court Theatre by Lillah McCarthy; both actresses gave energetic, large and whole-hearted performances. Many other players have attempted it, among them Dorothy Massingham, Sybil Thorndike, and Catherine Lacy. Louis Calvert as Undershaft was hardly to be surpassed, though he never really understood the part, which has been played by Nicholas Hannen, Cecil Trouncer, Charles Laughton, and others. In America it was first produced at the Playhouse, New York, on 9 December 1915.

It was the second Shaw play to be filmed by Gabriel Pascal in England. Shaw wrote a number of additional scenes for the film and put in several additional characters; it was first shown in London on 7 April 1941 with Barbara played by Wendy Hiller, and Undershaft by Robert Morley.

(16)
Passion, Poison and Petrifaction

OR THE FATAL GAZOGENE
(1905)

Written for the Actors' Orphanage at the request of Cyril Maude, who produced it at Regent's Park 'where it was performed repeatedly, with colossal success'.

In a bed-sitting room in a fashionable quarter of London a lady goes to bed (fully dressed). Thunder rolls and her husband enters with a dagger. Her lover enters in his new evening suit. They prepare to drink whisky together, but the husband has poisoned the gazogene (the apparatus making the soda-water): only the lover drinks and is poisoned. The lady says that all the affection she once had for her lover is now transferred to her husband for good, which so alarms the husband that he offers an antidote to the poison to the lover, which consists of lime, the handiest form of which is the plaster from the ceiling. So the lover is stuffed with plaster first in solid, afterwards in liquid form. The landlord and a policeman enter and the landlord is charged by the husband with poisoning the lover with a poisoned ceiling. The lover is turned into a statue. A doctor enters. Then a thunderbolt falls and lays out the landlord, policeman and doctor. The statue is lifted to its feet and blesses the united pair.

Characters

MAGNESIA, the lady, is, of course, beautiful.
PHYLLIS, her maid, is, of course, pretty.
ADOLPHUS, her lover, is, of course, handsome.
FITZ, her husband, is, of course, hideous.
THE LANDLORD is a monster.
THE POLICEMAN is a policeman.
THE DOCTOR is professional.

There is a choir of invisible ANGELS who sing 'Won't You Come Home, Bill Bailey'.

Production

The little piece is tomfoolery, written for an occasion. Attention needs to be given to absurdity and to nothing else, except exact timing.

(17)
The Doctor's Dilemma

A TRAGEDY
(1906)

The play contains an exposure of the medical profession, which, Shaw says in the preface, 'has an infamous character'. Most of its members 'have no honour or conscience'; they are not scientists, they practise the abominations of vaccination and vivisection, and exhibit man's 'specific lust for cruelty'. Called a tragedy it is written in a comic vein and is therefore tolerable, even to doctors; in fact it is tragi-comedy.

Shaw says in another preface attached to a volume of essays entitled *Doctors' Delusions*:

> Please do not class me as one who 'doesn't believe in doctors'. One of our most pressing social needs is a national staff of doctors whom we can believe in, and whose prosperity shall depend not on the nation's sickness but on its health.

While doctors can seldom have been so ruthlessly attacked as Shaw attacks them in the preface to this play, he is at pains to point out that 'the guilt is shared by all of us', and in the play itself the attack, though pointed, is not barbed. His practical remedy for the difficulty about doctors is a public medical service in which doctors are paid to keep people well. His practical advice to patients is:

> Use your health, even to the point of wearing it out. That is what it is for. Spend all you have before you die; and do not outlive yourself.

Forty years later Shaw's remedy, in theory at least, was applied in the National Health Service.

The play opens in the consulting room of Sir Colenso Ridgeon, who has just been knighted. His doctor friends call to congratulate him and discuss the cure for tuberculosis that has made him famous. There is plain speaking among themselves, for the doctors are not aware that they are overheard by an audience of patients! There are five of them in addition to Sir Colenso, and they perform here and throughout the play as a kind of Chorus to the hero. Sir Colenso is induced to see a persistent woman, Jennifer, who wants him to treat her husband, an artist, and, fascinated by her, he reluctantly agrees to see the man.

In the next act on the terrace of the Star and Garter, at Richmond, Sir Colenso has given a dinner to his friends, and the artist, Dubedat, is there. The latter, obviously a talented and exceptional man, has charmed them all; but when he has gone, they discover that he has been borrowing money from each of them, and that a waitress at the hotel claims to be his real wife. Thus for all his charm he is a worthless man. The doctor's dilemma arises from the fact that he can take only one more patient: shall he treat the artist, now clearly seen to be highly undesirable, or shall he treat Blenkinsop, an old friend, a sick and poor general practitioner, and a thoroughly decent fellow?

In the third act, which takes place in Dubedat's studio, the artist gives further evidence of moral depravity, showing himself capable of blackmail, and goes on to say:

> Look here. All this is no good. You don't understand. You imagine that I'm simply an ordinary criminal. . . . Well, you're on the wrong track altogether. I'm not a criminal. All your moralizings have no value for me. I don't believe in morality. I'm a disciple of Bernard Shaw.

Sir Colenso finally declares, 'I will not lift a finger to save this reptile'. He decides to treat Blenkinsop, leaving the artist to Sir Bloomfield Bonington who, he feels sure, will kill him.

The fourth act is in the studio and the artist is dying. 'B.B.'s' treatment has made the disease worse. 'An enormously interesting case', says the doctor, admitting that he does not know what has been happening. Dubedat makes a beautiful death; for when men have nothing more to live for, they have no reason to hate their fellows. 'I'm perfectly happy. I'm not in pain. I don't want to live. I've escaped from myself. I'm in heaven, immortal . . .' he declares. And he goes on to justify himself: 'I know that in an accidental sort of way, struggling through the unreal part of life,

I haven't always been able to live up to my ideal. But in my own real world I have never done anything wrong, never denied my faith, never been untrue to myself.' What better last words could the best man offer? Shaw, however, is always on the side of the artists and poets against the rest of the world, although he does not necessarily approve of their behaviour, and lets us see that the dying man is laughing at them all. 'Was that death?' asks Jennifer; she leaves them and her dead husband to return 'wonderfully and beautifully dressed', and to shake hands with them all. 'We have had a wonderful experience', she says; but she does not shake hands with Ridgeon. Shaw was much criticized for this death scene, which undoubtedly makes serious demands not only upon the actor and the other players, but also upon the audience. The play depends upon it, however, for the sake of the dramatist's aim, which is to make the artist acceptable. Dubedat is intended to be agreeable in his death. In answer to criticisms Shaw put a note in the programme at the Court Theatre in September 1906 when the play first went into the evening bill: 'Life does not cease to be funny when people die, any more than it ceases to be serious when people laugh.'

There is a fifth act in a Bond Street picture gallery, where an exhibition of the artist's pictures is taking place. Jennifer and Sir Colenso meet; he tells her that he did no go on with the case of her husband because he was in love with her. But she has already re-married. 'Then I have committed a purely disinterested murder', are Sir Colenso's last words.

The death of a worthless man does not make a tragedy, any more than does a play's construction in five acts.

Shaw started the play with Jennifer as the central character, possibly with the idea of tragedy, but soon discovered that his real concern was not with Jennifer and the problem of her husband, but with the doctor and the temptation with which he was faced, which might have led to tragedy. This explains the last act, which is unnecessary from any other point of view, for there must be no doubt about the doctor's 'comic' defeat. Jennifer is important, for the dilemma would not have arisen apart from her. The drama lies in the cross currents of human emotions. The brilliance of the writing is so great that the weakness of the plot, which cannot be denied, is overcome. Its weakness lies in Ridgeon's motive, which makes him absurd, thus the play is 'tragi-comedy', made tasteful by the splendid character drawing of the doctors.

Characters

SIR COLENSO RIDGEON, fifty, off-hand, sensitive, shy, younger than his years, self-conscious about his knighthood, an attractive and admirable man. The play is his, though there are strong characters competing with him.

JENNIFER DUBEDAT, an arrestingly good-looking young woman, dark, tall, slender, strong, impetuous in manner.

LOUIS DUBEDAT, a slim young man of twenty-three, 'pretty, though not effeminate', very observant, engaging, not shy. Attractive to everyone. Has a cough.

DR LEO SCHUTZMACHER, a middle-aged, well-dressed, Jewish doctor.

SIR PATRICK CULLEN, over seventy, downright, large build, an Irishman long resident in England, cordial and fatherly with Ridgeon.

CUTLER WALPOLE, forty, shortish, energetic, successful, a popular surgeon.

SIR RALPH BLOOMFIELD BONINGTON, in his sixties, tall, distinguished, self-assured, never tired of his own voice.

DR BLENKINSOP, about the same age as Ridgeon, clearly not prosperous, has a slight cough, indicating his illness.

MINNIE TINWELL, a pretty, fair-haired maid at the hotel, about twenty-five.

REDPENNY, a young medical student, who acts as the doctor's secretary and laboratory assistant.

EMMY, an old servant, with the manner of an old family nurse.

MAID at the doctor's house.

WAITER at the hotel.

NEWSPAPER MAN, a cheerful, affable, ignorant reporter.

SECRETARY of the picture gallery.

Production

The play makes heavy demands upon the actors. The casting calls for the utmost discrimination, and the acting throughout needs finish. Ridgeon must be interesting in himself, a man of character, but with a sense of humour, for his painful defeat does not knock him out. Jennifer must be able to charm all the men. Dubedat is burning. The style of playing is high comedy, and, while characterization is important, an elevated style and controlled timing must be maintained throughout. There should be nothing sentimental in Dubedat's death. The full effect of the death scene is in its serious comedy rather than in the artist's tragedy. Four sets are required, all fully described in the text. The period is 1908, and should be observed.

A Note on Productions

The first production by Vedrenne-Barker at the Court Theatre on 20 November 1906, under the dramatist's direction, would be difficult to surpass. The parts of the doctors received the skilful comedy playing they must have, with character acting on the highest level. Ridgeon played by Ben Webster was as polished as could be, Jennifer and Dubedat, played by Lillah McCarthy and Granville Barker, had, respectively, the right romantic quality, the artist being not only plausible but excitingly poetic. The play has often been revived, Ridgeon having been played by Felix Aylmer, D. A. Clarke-Smith, Barry Jones, Austin Trevor and others, while Jennifer has been played by Cathleen Nesbitt, Gwen Ffrangcon-Davies, Lydia Sherwood and Vivien Leigh. It was first produced in New York at Wallack's Theatre on 26 March 1915 by Granville Barker.

A Metrocolor film version made in 1958 attempted to do the play justice. The script was by Anatole de Grunwald and the direction by Anthony Asquith. No additions were made to Shaw's text, but it was severely cut. The production was glamorized and while the wit was preserved the drama was obscured. None the less it made an interesting and intelligent film, giving some idea of the quality of the work.

(18)
The Interlude at the Playhouse

(1907)

This was written for the re-opening of the Playhouse Theatre, London, by Cyril Maude on 28 January 1907. It was a piece for an occasion and was not included in the collected plays, and could be ignored, except that Shaw appears to have included it in the numbering of the plays.

(19)
Getting Married

A DISQUISITORY PLAY
(1908)

Shaw, provoked by being told that his plays were mere talk, wrote a play that is a single conversation from start to finish, without even the pretence of division into acts. The curtain falls twice during the conversation for the convenience of the audience; but there is no indication of these interruptions in the play. The puzzled critics on its first production regretted that it was not the equal of the author's previous works, and left it at that. But it is admirable conversation, an excellent dramatic work, and Shaw's acceptance of the challenge that his plays were talk resulted in a brilliant success.

As he says in a note in the collected edition, 'a return' is made in the play 'to unity of time and place as observed in the ancient Greek drama'; but he declares that he did not write the play as 'a deliberate display of virtuosity in form', but because the form was the most suitable to his purpose, as indeed it was.

It is a discussion about marriage in which various points of view, conventional and unconventional, religious and secular, are stated. The discussion is lively, witty and with many elements of surprise, for Shaw does not for one moment forget his playwright's cunning. The characters display themselves, and we are allowed to gain such knowledge of them that we get interested in the persons as well as in what they say. The conclusion of the whole matter is characteristically Shavian, for we are lifted on to another level:

MRS GEORGE: Hm! Like most men, you think you know everything a woman wants, don't you? But the thing one wants most has nothing to do with marriage at all. Perhaps Anthony here has a glimmering of it. Eh. Anthony?
SOAMES: Christian fellowship?
MRS GEORGE: You call it that, do you?
SOAMES: What do you call it?

There is no answer. The time is 1908, and the scene the Bishop of Chelsea's palace. Edith, youngest daughter of the Bishop, is to be married that morning. The relatives have gathered for the event. Marriage is, of course, uppermost in their minds and their own positions in relation to it emerge. One of the Bishop's brothers has just been divorced; he comes too, and so does the wife, who has divorced him, also the man she intends to marry again, who is the present bridegroom's best man. When the time arrives for the ceremony it is found that the bride has locked herself in her room; she is reading a pamphlet and refuses to be disturbed. Similar news arrives about the bridegroom. Then the bridegroom turns up to say that he was in utter ignorance of what he was letting himself in for when he undertook to get married. He had given his word and will stick to it; but if he is married it will be under protest. Immediately the bride appears in her dressing gown to find out what has happened to the young man, and jumps at the opportunity to throw the responsibility for cancelling the marriage upon him. She herself has no intention of entering into such 'a wicked contract'.

Here's a situation! The people are gathering in the church for the wedding and those concerned are arguing whether the ceremony should take place! The Bishop, an authority on the history of marriage, makes the rather cynical suggestion that the two should consider a marriage by contract; so an attempt is made to draw up such a contract, without success. They all give their opinions, even the greengrocer in charge of the wedding breakfast gives his, which is that it is better to argue about marriage after than before. 'It doesn't bear thinking about', is his philosophy. 'The great thing is to get the young people tied up before they know what they are letting themselves in for.' He recommends that his sister-in-law, the Mayoress, who is already in the church waiting for the ceremony, should be consulted: 'She has a very exceptional experience, and a wonderful temperament and an instinct in affairs of the heart.'

Mrs George, the Mayoress, is one of Shaw's great characters, she speaks for women, and in a trance reveals Shaw's feminine soul, the soul which is all men's, though not all of them realize it. This is what she says: the last, the best word that any man could say: 'I've been myself. I've not been afraid of myself. And at last I have escaped from myself, and am become a voice for them that are afraid to speak, and a cry for the hearts that break in silence.' After Mrs George takes the play into mystical realms, Shaw introduces knock-about fun as his custom is. The bride and bridegroom suddenly appear to say that they are married, and the divorced couple announce the reversal of their divorce.

Characters

THE BISHOP OF CHELSEA, the leading character, and, though the oldest, is 'younger by temperament than his brothers', slim, active, successful, very well spoken and always pleased with himself. He does not appear until after the play has well started but has quickly to gain and after to maintain his position. He is not a caricature.

MRS BRIDGENORTH, the Bishop's wife, is about fifty, a placid, gentle woman.

GENERAL BRIDGENORTH, about fifty, 'carefully trained' to be ignorant, stupid and prejudiced.

LESBIA GRANTHAM, a handsome women in her prime, fastidious, tolerant and amused.

REGINALD BRIDGENORTH, younger than the General, a likeable man, belonging to the English propertied class, 'muddled, rebellious, hasty, untidy, forgetful', tough physically and boyish in manner and speech.

LEO, his wife, is pretty, youthful, restless and charming.

ST JOHN HOTCHKISS is twenty-nine or thereabouts, very smart, energetic and gay in manner, who declares himself with much charm to be a professional snob, and has a great deal to say.

CECIL SYKES, the bridegroom, is an ordinary good-looking fellow, and his bride EDITH is the spoilt child of a clerical household.

FATHER ANTHONY SOAMES is the Bishop's Chaplain, self-composed, highly efficient, and never put out.

MRS GEORGE COLLINS is 'every inch a Mayoress', not afraid of displaying her status, or of colour in her dress; between forty and fifty, 'not a lady', a clairvoyant, once beautiful, now all her beauty is in her eyes. She has a trance and a long important speech in the trance.

WILLIAM COLLINS, greengrocer and alderman, is an elderly affable man, with the perfect manners of a shop-keeper, resembling William the waiter in *You Never Can Tell*.

THE BEADLE to the Borough Council.

Production

Although the plot is all situation and somewhat frivolous, none the less the play depends on high-comedy acting, finished, and pointed speaking, a display of admirable dialogue and fine sustained speeches. One of the problems of its production is to keep the Bishop well in the picture, for he is the most important man from every point of view, but Shaw has made him take a rather detached part in the action. Shaw said of Mrs Collins that the actress must combine inspiration with the broadest comic characterization. There is a single scene. The period, which is 1908, must be observed. The play is a *tour de force* of modern dramatic writing and should be played in the same spirit.

A Note on Productions

The first production showed the play at its best with a cast including Henry Ainley (the Bishop), Robert Loraine (Hotchkiss) and Fanny Brough (Mrs Collins). It was not revived in London for fourteen years, five times altogether, but has always succeeded, without always having had justice done to it. The first production in New York was at the Booth Theatre on 6 November 1916.

(20)
Press Cuttings

A TOPICAL SKETCH
(1909)

Written for the Women's Suffrage Movement the play was at first refused a licence because of its political references, but was afterwards licensed on condition that General Mitchener was re-named General Bones, and Mr Balsquith renamed Mr Johnson: a condition that would not now be enforced.

It opens in General Mitchener's room at the War Office. A suffragette has chained herself to the door scraper with a letter to the General from the Prime Minister asking him to see her at once. Reluctantly he has her released, and shown up to him, when she turns out to be the Prime Minister in disguise, who knows no other way to reach the War Office owing to the fierceness of the suffragette campaign! Martial law has been proclaimed and General Sandstone has resigned because his plan to exclude all women from an area within a two miles' radius of Westminster has been rejected. General Mitchener approves of the plan, but the Prime Minister says that public opinion would never stand it. The Prime Minister goes out to receive a deputation from the Anti-Suffragette League. In the meantime the General is interviewed by the office charwoman, who tells him that child-bed is more dangerous than the battlefield; afterwards he has to listen to his orderly who tells him that it is not fighting he objects to but soldiering. Then he has to receive the two ladies who form the Anti-Suffragette deputation. They come to support the Sandstone plan. They declare that what women want is not the right to vote but the right to military service – 'all the really strong men of history have been disguised women'. Their arguments convert the General to the suffrage cause, and they leave him in disgust. The Prime Minister returns to say that Parliament is in revolt, for one reason or another, but the General refuses to yield to clamour. The piece ends with everybody on the stage, and marriages being arranged all round.

Characters

GENERAL MITCHENER is a highly-connected commander.

HIS ORDERLY is an unsoldierly, slovenly, discontented young man.

BALSQUITH, the Prime Minister, is obviously neither Balfour nor Asquith, 'and cannot in the course of nature be both'.

MRS FARRELL, the office charwoman, is a lean, respectable Irishwoman.

LADY CORINTHIA, who forms one of the anti-suffragette deputation, is over thirty, beautiful and romantic.

MRS BANGER, the other member of the deputation, is a masculine woman of forty.

Production

The play is farce. One of Shaw's 'tomfooleries', it should be handled nonsensically as a topical piece belonging to a period now long past.

A Note on Productions

It was first privately performed at the Court Theatre on 9 July 1909, and first given in public by Miss A. E. Horniman at the

Gaiety Theatre, Manchester, 27 September 1909. It was first performed in the United States in Boston, 1 January 1912. It has been revived in London several times.

(21)
The Shewing-up of Blanco Posnet

A SERMON IN CRUDE MELODRAMA
(1909)

This one act 'religious tract in dramatic form' was censored because its references to the Almighty were considered to be blasphemous.

The play is the account of the conversion of a blackguard in the Wild West of America. A man takes a horse belonging to his step-brother considering that it really belongs to himself. As he could not hope to maintain his claim he intended to disappear with the horse, but on his flight meets a woman with a dying child and lets her have the horse to bring the child to a doctor, while he sits waiting for the men who are looking for him as a horse thief. He is an utterly worthless fellow, who in the ordinary way cared nothing for dying children or unhappy mothers. Why he gave up the horse to the woman, he does not know, except that God made him. The sight of the woman and the child was a revelation that his life was a rotten game.

At his trial the only people who had seen him with the horse were the woman with the child and a woman of the town. When the first woman is brought in, Blanco says she is not real, and when it is reported that the child has died he becomes hysterical. The woman, not recognizing him, says that Blanco was not the man. The other woman, disturbed by the mother's story, changes her mind and says she did not see him with the horse. The jury are determined to hang Blanco, but the Sheriff, touched by the behaviour of both women, sets Blanco free. Then Blanco delivers a sermon on everybody being rotten and the fact that he has found a great game to be played, which he intends to play in the future. It is a violent play, but its note is religious exaltation.

Characters

BLANCO POSNET is the disreputable but romantic hero in a state of incipient delirium tremens. A character of much energy, and sudden poetic elevation.

ELDER DANIELS, his step-brother, is much older, a sanctimonious Elder and the local store-keeper.

SHERIFF KEMP is a stout, heavy, powerful and commanding man.

STRAPPER KEMP, his young brother, is strong, selfish, sulky.

WAGGONER JO, an elderly carter.

FEEMY EVANS is twenty-three or twenty-four, battered good looks, and dirty-fine dress, the disreputable villainess who becomes a heroine.

THE WOMAN is the appealing mother.

THE FOREMAN OF THE JURY is a typical Western tough.

NESTOR, a juryman, is an old man and drunk.

BABSY is a bumptious young slattern.

LOTTIE is sentimental, neat and clean.

HANNAH is elderly and wise.

JESSIE is good-natured but sharp-tongued.

EMMA is a sneak.

There are two or three MEN with Strapper. Other WOMEN. Ten other JURYMEN. Other MEN in the crowd.

Production

The play is romantic melodrama. Its treatment should be realistic, with sharp, quick playing, careful timing, without undue emphasis on the sentimental aspects. The part of Blanco needs an actor with marked personality. The setting is a barn in Western America, and the period is not later than the beginning of the present century.

A Note on Productions

The play was intended to be done at the After Noon Theatre at His Majesty's Theatre in 1909, but a licence was refused by the censor, so the first production was that of the Irish Players at the Abbey Theatre in Dublin, where the Lord Chamberlain had no jurisdiction. Later the production was brought to London and given privately for the Stage Society. The Irish Players took it to the United States and performed it in Boston in 1911. It was licensed in 1916 and first publicly performed in England at the Playhouse, Liverpool, again by the Irish Players. Apart from an amateur production it was first publicly performed in London at the Everyman Theatre in 1912. Martin Harvey played Blanco in a London Coliseum performance in 1926, and the part has also been played by Esme Percy, John Slater and others.

(22)
The Fascinating Foundling

A DISGRACE TO THE AUTHOR
(1909)

This is another brief piece of tomfoolery. A young man calls at the Lord Chancellor's office to see him and does so after some high words with the Lordship's clerk. The young man is a ward in Chancery and demands that the Lord Chancellor shall start him on a stage career and also find him a wife old enough to be his mother. Having had a note taken of his requirements the young

man leaves, to be followed by a young woman, who is a foundling, who demands that the Lord Chancellor shall find her a
husband. As she makes her demand the young man returns for
his walking stick, she throws herself into his arms and he accepts
her on learning that she is a foundling.

Characters

MERCER is an elderly looking clerk.

HORACE BRABAZON is a smart and beautiful young man of
nineteen.

THE LORD CHANCELLOR is all that such an imposing official
should be.

ANASTASIA VULLIAMY is a beautiful and irresistible girl.

Production

The setting is the Lord Chancellor's office. The piece is farce and
needs to be played sharply, yet with sense of character to get the
full value of Shaw's humour.

A Note on Productions

The play was performed at the Arts Theatre Club on 28 January
1928, when it had forty-four performances.

(23)
The Glimpse of Reality

A TRAGEDIETTA
(1909)

A very old friar confesses a young girl. She is to be married to a
young fisherman, but has no dowry. She confesses that she is

about to commit a grievous sin: to get the dowry she intends to decoy a young nobleman to her father's inn, where he will be murdered, for there is a price of thirty crowns on his head. The friar turns out to be the young nobleman, in disguise; he threatens to fight the inn-keeper, for whom, however, he is no match with the sword. To gain time, the nobleman orders a meal, which all four (the fisherman having turned up) eat together; but it seems there is no way out of it, the inn-keeper does not intend to let him escape, and there are three to one. Then the nobleman, seeing that death is inevitable, says that 'There is nothing like a good look into the face of death . . . for shewing you how little you really believe and how little you really are.' He then attacks the inn-keeper, is overpowered, but spared, as they think he is cracked and it is unlucky to kill a madman.

The piece is not very convincing.

Characters
COUNT FERRUCIO, a handsome young nobleman.
GIULIA, a handsome girl.
SQUARCIO, her father, an inn-keeper.
SANDRO, a young lad.

Production
The period is the fifteenth century and the setting an inn on the edge of an Italian lake. The usual treatment for a Shaw farce.

A Note on Productions
Apart from amateur productions, the play was performed at the Arts Theatre Club on 20 November 1907, and revived there again on 20 June 1951.

(24)
Misalliance

(1910)

When this play was first performed at the Frohman Repertory season it passed over the heads of everybody. The critics without exception would have none of it, and the public was puzzled. The current opinion was that gradually Shaw was giving up being a dramatist. Everybody took him at his word and declared that it was talk and nothing more. Yet it holds the stage.

The piece is not described, but is a long debate about the relations between parents and children, with many other subjects touched on incidentally, including the independence of woman, the theme being the desire in a young woman for something to happen. The debate is enlivened by a rough and tumble and the fall of an aeroplane into a Surrey garden. Everything is given up to the most highly rhetorical, at times lyrical talk, operatic in manner, on the theme of love, with airs, duets, quartets and symphonic movements. But his characters so amuse Shaw that they run away with the theme and lose it. He had to write what he wanted to say about parents and children in a long preface, one of his longest and best.

The action is continuous, without division, though for convenience it can be divided into three parts. In Surrey, on the slope of Hindhead, lives John Tarleton, a prosperous manufacturer of underwear. Johnny, the son, is enjoying his week-end, when Bentley Summerhays, 'all brains and no body', arrives to interrupt him. Bentley is on trial at the office as a suitor for the daughter Hypatia's hand. The rough and tumble soon begins, and Bentley screams with fear of Johnny, to be protected by Hypatia and her mother. They take him away to comfort him, when Lord Summerhays, Bentley's father, appears, to sympathize with Johnny. They go off for a stroll. Bentley, who has returned, goes too, and the women then appear to be left alone to talk about the men; it appears that Hypatia wants to marry, but not for love: she wants something to happen. This long duet between mother and daughter is a feature of the play. Mrs Tarleton offers an apologia for common sense; her daughter states the case for youth and freedom: for her it is a heart-break house, and she is surprised by love as Ellie was in the later play. Then Tarleton – 'read Darwin' – comes in, full of vitality, and the debate gets fast and furious, rising to boiling point when Lord Summerhays and Johnny join in.

For relief, Hypatia and Lord Summerhays are left alone, and it becomes apparent that their relations are different from what might be expected, for his lordship is in love with the girl and she tells him he is an old woman, 'always on the shrink'. They are interrupted by the return of Tarleton, and when the girl goes the two men talk about their children, interrupted in their turn by the descent of an aeroplane on the greenhouse, and the appearance of the aviator, who is a friend of Bentley's, and his passenger, Lina Szczepanowska, who has travelled in the aeroplane because one member of her family has to risk his or her life every day, and it was her turn. (Remember the date – 1910.) Lina is an acrobat and juggler, and of course she sets the house upside down. Tarleton wants to make a fool of himself with her, and she takes him off to give him a few exercises on the parallel bars in the billiard room.

The room being left empty a strange young man appears and hides in a portable Turkish bath standing in the room, just unpacked. Hypatia and the aviator enter; she makes violent love to him, so that he runs away with her after him. Tarleton comes in, and the young man appears from the Turkish bath threatening him with a revolver. The young man intends to avenge his mother who died in poverty and was once Tarleton's mistress. Tarleton, however, can't remember her, but succeeds in talking until Lina comes in and the young man is disarmed. Then there is more talk about the young man, and what the young man saw taking place between Hypatia and the airman, until Mrs Tarleton discovers that he is the son of a girl who had once come to her in her trouble, when she mothers him, and he is given sloe gin, which makes him drunk; then he talks about socialism and capitalism until he is taken away. Finally they discuss the great question, whom does Hypatia want to mate with? Hypatia says, 'Papa: buy the brute for me' – the brute being the airman. This leads to more talk about parents and children. At last, Lina returns and says she will go off tomorrow with Bentley as her passenger. 'Is there anything else?' asks Mrs Tarleton. 'I suppose – er – I suppose there's nothing more to be said', answers her husband. 'Thank goodness', declares Hypatia, for the curtain to fall.

Characters

HYPATIA is a striking, dark, purposeful, handsome young woman, longing for she does not know what. Shaw's description of her should be noted. She is a formidable creature, but highly attractive. The play is hers, and the player needs the personality to carry it off.

JOHNNY TARLETON is an ordinary young business man of thirty or less.

BENTLEY SUMMERHAYS is a thin-skinned, delicate, assured and exasperating young fellow.

MRS TARLETON is shrewd and motherly, likeable and unaffected.

LORD SUMMERHAYS is an ex-Colonial Governor.

JOHN TARLETON is an immense and genial veteran of trade, weighty in appearance and speech: the pivot of the action.

JOSEPH PERCIVAL is a good-looking, highly efficient young airman.

LINA SZCZEPANOWSKA is a highly good-looking Polish acrobat, who brings decision into the action.

JULIUS BAKER, a young man, a clerk, who is called 'Gunner' because he carries a gun.

Production

The play is comedy with elements of farce, really a fantasy. The most accomplished acting is required, as in comedy, with the utmost precision of timing and emphasis. The absurd Tarleton carries the weight of the play, but is not the protagonist. Mrs Tarleton must be very likeable, for she is dear to him and to her daughter. Bentley's hysteria must not be overdone. The real difficulty is with Hypatia, who must convey mystery, the mystery of the female mind, yet not a mere calculating creature: she is a poetic creation. The love scenes are especially important. The action is supposed to be what a girl who cannot find anyone fit to marry imagines might happen to bring a dramatic change in her situation. Its realism, therefore, is the background for fantasy. A very difficult play to produce and act, because it calls for virtuosity of treatment throughout. The setting is a large hall in a well-furnished house, out of which leads a glass partition. The period is 1909 and the play should be treated as a period piece.

A Note on Productions

First performed in the Frohman Repertory season at the Duke of York's Theatre on 23 February 1910. The importance Shaw placed upon Hypatia is indicated by his efforts to get an actress of unusual personality to play the part in the original production. He wanted Mona Limerick, who was not available for the opening, but came in after the eighth performance. The play was too strong meat for critics and public. When produced at the Broadhurst Theatre in New York on 27 September 1917 it was much cut, to Shaw's disgust, and treated as a farce, with much popular success. This was repeated eighteen years later in the same city, when it was burlesqued and had a long run. These productions did the play injustice. It has been revived on six occasions in London but its problems of casting and interpretation have not always been solved.

(25)
The Dark Lady of the Sonnets

(1910)

This short play was written on behalf of the Shakespeare National Memorial Theatre as an appeal for funds. It relates an encounter between Shakespeare and Queen Elizabeth on the terrace of the Palace at Whitehall, where the poet had a rendezvous with Mary Fitton. The piece is spirited, and provides an opportunity for a piece of virtuoso playing by the actor who takes the part of Shakespeare. The story of Mary Fitton was got from Thomas Tylor, who identified that lady with the dark lady of the sonnets, Shaw having become acquainted with Tylor in the 'eighties in the British Museum, when they were both readers there.

Shakespeare is shown as a poet with a notebook. He is fascinated with the Queen and gets many queenly phrases from her, and finally begs of her to endow a great playhouse or National Theatre 'for the better instruction of your Majesty's subjects'.

Shaw wanted Ellen Terry to play the Queen.

Characters

SHAKESPEAR is a young poet, very self-assured, dignified, an ideal, not a naturalistic, Shakespeare.

QUEEN ELIZABETH is as she is in her portraits.
MARY FITTON is a handsome dark girl.
A BEEFEATER is on guard.

Production

The play is at night, by moonlight. Performed with the spirit in which it is written it makes an attractive short piece; its plea for the theatre should not be ignored.

A Note on Productions

At its first production Granville Barker played Shakespear, Suzanne Sheldon, Queen Elizabeth, and Mone Limerick, Mary Fitton. It has been revived many times. When first broadcast on the radio on 22 April 1938 Shaw wrote a prologue, which he spoke himself, explaining what he intended in the play.

(26)
Fanny's First Play

AN EASY PLAY FOR A LITTLE THEATRE
(1911)

This is certainly an easy play, the author calls it a 'pot-boiler'. He wrote it for Lillah McCarthy when she was about to go into management, and it so greatly pleased the public that it had a run of 622 performances. At first, Shaw did not put his name to the play, which was announced to be by an anonymous author. In an epilogue its authorship is discussed, when one of the newspaper critics finds in it 'the hackneyed old Shaw touch', but a second is quite sure that it couldn't be by him, for 'Shaw is physiologically incapable of the note of passion'. 'Yes, I know', agrees another, 'Intellect without emotion. That's right. I always say that myself. A giant brain, if you ask me, but no heart.' Many people did at first think the play to be by some other writer, which seems almost unbelievable.

It is about the awakening of the soul. 'I hate to see dead people walking about', Shaw says in the brief preface. 'Our respectable middle-class people are all as dead as mutton.' Shaw gives a picture of two respectable families living on Denmark Hill, whose children let themselves go one evening so far as to fall into the hands of the police, and get sent to prison. Shaw's comment is that 'the young had better have their souls awakened by disgrace, captured by the police, and a month's hard labour, than drift along from their cradles to their graves doing what other people do for no other reason than that other people do it'.

We see the Gilbeys anxious about their son, who has disappeared for fourteen days: they get no news until a girl, who announces herself as 'Darling Dora', calls to raise the amount of the fine required to get him out of prison. She was his companion in disgrace. The parents are ashamed and shocked. But their shame is mitigated when they discover that the Knox's girl, their son's fiancée, has also been missing. On the same occasion, which was the Oxford and Cambridge Boat Race night, she, too, had accidentally got into a disturbance with the police, and had been sent to gaol. The outcome of this experience is that the boy makes up his mind that he does not want to marry the girl, and she knows that she does not want him. In fact, they wake up. But the girl has awakened more completely; for her experience has meant more to her than the boy's to him. That is the Shavian touch, and a true one. In the end, the boy has his Darling Dora, who is a good sort, and the girl has the Gilbey's footman, who turns out to be brother of a duke. A Frenchman, who happened to be with the girl when the trouble occurred and gets sent to prison with her, is introduced to enable Shaw to contrast English with French respectability.

The play might have been accepted on its merits as a simple domestic piece, excellent of its kind, and highly amusing, had it not been that Shaw added an Induction and Epilogue to make the most of its anonymous authorship. Its separate story is that a girl has written a play, which she wants her father to see; he arranges for a private performance at his house, and invites the London critics to compose the audience. This provides Shaw with the opportunity of poking fun at the critics. The girl's object is to let her father know how her life has changed since she left his home in Venice – for he cannot stand England. She has become a Fabian and a Suffragette, and he declares, having seen the play, 'I feel now as when the Campanile fell.'

Characters

In the Induction: THE COUNT, who is Fanny's father, is a handsome man of fifty, a hundred years out of date in dress, habits, and ideas. CECIL SAVOYARD is a middle-aged theatrical agent. FANNY O'DOWDA, the authoress, is a charming girl of nineteen. MR TROTTER, the critic, represents A. B. Walkley of *The Times*, a man of fifty, wearing diplomatic dress. MR VAUGHAN is E. A. Baughan of the *Daily News*, a man of forty, and rather enthusiastic. MR GUNN is Gilbert Cannan, thirty, dry, satirical, very superior. MR FLAWNER BANNAL is the representative critic of the popular press who knows nothing and cares less about the drama, a cheerful, amiable, ignorant fellow. There is the Count's FOOTMAN.

MARGARET KNOX is a bright, energetic and intelligent girl of eighteen, audacious, resolute and very attractive: the action is seen through her eyes.

MR GILBEY is a respectable and prosperous tradesman of Denmark Hill, in the fifties, stoutish and rather short.

MRS GILBEY is about the same age as her husband, a placid, homely, kindly person.

JUGGINS, the Gilbey's footman, is thirty-five or threabouts, tall, good-looking but 'low spirited', and with the quiet and confident manners of an aristocrat, which in fact he is.

DARLING DORA is a gay and cheerful girl, very good-looking, affable and confidential in manner.

MRS KNOX is a plain earnest woman, dressed without regard to fashion, possessing an atmosphere of peace.

MR KNOX is about fifty, a troubled, fussy, worrying man, harder and uglier than his friend and partner Gilbey.

MONSIEUR DUVALLET is a good-looking young French marine officer.

BOBBY GILBEY is manly enough by nature but untrained, and suffering from having too-loving parents.

Production

The Induction is high comedy, to be smartly and sharply done, with attention to the differentiation of the critics. The play is domestic comedy in which attention must be given to actuality; it presents a marked contrast to the first part. The play itself has no difficulties, asking for straightforward treatment. The Induction can be played before the curtain if the forestage is wide enough: if not, a drop curtain can be used. There are two settings, the Gilbey's dining room and the Knox's drawing room, very conventional middle class. The period is 1911.

If the Induction is impracticable, there is an introduction by Shaw, to be spoken by Fanny, before the curtain.

A Note on Productions

At the first production, for which Lillah McCarthy was responsible at the Little Theatre on 1 January 1912, she played Margaret, and there was a first class cast which included Harcourt Williams, Christine Silver, Nigel Playfair, Dorothy Minto, and Cicely Hamilton, among others. After its first long run it was revived by Lena Ashwell in 1915, who played Margaret, and it has been performed many times since. It was first produced in New York at the Comedy Theatre on 16 September 1912.

(27)
Androcles and the Lion

A FABLE PLAY
(1911–12)

The central theme of the play is that men must have something worth dying for to make life worth living; because an end outside oneself – in other words a religious aim – is necessary for decent human existence.

In its inception the play was intended for children, and is, therefore, a short piece. Shaw takes the story of Androcles the Greek slave, who coming across a lion in the jungle suffering agonies from a thorn in his paw removes the thorn and goes on his way, to be captured some time after by the Romans and thrown to the lions in the Coliseum at Rome. There he meets the lion who recognizes him with joy, to the amazement of the audience. It is the time of the persecution of the Christians, which provides Shaw with the opportunity to present Christians, with the knowledge of their fate before them, who discuss their religion with Romans. One of the Christians so far forgets himself when turned into the circus as to slay six of Caesar's pet gladiators, which so delights the Emperor that he crowns the repentant man with laurel, pardons all the Christians, and proclaims Christianity as the State religion. Androcles gets thrown to the lions because he is not a Christian, for the people must not be denied their pleasures; but the lion saves him.

The central idea of the play is in the Christian woman's talk with the Roman captain:

THE CAPTAIN: Are you then going to die for nothing?

LAVINIA: Yes: that is the wonderful thing. It is since all the stories and dreams have gone that I have now no doubt at all that I must die for something greater than dreams or stories.

THE CAPTAIN: But for what?

LAVINIA: I don't know. If it were for anything small enough to know, it would be too small to die for. I think I'm going to die for God. Nothing else is real enough to die for.

THE CAPTAIN: What is God?

LAVINIA: When we know that, Captain, we shall be gods ourselves.

The leading character is Lavinia, not Androcles, and the action and all the characters are as she views them. Laurence Housman said that this play gave him his first incentive to write the *Little Plays of St Francis*.

Characters

LAVINIA is a good-looking young Christian woman who has plenty to say and says it well; she has personality, and needs to be played surely.

ANDROCLES is a small, thin man who might be any age, gentle, timorous, rather talkative.

MEGAERA his wife is a handsome shrew.

THE LION is an active and intelligent beast with a sense of humour.

THE CENTURIAN is the type of sergeant to be found in every army.

THE CAPTAIN is a handsome patrician of about thirty-five, a cold, distinguished, superior and romantic man who likes to hear himself talk.

LENTULUS and METELLUS are young Romans of fashion, one fair, the other dark.

FERROVIUS is a powerful man, impatient, quick-tempered, a convert to Christianity who finds difficulty in loving his enemies.

SPINTHO is the wreck of a once good-looking man, gone hopelessly to the bad, and described by the Centurian as an 'emetic'.

THE EDITOR is in charge of the arrangements at the Coliseum.

CAESAR is the young Emperor and must look his part.

There are a squad of ROMAN SOLDIERS, a large batch of CHRISTIAN PRISONERS of all ages and both sexes, GLADIATORS at the Circus, a CALL BOY, a MENAGERIE-KEEPER, ATTENDANTS at the Circus, and a SUITE for Caesar.

Production

Shaw denied that the play was a comedy and insisted upon its being a fable, which means that it should be done with some exaggeration; but the philosophy is not to be sacrificed to the fun. It should be regarded as fantasy, with spirit and without parsimony in numbers of players and dressing. The staging is complicated, the first scene being in the jungle, the next at the converging point of three roads to Rome, the third behind the Emperor's box at the Coliseum, the fourth in the amphitheatre, and the fifth the same as the third: there should be the minimum of interval between the fourth and fifth scenes, because the action must be maintained. The Lion is a highly important character and must be well played. For these reasons naturalism should never be attemped, and open stage treatment, in which the action can take place without pauses, should be aimed at.

A Note on Productions

The first production was at the Kleines Theater, Berlin, on 25 November 1912, in pursuance of Shaw's determination that the Continent should see his plays before London critics had condemned them. It was not seen in London until over nine months later when it opened the Lillah McCarthy-Granville Barker season at the St James's Theatre on 1 September 1913. Much trouble was taken with the settings and costumes by Albert Rutherston, and no expense was spared. The production was by Granville Barker, Shaw not attending rehearsals until the end. The result was not altogether satisfactory, for the two men had different methods, and the production had a sort of uneasiness. The play was fallen upon by the critics even more violently than ever, and aroused great controversy in the religious press. The comic genius in religion was not appreciated by all. But the play has become one of the most generally esteemed and agreeable of all the author's works and is revived with success.

It was filmed in Hollywood in 1955 but hardly lifted out of film commonplace by Gabriel Pascal, who was at that time near the end of his life.

(28)
Overruled

(1912)

A farcical comedy in one act on the theme of polygamy. 'It is a clinical story of how the thing actually occurs among quite ordinary people, innocent of all unconventional views concerning it.' The original title was *Trespassers*. Shaw told Mrs Patrick Campbell that she put the play into his head.

At a seaside hotel a lady and gentleman are sitting alone in the lounge on a summer night. They have recently met on a ship: each think the other to be unmarried. They discover the truth. Then two people enter. The newcomers are their respective husband and wife, so they disappear through the french window at the back. The second couple has also just returned from a voyage. They confess that they are married and that each is having a holiday apart from his or her respective partner. They approach the point of calling each other by their Christian names, but the lady rejects the gentleman's advances. Then the first couple reappear and the situation is discussed. The men are concerned about their mothers and their principles, the women about the practical issues; the conclusion to which the women force them is that 'we're human'.

Characters

GREGORY LUNN is under twenty-five, rather handsome and almost a dandy.

SIBTHORPE JUNO is a fussy energetic little man, a solicitor.

MRS JUNO is attractive, under twenty-five or over twenty-five.

MRS LUNN is tall, imposing, languid.

Production

The play is a farce to be done with reference to the situation. The contrast is between the two couples. The setting and scenes should be smart.

A Note on Productions

The original production formed part of a programme contributed to by J. M. Barrie and Arthur Pinero under Charles Frohman's management at the Duke of York's Theatre on 14 October 1912. It has been revived several times.

(29)

Pygmalion

(1912)

Although its background is phonetics, the play's theme is human relations; in particular, love, as the title suggests. A philosopher-scientist creates an image that falls in love with him, and what to him is a scientific experiment turns out to be an exercise in the natural affection of the human heart. The play is meant to speak for itself, and it is not without significance that Shaw wrote one of his shortest prefaces to it; but he also wrote a fairly long epilogue containing a sequel, as though the play were incomplete.

Its plot is simplicity itself, but its theme is the creative element, and the bones of the plot are well clothed and moved by intelligence. When the play opens, a group of people are standing under the portico of St Paul's Church, Covent Garden, waiting for the rain to stop. Among them are a lady, her son and daughter, a flower girl, Colonel Pickering and Henry Higgins, author of Higgins's Universal Alphabet, who professed to be able to teach anyone any dialect, including how to speak correctly. The Colonel and Higgins, knowing each other by repute, strike up an acquaintance. Higgins takes note of the Cockney accents he hears, and as he goes away throws a handful of money into the flower girl's basket.

Next day at Higgins's laboratory he and the Colonel are having a technical discussion when the flower girl, Eliza Doolittle, appears. She says she wants to be a lady in a flower shop, but can't get a job 'unless I can talk more genteel', so she has come to Higgins to teach her. To her alarm he pounces on her as an excellent subject, and undertakes to make a duchess of her in six months, and she is handed over to his housekeeper. Very soon the girl's father, Alfred Doolittle, a dustman, arrives to inquire about his daughter, whom he is not going to let go for nothing. He gets a five-pound note, which strikes him as generous.

In the third act, at Higgins's mother's house, on her at-home day, Higgins turns up unexpectedly to say that Eliza is coming. Mrs Higgins has no time to protest. Two guests arrive and Higgins recognizes them as the mother and daughter who were under the portico in Covent Garden. Their son Freddy also arrives, and the Colonel. Presently Miss Doolittle is announced, a lovely creature. She doesn't, however, keep to the weather and health, subjects Higgins had prescribed for her. When Eliza takes the hint to go, the famous conversation takes place in which the infamous word was first used on the stage, a word that has since become necessary to every play. The at-home breaks up. Mrs Higgins, after listening to her son and the Colonel on the subject of Eliza, can only say angrily 'Oh men! men!! men!!!'

In the fourth act, at the Wimpole Street laboratory, Higgins, the Colonel and Eliza return after her successful society appearance as a Duchess. The men are satisfied. 'Thank God it's all over', says Higgins. They find Eliza, however, not at all satisfied. She has been made a lady, and is fit for nothing else; she tells them what she thinks of them. Higgins loses his temper. Pygmalion has come to life and he does not like it.

In the fifth and last act, Higgins appears at his mother's house to tell her that Eliza has bolted. Without his knowing it, she has fled to his mother for succour. Immediately after him comes Alfred Doolittle, sent on from Wimpole Street, to complain that he has been left a legacy by an American language fanatic: he goes off to marry the woman who had lived with him as Eliza's step-mother. Higgins is finally left alone with Eliza. There is a remark-able sexual encounter in which those who say that Shaw has no conception of human feelings are confounded. It is thought to be left uncertain whether Eliza may marry Higgins. Shaw's idea certainly was that she did not, for Higgins was beyond such weakness – as such a marriage would have been in him. In the epilogue, which forms no part of the play, the dramatist makes clear that she did not, she married Freddy and became joint proprietor of a fashionable greengrocery business. Mrs Patrick Campbell had the last act rewritten in her own favour as actress and proposed to perform it in America, which Shaw, of course, forbade. In the film and musical versions, however, Higgins is left (possibly and quite falsely) a happy man. By allowing this in the film Shaw in some degree compromised with his own sense of dramatic fitness for the sake of pleasing his friend Pascal. He was not in a position to object to the same treatment in the musical version, *My Fair Lady*. In leaving the issue ambiguous he went as far as he could, and it was up to the audience to understand that Higgins and Eliza do not speak the same language.

Characters

HENRY HIGGINS is forty or so, robust, energetic, scientific, positive but also a very 'impetuous baby'. He is one of Shaw's most closely observed and deeply felt characters. The play is, of course, his presentation of the comic situation, and the part calls for the most highly competent comedy playing.

COLONEL PICKERING is elderly, soldierly and amiable – a foil to Higgins.

FREDDY EYNSFORD-HILL is a nice young man of twenty.

ALFRED DOOLITTLE is an elderly, vigorous, interesting dustman, one of Shaw's usually pleasing character parts.

ELIZA DOOLITTLE is under twenty, a Cockney flower girl who becomes indistinguishable from a Duchess; she must, therefore, be a personality, but not sentimentalized.

MRS EYNSFORD-HILL is well-bred and quiet.

MISS EYNSFORD-HILL, her daughter, is very much at home in society.

MRS HIGGINS is over sixty, and a pleasant but determined mother.

MRS PEARCE is Higgins's housekeeper.

PARLOURMAID at Mrs Higgins's.

A BYSTANDER under the Portico of Covent Garden, where there are several other pedestrians sheltering from the rain.

Production

The play is romantic comedy, and needs well rounded and full-blooded romantic treatment with Higgins presented in the terms of intellectual comedy. Eliza is true woman, a natural romantic type. Conflict between the two on the level of unconscious comedy-romance makes the play: Higgins belongs to the intellect, she has no mind at all; he has not discovered his heart, she is nothing but heart; he sees her for exactly what she is, but does not know himself. This gives the play poignancy. It is not Eliza's drama, however, but Higgins's and to overweigh the sentiment is to distort its theme. Doolittle is a comedy character. There must be nothing naturalistic in the play except the settings, which need not be naturalistic either. The playing requires much spirit from the players. The settings are the Portico at St Paul's, Covent Garden, at night, a laboratory-drawing room at Wimpole Street, and a drawing room in Chelsea. The period is not later than 1912.

A Note on Productions

The first production was in German at the Hofburg Theatre, Vienna, on 16 October 1913. It was presented in London by H. Beerbohm Tree at His Majesty's Theatre on 11 April 1914, with Tree as Higgins and Mrs Patrick Campbell as Eliza. It has always been one of the most successful of the author's plays, and has been revived many times. It was made into a highly successful film in 1938 by Gabriel Pascal, directed by Anthony Asquith, with Leslie Howard as Higgins, and Wendy Hiller as Eliza. Additional scenes were written by Shaw and the film was much praised. A few months before the centenary of Shaw's birth a musical version, *My Fair Lady* by Alan Jay Lerner (the music by Frederick Loewe), was presented in New York (on 15 March 1956) at the Mark Hellinger Theatre with Rex Harrison as Higgins and Julie Andrews as Eliza, which proved to be one of the most successful theatrical pieces ever produced, having a run that continued till 29 September 1962, 2,717 performances. It arrived at Drury Lane Theatre on 30 April 1958 and that run still continues. This version of the play, up to the expert standard of the best American musicals, shows how much lower and lacking in originality is that standard than that of Shaw's romantic drama. The libretto is poor, though the music is tuneful, whatever quality the dialogue possesses being entirely in what remains of Shaw's lines. Its popularity is deserved, for it rests squarely upon the theatrical effectiveness of Shaw's original work: had he been alive he would not have consented to a libretto by any other hand than his own.

(30)
Great Catherine

WHOM GLORY STILL ADORES
(1913)

Shaw told one of his favourite actresses, Gertrude Kingston, that she should play queens, and he had to write this small bravura piece for her to justify his remark. 'In the long run', he says, 'the actors will get the authors, and the authors the actors, they desire.' He did not pretend that the play was much more than tomfoolery.

The piece, excellent in its opening, becomes inconclusive and pointless.

There are four scenes. Prince Patiomkin, the Empress's favourite, is drunk and receives an English officer who comes with a recommendation to Her Majesty. They quarrel and the officer back-heels the Russian, who falls with a crash on the floor. The outcome is that Patiomkin takes the officer to Catherine. In the second scene Catherine is in bed with the Court in attendance; she has just got up when the officer is brought in. He pleases Catherine, which impresses Patiomkin. In the third scene, the officer on a terrace garden overlooking the Neva explains to his fiancée that the Empress has taken a fancy to him and they had better fly; but he has hardly spoken before the Empress's soldiers have entered to find and capture him. In the fourth scene the officer is brought back to the Palace where Catherine receives him, still bound. She tantalizes him, and as she is doing so, the fiancée appears, who is overcome by the extravagance of the Russian way of talking. The officer, released, gives Catherine some advice and is allowed to go.

Characters

THE EMPRESS CATHERINE II is handsome, imperious, a great woman.

PRINCE PATIOMKIN, gigantic, ugly, one-eyed, but a man to be reckoned with in every respect.

COSSAK SERGEANT, an old soldier.

VARINKA, Patiomkin's niece, a pretty young lady.

THE PRINCESS DASHKOFF, belonging to the Court.

NARYSHKIN is Catherine's Chamberlain.

CAPTAIN EDSTASTON, a handsome, strongly built English officer.

CLAIRE, a robust young English lady.

Production

The play is historical farce, to be played for situation. The period is 1776. The settings are in Patiomkin's bureau, the Emperor's bedroom, a terrace garden overlooking the Neva, a triangular recess communicating with the ball-room at the Palace. The properties are described in the text.

A Note on Productions

It was first produced at the Vaudeville Theatre, London, on 18 November 1918, with Gertrude Kingston as the Empress. It was made into an opera in Germany in 1932, with music by Ignaz Lillien.

(31)
The Music Cure

A PIECE OF UTTER NONSENSE
(1914)

'There is', says the author, in a note to this little play, 'no pressing reason why the thing should be performed at all.' It is a variety turn for two musicians.

A young man is crying convulsively on a sofa in a hotel drawing room. A doctor is trying to soothe him. The young man is an Under-Secretary at the War Office; he knew that the Army was going to be put on a vegetarian diet, and bought all the shares he could afford in the British Macaroni Trust. 'Any fellow would have done it', the young man declares. But the Opposition attacked him, and he had to go before a Committee of Inquiry, which had reduced him to his present nervous state. The doctor gives him an opium pill and leaves him to sleep. Then there enters a lovely lady who proceeds to play the piano. This arouses the young man, who wants her to desist. She, however, refuses, having been engaged to play by the young man's mother. When the young man tries to stop her she knocks him down. She is obviously his superior. He offers to marry her and to be a 'dear, little domesticated husband', which being what she is looking for she asks him to name the day.

Characters

LORD REGINALD FITZAMBEY is a pretty and fashionably dressed young man of twenty-two.

THE DOCTOR is a dozen years his senior.

STREGA THUNDRIDGE is a lovely lady and the strength of her left arm is as the strength of ten.

Production

The play is farce. The lady must be overwhelming. She is a famous pianist, and the young man is a pianist also. Shaw says that any musical instrument will do instead of a piano; but the play needs that instrument and competent players.

A Note on Productions

It was first performed in London as a curtain raiser to celebrate the 100th performance of *Magic* by G. K. Chesterton, at the Little Theatre, on 28 January 1914.

(32)
O'Flaherty, VC

A RECRUITING PAMPHLET
(1915)

'Incomprehensible as it may seem to an Englishman,' said Shaw, 'Irish patriotism does not take the form of devotion to England

and England's king.' The play is a comic presentation of a common soldier's attitude to the first world war; this Irish soldier gets into so much trouble with his mother and sweetheart that he is glad to return to the comparative peace and quiet of the battle front.

Private O'Flaherty, VC, has come home after being employed recruiting in Ireland as a hero of the war. He is nervous about meeting his mother because he has led her to believe that he was fighting in the German army, she having no idea that an Irishman would do anything but fight against the English. When she gets him to herself she flies at him for lying to her, and for shaking hands with the English king when he got the Cross. But he appeases her by saying that he joined the army that would pay her the biggest allowance. Tessie, his sweetheart, is interested in his pension, and when he gives her a gold chain, found on the battlefield, his mother gets furious and there is a row, which is ended by the women being forcibly ejected.

The point of the play is brought out in an entertaining and characteristically Shavian conversation between O'Flaherty and an Irish General.

Characters

O'FLAHERTY, VC, is an ordinary Irish soldier, who needs sufficient personality to carry the play.

GENERAL SIR PEARCE MADIGAN is an elderly baronet and landowner.

MRS O'FLAHERTY is an old-fashioned Irish peasant.

TERESA DRISOLL is a pretty Irish maid.

Production

The play is farcical-comedy, to be done with spirit, but with the comedy element uppermost. The old woman is a character part. The setting is at the door of an Irish country house in a park in 1915.

A Note on Productions

The play was too much politically for the Abbey Theatre, Dublin, where it was intended to be performed on 23 November 1915, the first world war being on. It was, however, as noted elsewhere, performed by Robert Loraine when in the Air Force in France in February 1917. It was first performed publicly in New York in 1920, and privately by the Stage Society in London the same year. Shaw made the piece his first radio broadcast on 20 November 1924. It is an easy and agreeable little play that deserves to be seen more often.

(33)
Augustus does his Bit

A TRUE-TO-LIFE FARCE
(1916)

The problem during the first world war was how to win it with Augustuses on the backs of our Government departments – 'well meaning, brave, patriotic, but obstructively fussy, self-important, imbecile and disastrous'.

In the Mayor's parlour of Little Pifflington, Colonel Lord Augustus Highcastle is reading the *Morning Post* when he is interrupted by the staff, an over-age clerk, whom they wouldn't have in the Army. After a slanging match between them, a lady appears. She is after a confidential list of gun emplacements. She gets it. Then she rings up Augustus's cousin at the War Office to say that she has won her bet.

Characters

THE LADY is young, charming, irresistible.

256

LORD AUGUSTUS is a well-preserved, typical, country house Englishman.

THE CLERK is a disreputable old man.

Production

The play is a topical farce, and makes fun of the English governing class. The piece depends on the lady, who must have personality.

A Note on Productions

The piece was first performed by the Stage Society at the Court Theatre on 21 January 1917, and first performed in America by amateurs at Washington on 10 December that year. It was produced at the Comedy Theatre, New York, on 12 March 1919 when it had 111 performances.

(34)
The Inca of Perusalem

AN ALMOST HISTORICAL COMEDIETTA
(1916)

The author reminds the reader that this play was written in the first World War when its principal character was still 'the Caesar whose legions we were resisting with our hearts in our mouths' ... and when 'anyone who breathed the slightest doubt of the perfection of German organization ... was called a pro-German'.

The little play has a prologue before the curtain in which an archdeacon is told by his daughter, widow of an American millionaire, that she cannot live on her allowance of £150 a year. He tells her that she had 'better become lady's maid to a princess until you can find another millionaire to marry you'. She says she will, and

257

disappears through the stage curtain, while the archdeacon goes grumbling through the auditorium.

In a hotel sitting-room the widow is interviewing a spinster Princess and engages herself on the spot, starting at once on her duties by finding fault with the tea brought to the Princess, also finding fault with the Princess's apartment, demanding a suite on the first floor. The Princess says she is to be married to one of the sons of the Inca of Perusalem, a boy she has never met. An officer from the Inca is announced and the maid undertakes to see him; when he appears he is the Inca himself, who thinks the maid to be the Princess. The maid sees through the disguise and when he yields to her fascination, and asks her to be his, she reminds him that he is married and he offers to embrace the Mohammedan faith. He then tells her that he had known all along whom she was. They go off for a ride round the town and a cup of tea at the Zoo.

Characters

ERMYNTRUDE is a fashionably dressed and handsome lady.

THE ARCHDEACON is just a clergyman.

THE HOTEL MANAGER is spruce and condescending.

THE PRINCESS is meek and mild.

THE WAITER was once an eminent medical man.

THE INCA is overpowering, and represents the German Kaiser.

Production

The piece is farce to be played for situation. Both Ermyntrude and the Inca must be overpowering in their respective ways.

A Note on Productions

First produced at the Birmingham Repertory Theatre on 7 October 1916, when Ermyntrude was played by Gertrude Kingston, who also played it on the first production in New York at the

Neighbourhood Playhouse on 14 November the same year. First publicly performed in London at the Bedford Theatre 30 May 1949.

(35)
Annajanska: The Bolshevik Empress

A REVOLUTIONARY ROMANCELET
(1917)

This is 'frankly a bravura piece', written for Lillah McCarthy for the variety stage.

At the General's office in a military station on the Eastern Front during the First World War, the General is lamenting the new disorder in which the Panjandrum has been exposed and learns that the royal daughter, the Grand Duchess Annajanska, has joined the Revolution, and eloped with a young officer. She has been captured and is brought in. The General is heartbroken and attempts to shoot himself. Annajanska gets possession of the pistol and drives everyone out but the General. She says she has come to save the Revolution, and the young officer is herself, as she proceeds to show the General.

Characters

ANNAJANSKA is handsome, strong, and knows her own mind.
THE GENERAL is old and an aristocrat.
THE LIEUTENANT is young and not important.
There are two SOLDIERS.

Production

The setting is supposed to be Beotia. The piece is farce, and depends on the lady.

A Note on Productions

The play was first performed in a variety programme at the London Coliseum on 21 January 1918 when Lillah McCarthy played Annajanska.

(36)
Heartbreak House

A FANTASIA IN THE RUSSIAN MANNER
ON ENGLISH THEMES
(1913–16)

A picture of 'cultured, leisured Europe before the War', ending with bombs falling, though nothing is said about bombs or war until they fall. It is an allegory of national affairs in the hands of governors who trust to Chance, which they call Providence, without troubling to learn their business. 'What may be my business as an Englishman, pray?' asks the head of the English country house, which is the setting of the play: 'Navigation', is the stern answer; 'learn it and live; or leave it and be damned.' Thus it is a play of democracy addressed to those who consider themselves to be 'self-rulers'. It is a stern comedy meant by Shaw as a warning to his generation.

We need not take too seriously the 'Russian manner'. Shaw refers to Chekhov and Tolstoy in his preface, and was undoubtedly influenced by Chekhov and *The Cherry Orchard*. But the Russian play is satire, while Shaw's is comedy. There is no attempt to imitate the Chekhov technique, subtle, indirect, intuitive, realistic. Shaw's is sharp, hard, brittle, poetic and unrealistic, very easily ruined (as indeed is Chekhov's) by clumsy performance. The Irish comic genius is not translatable into the tragi-comedy of the Russian world. Its protagonist is the girl Ellie, a somewhat withdrawn and negative character, and the characters and action are from her standpoint. That the play is a dream is clear enough, for Ellie falls asleep as soon as it opens. For that reason, Shaw's attack upon the audience becomes rather more indirect than usual, and even his Irish volubility is a little held in check. It is a play to leave hearers guessing; for it has the appearance of a joke: but few will see it without being conscious of the intense feeling with which it was written. There is no joke in its theme, which is as serious as the writer could make it. A notable feature of the work is that it is not a comedic treatment of the English, but international in its viewpoint, and the people might equally be German or French or American.

The structure of the play is romantic-melodrama: love in conflict with good and evil; but the writing is pure comedy. The characters are the leisured middle-class, the people with whom 'the pleasure of music, art, literature and the theatre had supplanted hunting, shooting, fishing, eating and drinking. . . . They hated politics. They did not wish to realize Utopia for the common people . . . when they could, they lived without scruple on incomes which they did nothing to earn.' Heartbreak House was an 'idle house', a house inhabited by those who 'did not know how to live'.

Shaw is not, however, attacking mere idleness or people of wealth, but lack of purpose, restating in another context the great theme of *Man and Superman*. He is attacking the cruelty, inhumanity, callous financial competition and political destructiveness engendered by nineteenth century science and economics, with their doctrines of limited wealth and the struggle for existence. He is attacking the lack of religious motive, which resulted in the 'half century of the drift to the abyss', bringing Europe to the First World War, and from the effects of which Europe will not escape until the people of all the nations desire life rather than

261

death, and learn to be master of their own destiny so that they are with confidence 'headed for God's open sea'.

The action takes place at a country house in Sussex on a fine evening in September. The house belongs to an old man, Captain Shotover, and is the home of Mrs Hushabye, his eldest daughter, her husband, Hector, and their children. Mrs Hushabye has invited to the house her young friend, Ellie Dunn, her father, Mazzini Dunn, and her fiancé, Mr Mangan; there also arrives straight from abroad, Ariadna, Mrs Hushabye's younger sister, whom she has not seen for twenty-three years, wife of Sir Hastings Utterword. Randall Utterword, Sir Hasting's man-about-town brother, turns up uninvited, and another unexpected guest is a burglar. These people talk and (except for the burglar) make love. All, except Ellie, are larger than life, and none of them is exactly what he or she appears to be.

Mrs Hushabye wants to break off Ellie's engagement to the financial magnate, Mangan, because he is too old: she finds Mangan ready to make love to her, and finds too that her husband, Hector, had already made love to Ellie. The complications of the personal relations make sufficient action for the play's development. When out of a clear sky a bomb from an enemy plane falls upon Mangan and the burglar, the play ends with our gaining some conviction of the existence of justice in the heavens. There is no reference to the war in the play, and the action is not fixed to time or place. It is not only international but timeless.

The philosophy of the play is expressed by the old Captain, who appears to be mad, though there is the suggestion that he is the sanest of them all. He says 'Youth – beauty – novelty – they are badly wanted in this house', and is answered before the evening is out when Ellie, the youngest of those present, falls in love with him; for she is youth searching for wisdom. She says: 'Life with a blessing! that is what I want.' Thus the play becomes an allegory of youth. Youth, which gets no help from its elders, lost in the maze of events, having no faith in the future, and forced to accept the makeshift offered by practical men as the one certain thing in life; but youth is ready, so Shaw says, to give up the easy way if but a single word of wisdom falls upon its ears. Thus Ellie gives up Mangan and his millions when the aged captain who has no security to offer points out to her a way of life. Ellie's symbolical marriage to the Captain represents youth and age in right relations, not a marriage in the flesh but in the spirit.

This play is unmistakably one of the great works of our age, for it sets the time's essential problem in a burning light.

Characters

ELLIE DUNN is pretty, slender, fair, intelligent, 'not a smart idler'. As the protagonist, representing youth, she must be given her rightful place. She is romantic but earnest, and appears to be not wholly awake, as though she were sleep-walking.

CAPTAIN SHOTOVER is eighty-eight years old; hardy and active, but finds it to suit him to pretend to be deaf and senile; he has a white beard and wears a reefer jacket with a whistle hanging from his neck, which he frequently uses. He is older than his years, and more magnificent than life: he must not be played in a naturalistic manner, despite the obvious temptation to do so.

NURSE GUINNESS is an old servant who has the privilege of outspokenness.

HESIONE HUSHABYE is forty-four, dark and extremely handsome, a 'gorgeous woman' a 'siren', 'born to lead men by the nose', more fascinating than is humanly possible. She is rather slack in dress but creates confidence by her natural ease and self-command. She is very sympathetic with Ellie.

LADY UTTERWORD is forty-two, blonde, very smart and handsome, a typical Governor-General's wife.

MAZZINI DUNN is a little elderly man, the inventor type, sincere, genuine, a sympathetic character.

HECTOR HUSHABYE is fifty, tall and handsome, well-mannered, more wonderfully romantic than anything but opera could provide.

BOSS MANGAN is fifty-five but looks much younger, frock-coated and excessively commonplace, the complete expression of worldly success.

RANDALL UTTERWORD is over forty, well bred, useless but agreeable.

THE BURGLAR is old and villainous.

Production

The play starts with Ellie falling asleep, which should be treated as the opening of the dramatic action which takes place in her dream. The style is comedy, with marked elevation, demanding the utmost polish and distinction throughout, speech requiring to be made luminous. The symbolical nature of the play, suggested by the names of the characters, should be kept in mind, and the element of heartbreak must be brought out. Naturalism is entirely out of place. The players must virtually sing their long speeches. The entire piece should be thought of as music. The last act is in the soft, cool, summer moonlight of contemplation, broken into but not shattered by the enemy bomb.

The first act is a sitting-room built to resemble the after-part of a high pooped ship with a stern gallery. The time is late after-noon. The second act is just before dinner the same day. The third act is in the garden after dinner.

The play is not dated except as to its writing and can rightly be treated as contemporary.

A Note on Productions

The first production was by the Theatre Guild in New York on

10 November 1920, when it had 120 performances. It was first produced in London the year after by J. B. Fagan at the Court Theatre on 18 October 1921, and was not revived there until just over ten years when Barry Jackson brought it from Birmingham to the Queen's Theatre on 25 April 1932. Captain Shotover and Hesione Hushabye are treated as the star parts and they have been played in London by Brember Wills, Cedric Hardwicke, Cecil Trouncer, Robert Donat, Walter Fitzgerald, and Mary Grey, Edith Evans, and Catherine Lacey respectively. Usually, insufficient attention is given to Ellie. The play has always been received with much respect and has always made a great impression; of its first performance *The Times* said that it was 'of all Shaw's plays the most responsible to sentiment, the most sensitive to the feelings of the average, sensual man'. It is by no means an easy work, however, for actors or audience.

(37)
Back to Methuselah

A METABIOLOGICAL PENTATEUCH
(1918–21)

This is Shaw's longest and most important play in aim and scope. It is five plays in one, and requires a different theatre from any that exists at present. He had already written *Man and Superman*, a 'dramatic parable in Creative Evolution', but, he says, 'being then at the height of my invention and comedic talent, I decorated it too brilliantly and lavishly', with the result that 'Nobody noticed the new religion in the centre of the intellectual whirlpool'. Much more needed to be said on this new religion, so when the war ended he started on this large work and laboured at it for more than two years.

Shaw had always been an anti-Darwinian, and when the First World War came the doubt was confirmed in his mind as to whether the human being, 'as he exists at present, is capable of solving the social problems raised by his own aggregation, or, as he calls it, his civilization'. There are plenty of people with good intentions, but there is no political science. What is required are men who are masters of such a science, who know the art of living together. Such men cannot be produced by our present methods of education, for 'our schools teach the morality of feudalism corrupted by commercialism, and hold up the military conqueror, the robber baron, and the profiteer, as models of the illustrious and the successful'. The only hope for man is that he should surpass himself and create a new man. This means conscious evolution. Man must decide upon his own perfection and help himself. 'Nature holds no brief for the human experiment: it must stand or fall by its results', and if man stays where he is he will be replaced. Therefore, let us resolve to live, and to live longer than we do now, so that we can do more, is the play's theme.

Thus the play is a biological treatise 'a contribution to the modern Bible', required for 'the genuinely scientific religion for which all wise men are anxiously looking'. The first word of that religion is that the universe makes itself out of nothing, and therefore man can make himself out of what he is. That is Creative Evolution. It is belief in the future and in the endless possibilities of man. Shaw propounds that at length in the preface to the play, arguing against the sceptics and mechanists and neo-Darwinians. It is a religion without miracle, except the great miracle of life.

Back to Methuselah is a legend of Creative Evolution, in which its author sounds rather a pathetic note at the end. 'My sands are running out' – he was sixty-five when the play was written – 'the exuberance of 1901 has aged into the garrulity of 1920 . . . I am doing the best I can at my age. My powers are waning. . . .'

But the play showed him to be as intellectually alive as ever.

Dramatically, the play is overwhelmed by its theme. There is no action and the talk hardly moves it, but the entire work glows with intellectual light. The play is more alive than the preface, and those who say that Shaw is better in his prefaces than in his plays find no support for their argument here. Shaw wrote it, as he indicated, under inspiration, and though some of it seems little more than an amusing satire on contemporary ideas and persons it rises to heights of eloquence he had never surpassed.

The play opens in the Garden of Eden. Adam has found a dead fawn and learns what death is. This disturbs him. Hitherto he had been troubled by the thought of having to exist for ever, 'the horror of having to be with myself for ever'. Now he has another troubled thought, death. The Serpent whispers to Eve that there is a way of escape, that death can be overcome by birth, and in birth man can for ever renew himself. The two choose this way of escape; and their son Cain having killed Abel discovers that he does not know what he wants . . . 'except that I want to be something higher and nobler than this stupid old digger'. What is there left for man? Only hope of dreams coming true. 'Man need not always live by bread alone', says Eve. 'There is something else.' There we leave them.

In the Second Part we are in the first years after the First World War when Conrad Barnabas makes the discovery, and writes a book upon it, that man would live as long as he pleased if he were to will it strongly enough. He and his brother have an interview with the leading politicians of the day with a view to trying to get this discovery taken up as a national programme aimed at extending the term of human life to three hundred years. But they make it clear what sort of willing they mean:

Do not mistake mere idle fancies for the tremendous miracle

– working force of Will nerved to creation by a conviction of Necessity. I tell you men capable of such willing, and realizing its necessity, will do it reluctantly, under inner compulsion, as all great efforts are made. They will hide what they are doing from themselves: they will take care not to know what they are doing. They will live three hundred years, not because they would like to, but because the soul deep down in them will know that they must, if the world is to be saved.

This is Shaw speaking with all the conviction of his being that if only men would will what they are capable of doing, life would be transformed. But while the Liberal leader Lubin (Asquith) finds the Barnabas' idea, so stated, to be moonshine, the other popular politician Burge (Lloyd George) is ready to adopt it as an electioneering cry. The brothers are disgusted: 'We had better hold our tongues about it', says Franklyn Barnabas.

The Third Part is in the year A.D. 2170: 'The Thing Happens'. Two persons, a clergyman friend of the brothers, and their parlourmaid, have taken seriously the idea of extending their lives. After two hundred and fifty years they are still alive, one an Archbishop, the other Domestic Minister of Britain. Their secret has hitherto been kept, but in the parlour of the President of the British Isles it is brought to light. Television is common, and people see each other at a distance as easily as they use the telephone – a prophecy now near realization. The two young-old people contemplate marriage when they meet.

The Fourth Part is in the year A.D. 3000. An elderly gentleman on the shore of Galway Bay in Ireland has come from the capital of the British Commonwealth in Baghdad to visit his ancestral shores. He is not unlike the Bernard Shaw we know; but, old as he is, he is one of the expiring race of short livers; for at this time a new race of men and women exist who live as long as they please, and possess extraordinary powers over nature. This part is in three acts in which the conflicting politics of the short-livers and the long-livers is the theme. In the course of the discussion the elderly gentleman explains what he means by the soul:

My body is dust, madam: not my soul. What does it matter what my body is made of? the dust of the ground, the particles of the air, or even the slime of the ditch? The important thing is that when my Creator took it, whatever it was, He breathed into its nostrils the breath of life; and Man became a living soul. Yes, madam, a living soul. I am not the dust of the ground: I am a living soul. That is an exalting, a magnificent thought. It is also a great scientific fact. I am not interested in the chemicals and the microbes: I leave them to the chumps and noodles, to the blockheads and the muckrakers who are incapable of of their own glorious destiny, and unconscious of their own divinity. They tell me there are leucocytes in my blood, and sodium and carbon in my flesh. I thank them for the information, and tell them that there are black beetles in my kitchen, washing soda in my laundry, and coal in my cellar. I do not deny their existence; but I keep them in their proper place, which is not, if I may be allowed to use an antiquated form of expression, the temple of the Holy Ghost.

The elderly gentleman wants to stay in the land of the long-livers and is told: 'If you stay with us you will die of discouragement.' He answers, 'If I go back I shall die of disgust and despair. ... It is the meaning of life, not of death that makes banishments so terrible to me.' So, permitted to stay, he dies on the instant.

The Fifth and last Part is 'As Far as Thought can Reach', in the year A.D. 31920. By that time people are born fully developed from eggs. There is no childhood – a time hateful to Shaw – but young men and women appear on the earth at about the age of eighteen, having attained consciousness, moral sense, and intelligence before birth in the egg! People die only by accident. As they grow old, their lives change from pleasure to ecstasy, and they learn that their true creative powers are over themselves. One of the young artists has discovered how to make human beings, but these creatures are automata responding only to stimuli from without. The Ancients cause the automata to die.

The Ancients look forward to the escape from the body, and from the deception to which those in the body still are subject – 'None of us now believe that this machinery of flesh and blood is necessary', they say. This part contains an admirable expression of Shaw's attitude to art and artists, and to science, and his presentation of mere youth is, for once, satirical.

At the end, in the darkness, Adam, Eve, Cain and the Serpent reappear as shadows, and Lilith, 'in whom father and mother are one', comments on human life as it has developed: she says that because man is still reaching out towards the future she will have patience with him still. In noble rhetoric she concludes:

> Of Life only is there no end; and though of its million starry mansions many are empty and many still unbuilt, and though its vast domain is as yet unbearably desert, my seed shall one day fill it and master its matter to its uttermost confines.

The last words are hers, male and female in one, she who is to be superseded. This was Shaw's attempt to get free from the limitations of the natural world, the world of the senses, and the course of natural life. The theme is not longevity as an idea in itself, but longevity as a means of transcending the present period of short aims and disbelief in the future. So far as it is possible to put the vision of the future into a play, Shaw, perhaps, does it.

If what he shows us is unsatisfactory, as undoubtedly it is, that is because the future is unknown and cannot be expressed in words. 'It is enough that there *is* a beyond.' The weakness of the play is that its integrity depends wholly upon a theme too impersonal to be developed as drama. It has no protagonist or single personal element, which is the essential element in drama, and this fact accounts for its stage weakness as a whole. In its parts, however, it is admirable, and while dramatically defective it lives through the energy of its thought and the glittering language in which it is expressed. There are many passages that are equivalent to the dramatist's personal confession.

Characters

PART I. 'In the Beginning.'

THE SERPENT has the voice of a woman.

ADAM is young, strong and handsome at first, and grows older.

EVE is young, strong and lovely at first, and grows older.

CAIN is a strong, sullen man.

PART II. 'The Gospel of the Brothers Barnabas.'

FRANKLYN BARNABAS is an impressive looking man of fifty with the appearance of a popular Nonconformist minister.

CONRAD BARNABAS, his brother, two or three years younger, shorter and with much less style in his bearing.

REV WILLIAM HASLAM is a schoolboyish clergyman.

SAVVY BARNABAS is a vigorous, sun-burnt, pretty, dark girl.

JOYCE BURGE is a well-fed man past fifty, broad forehead, grey hair worn long, rather like David Lloyd George.

LUBIN is at the end of his sixties, a Yorkshireman, white hair, unassuming, undistinguished, rather like Herbert Henry Asquith.

THE PARLOURMAID is young.

PART III. 'The Thing Happens.'

BURGE-LUBIN is rather like a composite portrait of a younger Mr Burge and a young Mr Lubin, stoutish, middle-aged, good-looking, breezy, genial.

BARNABAS is rather like Conrad Barnabas but younger and more commonplace.

CONFUCIUS is a Chinese sage.

THE NEGRESS is a handsome creature with a good figure.

THE ARCHBISHOP OF YORK is older than the Rev William Haslam but recognizably the same man, no longer boyish, with an air of authority and self-possession.

MRS LUTESTRING was once the parlourmaid, now a handsome woman in the prime of life.

TELEPHONE OPERATOR, a voice.

PART IV. 'Tragedy of an Elderly Gentleman.'

THE ELDERLY GENTLEMAN is rather like Bernard Shaw, tall, white whiskers and eyebrows, energetic, talkative.

FUSIMA has the appearance of a young girl but the manner of a mature woman.

ZOZIM has the appearance of a boy but is a grown man.

ZOO is rather like Savvy Barnabas, but looks, if anything, younger.

GENERAL AUFSTEIG is short, saturnine, rather like Napoleon.

THE ORACLE is a handsome woman of majestic carriage.

AMBROSE BADGER-BLUEBIN is the British Envoy, a typical politician, 'who looks like an imperfectly reformed criminal disguised by a good tailor'.

MRS BADGER-BLUEBIN is his wife.

MISS BADGER-BLUEBIN is his pretty daughter of eighteen.

PART V. 'As Far as Thought can Reach.'

STREPHON is a graceful youth of eighteen.

CHLOE is a graceful nymph of eighteen.

ACIS is another graceful youth but older than Strephen.

THE HE-ANCIENT in uprightness of physique and manner seems to be in the prime of life, but is hairless, except for his eyelashes, and his face is exceedingly wrinkled.

THE SHE-ANCIENT is upright and vigorous, but hairless, with manly breasts and her face also deeply creased.

AMARYLLIS is the Newlyborn and appears to be seventeen, very pretty indeed.

ECRASIA is a handsome nymph older than the other nymphs, with authoritative bearing.

ARJILLAX is a bearded sculptor.

MARTELLUS is a beardless and sardonic sculptor.

PYGMALION is a laboratory product, a square fingered youth, whose face seems to be made of horizontal blocks, clumsy, with a fixed smile.

OZYMANDIAS and CLEOPATRA-SEMIRAMIS are a synthetic couple, automata, handsome and impressive.

GHOST OF ADAM is the shadowy figure of Adam.

GHOST OF EVE is the shadowy figure of Eve.

GHOST OF CAIN is the shadowy figure of Cain.

GHOST OF THE SERPENT is the shadowy figure of the Serpent.

GHOST OF LILITH is the shadowy figure of the female-male who came before the Serpent.

There are many YOUTHS and NYMPHS.

Production

The play is epic drama intended to be handled on the grand scale. It should not be necessary to say that naturalistic treatment even in its most realistically written episodes is entirely out of place. Throughout it must be kept in the realm of fantasy and make-believe, the poetic and prophetic elements informing the entire productions, though there are elements of farce, introduced to make the play easier for the audience and more palatable. It is possible to mistake the silliness for seriousness, and vice versa, with disastrous results. It should not be performed slowly with over-elaboration of business, but with as much quickness and in as spirited a manner as possible. Good speaking is essential, as in all of Shaw's plays. Elaborate and careful staging and dressing are required, the details of which are fully described in the text.

The five parts were originally given at five performances. The first part 'In the Beginning: 4004 B.C.' is the shortest. It is in two acts. The next part 'The Gospel of the Brothers Barnabas: Present day' is about half as long again and is in one act. The third part 'The Thing Happens: A.D. 2170' is between the two in length. The fourth part 'Tragedy of an Elderly Gentleman: A.D. 3000' is in three acts and is rather longer than the second part, and the fifth part in one act is approximately as long as the second part. An entire day should be given up to its performance. Alternatively, it could be done with advantage in two performances, the first taking slightly longer than the normal two and a half hours, and the second starting early in the evening.

The settings are Part I 'In the Beginning'. The Garden of Eden; an oasis in Mesopotamia. Part II 'The Gospel of the Brothers Barnabas' (A.D. 1969). A Study. Part III 'The Thing Happens' (A.D. 2170). The official parlour of the President of the British Islands. Part IV 'Tragedy of an Elderly Gentleman' (A.D. 3000). Burrin pier on the south shore of Galway Bay, Ireland; a courtyard before the portico of a temple; inside the temple. Part V 'As Far as Thought can Reach' (A.D. 31920). A sunlit glade at the foot of a wooded hill.

A Note on Productions

The first production by the Theatre Guild in New York on 27 February 1922 was given in three parts at weekly intervals: Parts I and II, Parts III and IV, and Part V. When first played by

Barry Jackson at Birmingham in 1923, the five Parts were given separate performances, this was repeated when the production was brought to the Court Theatre, London, the following year. A year later Parts I and V were given at separate matinees at the same theatre, and two years later at the same theatre the entire play was given in three performances (as in New York) with extra performances of Parts I and V. For all these performances Barry Jackson was responsible to whom Shaw wrote when he was asked for permission to do the play originally 'Is your family provided for?' When the play was submitted to the Lord Chamberlain for licence three conditions were imposed: (1) that the parody of the Athanasian Creed in Part V be omitted in performance, (2) that Burge and Lubin should not be made up to resemble D. Lloyd George and H. H. Asquith, who were alive at the time, and (3) that the usual conventionalities of dress be observed in representing the other characters, with reference to Adam and Eve in Part I. Shaw made no difficulty about these points, though he demurred to 'the serious purpose and significance' of his paraphrase of the creed being described as a 'parody'. 'I suppose the word was used in pure thoughtlessness', he said, 'I suspect the Lord Chamberlain of being a bit of a Mechanist himself.' And he thought the two statesmen would not thank the Lord Chamberlain for his delicacy. He considered the third condition to be 'out of the question, because "the usual conventionalities of dress" in the Garden of Eden . . . are no dress at all', which no one thought of adopting! In 1947 the play was given in four separate performances at the Arts Theatre Club in London, and during the same occasion the entire play was performed in one day, starting at 2.30 p.m. A condensed version was presented in New York under the auspices of the Theatre Guild in March 1958. Shaw being dead, violence was done to his work. It had been toured in a number of American cities by Tyrone Power, Faye Emerson and Arnold Moss, but the critics treated it with contempt 'as more or less of a joke', as it deserved.

(38)
Jitta's Atonement

Included in the *Tomfooleries* volume, this is a version of a play entitled *Frau Gittas Sühne* by Siegfried Trebitsch, an Austrian novelist and playwright, who earned Shaw's gratitude by becoming the translator of his plays into German. 'My personal debt to him is incalculable', said Shaw. The original play was first performed in Vienna on 3 February 1920. Without claiming knowledge of German nor pleading ignorance of it, Shaw says:

> It was not by any process known to men of learning, but rather by some telepathic method of absorption, that I managed at last to divine, infer, guess and co-invent the story of Jitta.

In fact, it was a Shavian acknowledgment of the original, not a translation by any means. The play opens in the drawing room of a flat in Vienna. Jitta, wife of a University professor, is in love with one of her husband's colleagues and the flat is their place of meeting. The professor is ill and may die suddenly; he tells Jitta about the manuscript of a book, which, when he is dead, he wants her to publish under her husband's name and he forces her to promise to do so. He dies, and she, utterly scared, goes hurriedly away.

In the second act a week later, Jitta's husband is Bruno's executor and is curious about the lady who is said to have been with him when he died. He asks Jitta if she knows who the woman was. Bruno's wife and daughter arrive. Jitta and the daughter talk together, and the daughter says she wants to find the woman who had made her father happy. Jitta's husband says he will not have the book published under his name and presses Jitta about the woman: she confesses that she and Bruno were lovers for three years. She says that unless he will publish the book as his she will make public the scandal about herself which will ruin him.

In the third act, the daughter is still endeavouring to find some clue to the identity of the mysterious woman. The widow is searching for a missing manuscript of a book. The daughter tells her fiancé of her longing and the widow tells Jitta that she has the silly idea that she is the woman; she laughs with Jitta and says that she is half disappointed that it wasn't. The daughter is told the truth by Jitta and is happy. Her husband confesses his own infidelities to Jitta; he refuses to publish Bruno's book as his own as he regards it as 'tommy rot'; but he agrees to edit it for Bruno's widow. So everybody is happy.

Characters

JITTA is handsome, refined, and in the early forties.

MRS BILLITER is an elderly housekeeper who looks after Bruno's flat, she appears to be undomesticated.

PROFESSOR BRUNO HALDENSTEDT is about forty-five, he is Jitta's lover, and suffers from angina pectoris.

PROFESSOR ALFRED LENKHEIM, Jitta's husband, is between forty and fifty, a prosaic don.

DR ERNEST FESSLER, engaged to Bruno's daughter, is an ordinary nice-looking young man.

AGNES HALDENSTEDT is a little older than Jitta, a good bourgeoise.

EDITH, her daughter, is pretty, and ingenuous with a strong character.

There is a FLOWER GIRL and a MAID.

Production

The play is comedy: Jitta's. There are three settings: a drawing room; Professor Lenkheim's study; Mrs Haldenstedt's sitting-room. The properties are described. The period is 1920.

A Note on Productions

The piece was first produced in Washington at the Shubert-Garrick Theatre on 8 January 1923, afterwards at the Comedy Theatre, New York, the same month. In London it was first done at the Grand Theatre, Fulham, on 26 January 1925, and privately at the Arts Theatre Club on 30 April 1930. It does not appear to have been taken very seriously anywhere.

(39)
Saint Joan

A CHRONICLE PLAY IN SIX SCENES AND AN EPILOGUE
(1923)

In writing *Saint Joan* Shaw did what he had often done, allowed some external stimulus to influence him to write. That was not because he had need for a subject, for subjects were always there, but he needed first the impetus and secondly the forms in which to express it. The Maid of Orleans was canonized in 1920, and amid the celebrations of that event Sydney Cockerell of the Fitzwilliam Museum, Cambridge, told Shaw that Saint Joan would make a good subject for a play. This appealed to him for many reasons, not the least important of which was that he liked to have a woman as his central character.

The play is a record of what mankind does to its geniuses and saints. Man wants neither, and the hatred men have for each other flares up intensely against great souls. So this remarkable creature,

Joan, who lived as God told her, yet was a simple maid, who delivered her country from confusion, yet claimed nothing for herself, who was a leader of men, yet no more than a girl, is taken as an example of how the chief instruments of human society, the State and the Church, combine in natural hatred to crush goodness, purity and the voice of truth when men are inconvenienced or made uncomfortable by them. Shaw is at pains to present Joan, adored by millions, as a peasant girl, though not ignorant or entirely uncultured, made extraordinary because of her heavenly visions and her obedience to them. Though there were no angels speaking to her, he says, for the bells were bells, what came to her in the voices and visions was none the less true. Shaw is certain of that. The play is remarkable because in it Shaw states the case against heresy – the heretic being a believer who resists authority – himself a congenital heretic.

Certainly the appeal of Saint Joan to Shaw was that she was 'in fact one of the first Protestant martyrs', by which he meant that she chose to put her conscience against the judgment of the Church. His play turns upon the argument between herself and her accusers as to whether her conviction that her 'voices' were the voice of God was to be accepted or the Church's judgment that they were not. She could not accept the Church's decision that she was deceived, so she was condemned; thus, says Shaw, she was a martyr for conscience and God's truth. That statement of the facts is disputed by Catholic critics, who say that Joan was not in fact tried by the Church but by the civil power using the processes of the Inquisition for its own purposes, and that Joan did indeed make constant appeals to her judges that her case should be submitted to the Pope. In other words, the critics allege that Joan was a victim not of an intolerant Church and her own stubborn will but of self-seeking and corrupt men. It is true that by the first quarter of the fifteenth century the Inquisition, that terrible weapon of the Church, had degenerated into a political instrument. The Church itself was then divided as Europe itself was, and there was confusion everywhere; and the Church's argument in this matter that she did not make a mistake is not wholly convincing.

Although Shaw scrupulously based himself upon the documents, it may be admitted that his account of the trial is not literally correct, without, however, reducing the truth of his drama. What Shaw shows in his play certainly belongs to the truth: that one who believed she has a message from God was required by the powers that be to deny it, and refused. That the heroic girl could not in conscience do what was required of her and was bound to suffer the consequences, was then and is still good Catholic doctrine, for conscience must be obeyed whatever the consequences; for conscience is not mere private judgment, it is the voice of God. Though, of course, one may be mistaken about one's conscience, and what is commonly called conscience is only too often little but custom, or fear of the opinions of others, or sheer self-will.

The play relates how Joan the peasant girl demanded of the ruler of her country to be sent to Orleans in the company of soldiers, dressed like them, to raise the English seige, to crown the Dauphin in Rheims Cathedral and to expel the enemy from France. She is naturally regarded as mad, but the Captain to whom she appeals is so impressed by her that he does what she asks, and she is given a guard of men, armour and a horse and goes off to the Dauphin. He is likewise impressed, and gives her command of the forces at Orleans. At Orleans she is told that the army needs a west-wind to enable it successfully to attack the English, and Joan is certain that St Catherine will send that wind. She does, and the enemy is driven away. The English are much disturbed by the Maid's leadership, and, with the aid of the Bishop of

Beauvais, who is on the English side, it is agreed that an attempt be made to capture her and get her condemned by the Inquisition as a sorceress. The discussion between the English Earl, an English Priest and the Bishop provides Shaw with the opportunity for one of his most brilliant displays of dramatic dialectics on nationalism, protestantism, aristocracy and English characteristics. When Joan has crowned the Dauphin she wants to return home, but is warned that the English have put a price upon her head, and that if she is captured neither the King nor the Church will be able to save her. Nine months after, she is captured and sold to the English, brought to trial and condemned. In the course of the trial Shaw lets all those concerned speak for themselves, and his exposition of the Church's point of view is a remarkable piece of writing.

In the epilogue, twenty-five years after she was burned, Charles the Victorious, once known as the Dauphin, dreams about Joan and her accusers, and of the course of history up to her canonization. This part of the play has been greatly objected to, for it interferes with the play as sentimental melodrama or mere narrative, but it contains the core of the drama, without which the play would lack the greatness and purity it possesses. Shaw left no one in doubt that it was essential, for without the comic spirit the play as Shavian drama would be incomplete. In this work, which is essentially tragic, Shaw's strength as a dramatist is demonstrated, for the undertones of comedy are raised to their highest pitch within the framework of the tragic conception, so that the entire work modulates in unison. The epilogue is one of the most moving and beautiful scenes he ever wrote. 'Mortal eyes cannot distinguish the saint from the heretic', says the Bishop; and indeed that is true, for the essence of drama is not in what is seen by mortal eyes but in vision.

The play is a fine piece of dramatic craftsmanship; for the action as it moves forward gains substance, gathering together the characters in emergency of emotion to the culminating trial, in which fundamental beliefs are challenged and brought to judgment. Although the trial is the outstanding feature, one of the play's best scenes is after the coronation where in the name of friendship the voices of the world are raised against the girl's pure faith. Its weakness is in Joan's outburst at the end of the trial when she tears up her recantation, for more seems to be demanded here in sheer writing than the rhapsody provided by the playwright: it makes a problem for the player.

Characters

JOAN is a country girl of seventeen or eighteen, uncommon, because enlightened by her visions and transformed by faith; vigorous, simple, with wisdom that gives her courage confounding all whom she meets. An actress of exceptional personality is required; for utter simplicity has to be combined with luminous faith and strength of purpose. The girl is a wonder, not a pretty young lady. While the earlier scenes must not be overplayed the later cannot be. The play is her vision throughout, including the epilogue, which should be understood as her meditation.

ROBERT DE BAUDRICOURT, a military squire 'with no will of his own', a typical professional army captain.

BERTRAND DE POULENGEY, a lymphatic French gentleman-at-arms.

THE ARCHBISHOP OF RHEIMS, about fifty, a well-fed political ecclesiastic.

MONSEIGNEUR DE LA TRÉMOUILLE, the Lord Chamberlain, 'a monstrous arrogant wineskin of a man'.

A COURT PAGE, a young boy.

GILLES DE RAIS, a smart young man of twenty-five, with a small beard, dyed blue, a maker of fashions, and romantic.

CAPTAIN LA HIRE, a mere soldier.

THE DAUPHIN, twenty-six, no physique, ugly, rather hang-dog, yet he has to stand out as a man in the play, for he is as Joan sees him.

DUCHESSE DE LA TRÉMOUILLE is the grand lady.

DUNOIS, twenty-six, handsome, good-natured, capable.

DUNOIS'S PAGE is a young boy.

RICHARD DE BEAUCHAMP, the Earl of Warwick, is an imposing nobleman of forty-six.

CHAPLAIN DE STOGUMBER is a bull-necked English chaplain of fifty.

PETER CAUCHON, the Bishop of Beauvais, is a distinguished, dry, hard man of sixty.

WARWICK'S PAGE is a young boy.

THE INQUISITOR is a mild elderly monk with reserves of authority and firmness, of the Order of St Dominic, and has the great speech in the play.

D'ESTIVET, Canon of Bayeaux, is the Prosecutor, under forty, very bitter.

DE COURCELLES is Canon of Paris, a young priest of thirty.

MARTIN LANDVENU is a pleasant spoken monk.

EXECUTIONER.

A STEWARD in the first scene.

ENGLISH SOLDIER in the Epilogue.

GENTLEMAN, a cleric, in the Epilogue.

There are English and French SOLDIERS.

Production

The play is historical, and its production calls for heraldic and ecclesiastical study. It is chronicle-tragedy in subject matter with an exalted dramatic theme given serious comic treatment involving the central problem of conscience, but it is not pure tragedy. The maid should be treated not as a sentimental heroine, but as a heroic character, martyred for her faith; yet in her vision, which constitutes the dramatic action, the affair has the gravity of the spiritually comic. The play is wholly hers, and it is essential that it should be understood that every character is presented through her saintly but candid eyes. It should be treated in the classic manner, severely, the staging formal, not naturalistic. It is Shakespearean in style. The difficult scenes for Joan are the first and second acts, the last act virtually acts itself so long as Joan is sincere and wholehearted; but in the earlier acts she is in the energy of possession by her voices and the conviction of her mission, exalted by ecstasy. It is a mistake to emphasize the rusticity of the girl, for the country woman is transfigured by her faith into a creature of unearthly beauty. She sees herself so and is so seen by others. In the last act the earthly beauty has gone, she is broken by her sufferings, but the heavenly light remains and she glows with inner brilliance.

The settings are: a chamber in the castle of Vauconteurs; in the throne-room of the castle at Chinois, in Lorraine; on a bank of the river Loire; a tent in the English camp; the ambulatory in the Cathedral of Rheims; a hall in the castle at Rouen; the King's bedroom in a royal chateau. The period is from 1429 to 1456. The properties are described in the text. The Epilogue is a dream; in it Joan remains central, for each of the characters is present still through her eyes, although this is not apparent at the start. She should be radiant.

A Note on Productions

The play has always been popular. It was first produced by the Theatre Guild, New York, on 28 December 1923, and its first production in London was at the New Theatre, three months later, on 26 March 1924. Saint Joan was played by Winifred

Lenihan in New York and by Sybil Thorndike in London. It was translated into French and produced in Paris by the Pitöeffs on 17 April 1925, afterwards in London. Shaw thought the production 'excessively clever', and Ludmilla Pitöeff, 'too intelligent', with 'too much sex in the part'. Revivals have taken place in London in 1926, 1931, 1934, 1939, 1945, 1946, 1947, 1954 and 1960, the character of Saint Joan being played by Sybil Thorndike (four times), Mary Newcombe, Constance Cummings, Ann Casson, Celia Johnson, Siobhan McKenna, and Barbara Jefford. A film version, for which Graham Greene was responsible, was made by Otto Preminger and shown on 12 May 1956. With a young American Saint Joan, able to suggest none of the qualities of genius, and with a script that was perhaps intended to be faithful but upset the construction of the play, it deservedly failed in Paris where it was first exhibited, a failure repeated in London and New York.

(40)
The Apple Cart

A POLITICAL EXTRAVAGANZA
(1929)

Upsetting apple-carts had ever been one of Shaw's main occupations, and in this play he upset the apple-cart of democracy. Not that he had not upset that particular apple-cart before; but here he upsets the apple-cart of royalty too, exposing 'the unreality of both democracy and royalty as our idealists conceive them'. He says little more about democracy than he had already said, which is that men and women must be educated for it; but he does say more about royalty, attacking 'the figment called a constitutional monarch', arguing in favour of men trained to rule. In the play, his monarch gets the better of his democratically elected ministers; but Shaw points out that he is left in a worse plight than they, for he wins by making a desperate bid for dictatorship; and dictatorship, much as Shaw admires the efficiency of its action, is, as he says, no more than a personal victory, which must end in the dictator's death or collapse. The alternative is to construct 'a political system for rapid positive work instead of slow nugatory work, made to fit into the twentieth century instead of the sixteenth'.

What the new system should be depends on people trained both for government and citizenship: people controlled by their consciences. It requires the enlargement of units of local government and the establishment of regional federal legislatures; also the abolition of national frontiers. 'Had we not better teach our children to be better citizens than ourselves?' is his generalized conclusion.

The play is set in the palace of King Magnus of England in the last quarter of the twentieth century. Politics has become a matter to which none but a few people give attention: only seven per cent of the electorate had bothered to vote at the last general election. Poverty has been abolished and everyone is comfortably off, for England is supplying the chocolate creams and other luxury articles of world commerce, and the country is securely in the hands of big business, which has discovered the secret of making everyone comfortable: a prophecy of the Welfare State. Yet all is not well, for the Cabinet is in revolt, because the king has been making speeches that show marked personal independence. He has been criticizing the Government and expressing his own opinions. That his Labour Government will not have; so he is presented with an ultimatum to the effect that he must make no more speeches, have no more contact with the Press, and surrender the royal veto. He asks for a few hours in which to consider the matter. After an exhausting meeting with men who are in every respect his inferiors, he spends the afternoon with his mistress, which enables the intimate aspects of royalty to be displayed, and much more; for the theme of the play, the conflict between human intelligence and natural instinct, is continued in other terms. Afterwards he meets the Cabinet again. Before this meeting, he receives the American Ambassador, who brings the momentous news that the United States has decided to cancel the Declaration of Independence and to re-join the British Empire. The members of the Cabinet will not, however, consider that red-herring: they want to know what the King intends to do about their ultimatum. His answer is that he intends to abdicate. Startled, they accept the decision. Then he tells them that he proposes to enter politics as a private gentleman and stand for the Royal Borough of Windsor at the forthcoming General Election. That is the upsetting of the apple-cart. They cannot permit him to become the virtual dictator of Britain by the votes of the people, so they withdraw the ultimatum and things remain as they are. As for the offer from America, it is not even considered!

The play consists of two long discussions in which the characters sit in a semi-circle, the debate suspended for the sake of the amatory episode, which separates the two acts, a piece of brilliant dramatic relief. With what wickedness Shaw arranges the stage to confound his critics, who endlessly complain that his plays are nothing but talk! Here he makes no pretence of physical action, but the dialogue is alive with movement, and the audience is charmed into listening, and, to prevent anyone from getting tired, the rough-and-tumble interval shakes everyone up. Though a topical piece, its relevance will remain, for it raises questions of political aims and behaviour that continue to be alive.

Characters

KING MAGNUS is tall, smart, self-possessed, with the easiest possible manner, and a man of thought. He is the apple-cart-upsetter, and the play is his, every character appearing from his point of view, including himself.

SEMPRONIUS, a 'smart and still presentably young' Royal secretary.

PAMPHILIUS, a smart, middle-aged secretary.

BOANERGES, President of the Board of Trade, a trade union official, fifty, heavily built and self-assertive, a strong man in his own eyes, not smart.

THE PRINCESS ROYAL, a pretty and impetuous young lady.

PROTEUS, the Prime Minister, is a distinguished-looking, well-mannered man, expert at sitting on fences, and keeps his team together by threatening to resign.

PLINY, Chancellor of the Exchequer, 'good-humoured and con-ciliatory'.

NICOBAR, Foreign Secretary, 'snaky and censorious'.

CRASSUS, Colonial Secretary, elderly and anxious.

BALBUS, Home Secretary, 'rude and thoughtless'.

AMANDA, Postmistress General, merry and high spirited.

LYSISTRATA, Powermistress General, a grave lady, with the manners of a schoolmistress.

ORINTHIA, the King's mistress, a romantically tall, strong beauty.

THE QUEEN is queenly, motherly, practical, a very agreeable woman as her husband sees her.

MR VANHATTAN, an effusive, all too typical, American Ambassador.

Production

The piece is high comedy and should be played as such throughout; thus it depends upon accomplished speaking, realization of the flavour of words, and smooth and skilful acting; in fact, acting virtuosity, for it is a mistake to look upon it as easy because the characters merely sit and talk. The dialogue is itself active, and a static impression is made only when it is delivered without sufficient attention to its movement. Note the names of the characters, which place the play outside natural life. The members of the Cabinet must be strongly differentiated, and characterisation can be studied from the composition of the various Labour Governments, though caricature is not intended. The middle episode must be done for all it is worth, and is meant to strike a note of relaxation and intimacy markedly different from the sustained artificiality of the rest of the play. The settings are: an office in the royal palace; Orinthia's boudoir; the terrace of the palace. In the properties and dressing of the piece the supposed date, which is towards the end of the century, should be taken into account; the King and his ministers are in uniform.

A Note on Productions

First performed in Warsaw, in Polish, on 14 June 1929, and first played in England at the Malvern Festival on 19 August 1929. The Malvern production was afterwards taken to the Queen's Theatre, London, on 17 September 1929 where it had a run of 258 performances. The King was played in Malvern and London by Cedric Hardwicke, and Orinthia by Edith Evans. The Theatre Guild produced it in New York at the Martin Beck Theatre on 24 February 1930. It was revived in London in 1935, 1936, 1949 and 1953, when the King was played by Esme Percy, Jack Hawkins, Oliver Burt and Noel Coward, and Orinthia by Oriel Ross, Emma Trechman, Joan Geary and Margaret Leighton.

(41)
Too True to be Good

A POLITICAL EXTRAVAGANZA
(1931)

Having written about the effect of the capitalist system upon the poor, Shaw writes a play about its effect upon the rich. Poverty is a sin, according to *Major Barbara*; riches are no less sinful, according to this play. Because many people were seriously annoyed by it, the play aroused perhaps more animosity against its author than any other of his works; for he had the audacity, it seemed, to contradict himself. The critics called it a pessimistic play, because they saw Shaw giving up his cause as reformer as hopeless. Of course, he did nothing of the kind: his confidence was never exhausted, any more than was his dramatist's skill.

The preface written in 1933 is unusually short; it contains parts of a broadcast address given in 1929 and of some articles Shaw had written on democracy.

The play is a story of three reckless young people who come into possession of money and have a good time, only to find themselves miserable. Its mechanism is that of a dream, reminding one of *Heartbreak House*. A girl is in bed with a high temperature, suffering from measles. She is one of the idle rich, has always been molly-coddled by her mother, and always been considered delicate. In her dream, or delirium, she sees the microbe which is supposed to have made her ill, though in Shavian truth it is she who has made the microbe ill. The night nurse turns out to be a crook, and admits into the bedroom a man who proceeds to steal the girl's jewellery. The girl finds herself jumping out of bed and laying out the thief. She is not only well but full of health, and quickly agrees to join the thieves – the burglar convincing her that he is a clergyman – in stealing the jewels and escaping from home.

In the second act the dream fantasy continues. The girl crook has turned herself into a countess, the rich girl into a native servant, and the burglar into the countess's half step-brother. They are in the company of a military detachment sent into the mountains of Northern India to rescue a girl who is supposed to have been abducted by brigands who are demanding a heavy ransom. The abduction is all part of the fraud, for there are no brigands and the ransom is demanded by the burglar and his accomplices. In the third act the girl's mother arrives, does not recognize her daughter and engages her as a companion. The play ends with a long sermon by the pretended clergyman.

Into this fantastic framework Shaw introduces what he has to say about health, riches, idleness, the army, and the meaning of life. He does this through a burglar, who is a professional preacher; through a private soldier who is more efficient than his colonel; through a sergeant who is a student of the Bible and Bunyan; and through the burglar's father who is a disillusioned secularist; in fact through each of the characters. 'I have found myself out thoroughly in my dream', says the girl. She has found out that she wants 'something sensible to do'. She has everything but a job of work. 'I am free; I am healthy; happy; and I am utterly miserable. . . . I am a lost dog; a tramp, a vagabond. I've got nothing to do.' The sergeant sees the world as the City of Destruction. The Elder presents 'the supreme tragedy of the atheist who has lost his faith'. The clergyman-burglar declares 'We have outgrown our religion; outgrown our political system, outgrown our own strength of mind and character'; he must have affirmations to preach: 'The preacher must preach the way of life. Oh, if I could only find it.'

Those who saw in the play a discouraged Shaw have not

observed that the meaning of the play is that every man can discover the way of life for himself by finding his work.

Characters

THE PATIENT is a young, handsome, essentially healthy girl, typical of the young people of the time. She is the central character, for the play is her dream and the characters her dream creation.

THE MONSTER is a microbe, infected by the patient, and but for the consequent depression should, one can suppose, be very lively.

THE DOCTOR is young and represents the professional man who is merely professional.

THE MOTHER is elderly, the suburban middle-class woman, prosperous, empty-headed, a young girl's vision of her parent.

THE NURSE is young and attractive, a chambermaid who has got lifted up in the world.

THE BURGLAR is in the early thirties, good looking, lively, and an accomplished talker, having been a clergyman. Although he is not the leading character, to the extent that the theatricality of the play depends on any one actor, it depends on him.

COLONEL TALLBOYS, VC, DSO, is a typical military man, tall, handsome, and, of course, stupid.

PRIVATE MEEK is modelled on T. E. Laurence, a small, insignificant, but active and resourceful man, though not particularly likeable.

SERGEANT FIELDING is a well-built handsome man getting on for forty, a student of Bunyan and the Bible. The part gives solidity as well as variety to the comic element.

THE ELDER is tall and gaunt, hard, inflexible, and a talker.

Production

The weakness of the play dramatically is that none of the ten characters is outstanding; all are mouthpieces or types rather than individuals. Thus the play remains talk, the action slight, mostly knock-about. This means that the actors are required to speak rhetorical dialogue and to give polish to their speech: there are no exceptions. It is essential to bear in mind that the play is a dream; Shaw calls it an extravaganza. The girl says 'My dream has become a nightmare'. The entire play must, therefore, be fantastically treated, for everything is absurd, nothing is rational. The girl's bedroom should appear to be an ordinary room at the start, but after the mother goes out it should become part of the dream world. The Indian scenes are to be made as fantastic as possible: nothing natural appears or takes place.

A Note on Productions

The play was first produced by the Theatre Guild at the National Theatre, Boston, Mass, on 29 February 1932, and in the following April by the same organization at the Guild Theatre, New York. It was produced in Warsaw in Polish on 4 June. Barry Jackson presented it at the Malvern Festival on 6 August the same year, and by the same company at the New Theatre on 13 September. It ran in London for forty-seven performances. It was revived in London in 1944 and 1945. So far as I am aware, the dream element has never been perceived, despite Shaw's insistence upon it.

(42)
Village Wooing

A COMEDIETTINA FOR TWO VOICES
(1933)

Written by the author when on a world tour, as was the previous play and the one after it, this is one of the few unprefaced plays.

It is hardly a play at all, being a duologue, without action, in the form of three conversations. But the piece stages well, for Shaw cannot help writing dramatic dialogue, and the theme is the ever pleasing one of the relations between a man and a woman, and the pursuit of one by the other.

The first conversation is on the deck of a pleasure ship and is between a pale looking man under forty and a young woman. The young woman forces her conversation on the reluctant man, who desires to be left alone to get on with his work of writing. She tells him about herself. She is an assistant in a village shop and has won first prize in a newspaper competition. She gets out of the man that he is a widower, but he does not look at her. The second conversation is in a village shop on the Wiltshire Downs six months later. The young woman is at work, and the man comes in for some chocolate and other eatables, being on a hike. He doesn't recognize the girl, but she recognizes him. She talks him into agreeing to buy the shop and engaging her as his assistant. The third conversation is in the village shop three months later, and the end of it is that he agrees to marry her.

Characters

A is under forty, a literary man.

z is a presentable and pushing young woman.

There is a STEWARD on the ship.

Production

There are two settings, the deck of a ship and the interior of the village shop at Ayot St Lawrence. The play is comedy, though the situation is farce; it needs to be spoken with great spirit, requiring two actors with personality. It makes only half a programme.

A Note on Productions

It was first presented by the Dallas (Texas) Little Theatre Company on 16 April 1934, when *The Man of Destiny* was also performed. This was at the time when the Shaws visited America, though he was not at the performance. It was first played in England by the Repertory Players, produced by Christopher Fry, at Tunbridge Wells on 1 May 1934, when a short play by Christopher Fry was also done. It was first played in London at the Little Theatre on 19 June 1934 with John Galsworthy's *The Little Man* (not a very good programme), and has been successfully revived a number of times, usually with another Shaw play.

(43)
On the Rocks

A POLITICAL COMEDY
(1933)

There is significance in the fact that Shaw sees comedy in the sight of Western civilization driven on the rocks. Neither he nor any other dramatist has been able to present that situation as a tragic one. In this play the people of England are threatening to revolt, but there is no one to lead them, and no one to answer their demands, except the armed forces. There is nothing tragic in this, as Shaw sees it, because the revolt can be put down and the nation will remain upon the rocks. This is, indeed a comic situation, matter for laughter. Tragedy arises when in intense suffering and in loss men prove themselves greater than events.

There is no falling off in mental power or technical skill in this play, written in his seventy-seventh year, though Shaw is careless about the plot; but the characters are drawn with as sure a hand as ever, and the dialogue sparkles as in the plays of his prime.

The scene of the play is the Prime Minister's room in Downing Street. Sir Arthur Chavender, head of the National Government, is preparing a speech on the 'family' to be delivered that afternoon at Church House. He is interrupted by Sir Broadfoot Basham, the Chief Commissioner of Police, for whom the Prime Minister has sent to ask if he cannot stop the street-corner meetings that are going on everywhere among the unemployed. Sir Arthur would like the police to prohibit them; Basham looks upon them as necessary safety valves for public feeling. When Basham goes, Sir Arthur is interrupted by his wife who wants him to see a lady doctor, for she is convinced that he is over-working, and she induces him to consent. Then he receives a deputation from the Isle of Cats, who want something done about unemployment. Sir Arthur assures them that 'What mortal man can do, this Government has done', and when the deputation has withdrawn one of them, Mr Hipney, the Labour leader, has a heart to heart talk with him, in which the humbug of politics is the theme.

Left alone the Prime Minister discovers that a woman dressed in grey is in the room. She is the lady doctor, who diagnoses his trouble as 'that very common English complaint, an underworked brain'. He thinks she is mad, but he is no match for her in argument, and the result is that he agrees to go to her sanatorium, taking with him there the complete works of Karl Marx.

In the second act, four months later, the Prime Minister has returned from his visit to the sanatorium, and has just made a speech at the Guildhall, which has horrified the country. Sir Dexter Rightside, leader of the Conservative Party and Foreign Secretary in the National Government, calls upon him next morning before he is out of bed to know what he means by the announcement of a programme of nationalization for next session.

Rightside and Basham want to know if he has gone mad. Sir Arthur tells Basham that he has promised to restore the cuts in the pay of the police, which immediately wins Basham over. Sir Bemrose Hotspot, head of the Admiralty, arrives to congratulate the Prime Minister – 'What the country wants straight orders, discipline, character, pluck, a big navy', and so on. Then comes Mr Glenmorison, President of the Board of Trade, who is also very pleased at the proposals to abolish rates and open municipal banks, for they will make his seat safe for ever. While they are talking a Cingalese plutocrat enters, Sir Jafna Pandranath, who declares that he is with Sir Arthur to the last drop of his oriental blood, for he sees larger profits in nationalized land, compulsory labour, strikes made criminal and the rest of the programme. The Duke of Domesday comes to thank Sir Arthur for promising that the State will buy his land. Finally the Labour deputation from the Isle of Cats gets into the room to tell the Prime Minister that Labour will have none of his programme.

Then Sir Arthur declares that he proposes to enforce his proposals upon Parliament, confident that the country will accept them – 'They are sick of me and sick of you and sick of the whole lot of us. They want something done,' he says. The result is that his colleagues desert him; only old Hipney returns to say that he will follow anyone who will give him a good lead, 'and to blazes with your elections and your Constitution and your Democracy and all the rest of it'. However, Sir Arthur gives up, he sees what has to be done, but 'I don't feel that I am the man to do it'. He is a talker, not a man of action: someone else must do it. And at the end the unemployed break into Downing Street singing 'England Arise!' 'Suppose England really did arise!' is the Prime Minister's reflection as the curtain falls.

A love interest is intended to please the groundlings: the

Prime Minister's son gets engaged to the Marxist girl member of the Isle of Cats deputation and his daughter engages herself to the plutocratic member of the same deputation. Disillusionment is the note of the play with a powerful undercurrent of distorted actuality, for the dream element persists throughout; all the same and discursive as it is, this is an inspiring work, for it leaves a sense of direction, not ultimate defeat, despite the Prime Minister's weakness.

Characters

SIR ARTHUR CHAVENDER, the Prime Minister, is fifty but looks younger, buoyant, genial, and has an aristocratic air: it is his play.

HILDA HANWAYS, his secretary, is reasonably young, attractive, and capable.

SIR BROADFOOT BASHAM is efficient in the military sense, a gentleman, with fairly pleasant manners.

MISS FLAVIA CHAVENDER, the Premier's daughter, is nineteen and of the period.

LADY CHAVENDER is domestic, a nice woman, good looking, but bored with other people.

DAVID CHAVENDER is eighteen, slight, refined, less effective than his sister.

THE MAYOR OF THE ISLE OF CATS is thick and elderly.

ALOYSIA BROLLIKINS, member of the deputation from the Borough Council, is a smart, unladylike, confident woman of the people.

VISCOUNT BARKING, another of the deputation, is a loud-voiced revolutionary product of Oxford University.

ALDERMAN BLEE, a thin, small, middle-class young man.

MR HIPNEY is a sunny, comfortable old chap.

THE LADY DOCTOR, firm, competent, entirely self-possessed.

SIR DEXTER RIGHTSIDE, Foreign Secretary, elderly and explosive.

SIR BEMROSE HOTSPOT, First Lord of the Admiralty, a half-witted admiral, breezy and contented.

MR GLENMORISON, President of the Board of Trade, is a Scot, and not beyond middle age.

SIR JAFNA PANDRANATH, an elderly Cingalese plutocrat, small and elegant.

THE DUKE OF DOMESDAY, an elderly, delicately built, aristocrat of seventy.

Production

The play is high comedy with the strong elements of farce intended to be played for what they are worth, and some fantasy. It needs firm production, and exact timing, for nothing must be allowed to drag. The setting is its major difficulty, the Cabinet Room in No. 10 Downing Street; its chief feature the large table filling the centre of the room so that movement can take place only on the outskirts of the table, which tends to slow down the action and to enforce mere naturalistic playing; both tendencies must, however, be resisted. The play is in two acts. Its weakness is the weakness of the leading character, for the Prime Minister is essentially a weak man.

A Note on Productions

The first and only production in London was at the Winter Garden Theatre on 25 November 1933. In New York it was performed at Daly's Theatre on 15 June 1938. Its neglect on the stage is not deserved, despite its topical setting, for its theme is perennial.

(44)
The Simpleton of the Unexpected Isles

A VISION OF JUDGMENT
(1934)

The comparatively short preface is on 'Days of Judgment', in which the author explains that the fable of the play is that 'every day is a day of judgment; and its recognition as such is not the end of all things but the beginning of a real civilization'. The inquiry in such days of judgment is 'whether you are a social asset or a social nuisance'. It is the same inquiry, though expressed differently, as that made by Ibsen's Button Moulder in *Peer Gynt*, as Shaw points out.

The Prologue, in three scenes, opens in the emigration office at a tropical port in the British Empire into which comes a young woman who makes the emigration officer show her round; when they go out, the clerk, who had dreams of himself as an Empire builder, blows out his brains. After this the play proceeds as vision. The second scene discloses the young woman and the emigration officer on the cliffs overlooking the sea; the man tells the girl that he wants to do himself in, and is on the point of throwing himself over the cliff when a native priest appears who tells him that the cliff is holy and that he must not die there. When the young man tries to jump he cannot; the priest, however, helps him by a kick behind, explaining to the wondering girl that there are nets below and a palisade to keep out the sharks. The third scene shows an alcove on the cliff, half way down, where the young woman and the priest are feasting with a young priestess. The emigration officer appears, cured of his thoughts of death; and when left alone with the young woman throws her over the cliff.

Act one is in a garden on the Unexpected Isles. There are four shrines, two containing girl-goddesses, two with youthful gods. A young English clergyman appears and tells the Priest in the prologue, now twenty years older, that he has been chaplain in a pirate ship and has just escaped; left alone in the garden, and thinking the girl goddesses to be images, the young clergyman, whose name is Iddy, kisses one of them, with results that astonish his simple soul. The Governor of the Isles, with his wife, and the Emigration officer, now political secretary to the Isles, and his wife, who was the young woman in the prologue, then appear. They explain that the four divinities are the children of a group marriage of six parents, and are perfect in every way except that they do not possess moral consciences. A union is proposed between the clergyman and the two goddesses, which may make good the latter's deficiencies; the proposal, naturally, overwhelms Iddy, and, though he confesses that he is under some sort of enchantment, he rebels against matrimonial behaviour that is 'poison' to an Englishman; but left alone with the two goddesses his rebellion vanishes, for they quickly melt his heart.

The Second Act opens some years later. The garden is unchanged; but the harbour is crowded with British cruisers. It seems that the clergyman's behaviour has convulsed the Empire, which will not tolerate such conduct, though, in fact, he has proved himself to be an impotent simpleton. To gain time for him and the islanders, the naval commander is told there is an outbreak of smallpox in the port, and the ships vanish.

When the ships have gone, in a second scene, we find Iddy and his two loves discussing the situation. Iddy says that too much love is making him wonder if they may not soon come to hate each other, and the goddesses admit that they hate Iddy already, which brightens him up, for he can go on loving them if they won't love him in return.

The news arrives that England has left the British Empire, so the Governor contemplates creating the Isles an independent republic, when an angel appears to announce the Day of Judgment. 'The lives which have no use, no meaning, no purpose, will fade out. You will have to justify your existence or perish', he says. The Day of Judgment, declares the angel, is not the end of the world but the end of its childhood. The angel flies away; the divinities fade out, representing as they do 'the artistic, romantic and military ideals of our cultured suburbs', which have no real existence; the others, except the native Priest and the Priestess, go away, wondering if they may fade out too. Prola, the Priestess, summing up the play, says, 'We are not here to fulfil prophecies and to fit ourselves into jigsaw puzzles, but to wrestle with life as it comes. . . . I tell you this is a world of miracles . . . in the Unexpected Isles there is no security; and the future is to those who prefer surprise and wonder to security.' So the play ends with the two awaiting 'the life to come'.

The theme is that nothing matters but life as it is, and making the most of it. It leads to the conclusion that 'all plans fail', for Pra and Prola find their eugenic aims to fail. There must be an end of ease, of comfort, and of security, and we must look upon ourselves as living on an Unexpected Isle in which anything may happen, where we are to be prepared for everything, and where all things are possible because we can make them so.

The play is rich in dramatic content, but not consistent in its dramatic structure, for the protagonist does not fulfil his function, and the tension is either merely amusing and satirical or talked about and abstract, rather than immediate and concrete. It is entertaining, and, in a high degree, moving, but on the whole unsatisfying. In short, it is a theme for a poetic drama, which Shaw does not attempt.

Characters

AN ENGLISH EMIGRATION OFFICER, an unsatisfactory young
man of unhealthy habits, who becomes Hugo Hyering, CB. He
is, technically, the leading character, but his function is hardly
fulfilled.

WILKS, his clerk, an older and equally unsatisfactory man.

A YOUNG WOMAN, who becomes Mrs Hyering, handsome and
domineering.

THE STATION MASTER, another old man.

JO, whose voice only is heard.

PRA, a priest, handsome well dressed and well spoken.

PROLA, a priestess, young and beautiful.

LADY FARWATERS, a bland and attractive matron.

SIR CHARLES FARWATERS, young middle age, pleasant and
affable.

IDDY HAMMINGTAP, a baby-complexioned clergyman: the
'Simpleton'.

JANGA, an idealized youth.

KANCHIN, another idealized youth.

MAYA, a beautiful girl.

VASHTI, another beautiful girl.

THE ANGEL, a male angel.

Production

The play is satirical comedy, calling for well-studied but quick
playing, in a wholly fantastic setting. The Prologue should be
played as the entrance into memory of the future as well as the
past. There are four settings, three in the Prologue and one for
the play itself. Settings and playing should be a whole; the play
is essentially in the realm of the non-realistic: the world of
imagination.

A Note on Productions

The first production was by the Theatre Guild in New York on 18 February 1935. The same year Barry Jackson presented it at the Malvern Festival on 29 July. It has not been publicly performed in London, though performances were given at the Arts Theatre Club in March 1945.

(45)
The Six of Calais

A MEDIEVAL WAR STORY
(1933)

A trifle, in one act, in which Shaw repeats what he had often done before. He claims Jean Froissart and August Rodin as his collaborators, but declares that Froissart got the story all wrong and did not understand women, while Rodin's manner of creation was that of a sculptor, so that 'Nothing remained for me to do but to correct Froissart's follies and translate Rodin into words.'

On the 4 August 1346, Edward III of England, in his camp before the walls of Calais, has demanded that the six leading burghers should be surrendered to him, clad in their shirts, with ropes around their necks. The wretched men appear before him. One of them, Piers de Rosty (nicknamed Hardmouth), is insolent, and defies the King, who has him gagged and bound. The King orders the other five away to be hanged; but before they go his wife Queen Philippa comes out of her tent and assumes that the starving men are to be fed and honoured. When she hears their fate, she begs for their lives, and when the King is obstinate she weeps copious tears and gives him no peace until he consents. The King squirms and yells with anger at her persistent nagging, but has to let her have her way. Even a King, it seems, because he is

a man, can be made into a ninny by a woman. This King plucks
at his beard, looks fierce, swears, stamps his feet; but gives in.

The sixth burgher when he is untied and ungagged is by no
means grateful. He jeers at the King for being wife-ridden, and
annoys the Queen so much that she demands that he should be
hanged forthwith. Then the King turns the tables on his spouse,
and with the identical arguments she had used, declares that the
man must go free with the others. The play is no more than a piece
of fun. Shaw topples the King and Queen off their thrones,
exhibiting them as any ordinary foolish man and wife.

Characters

KING EDWARD III was thirty-five at the time of the play and the
author does not permit him any kingliness.

QUEEN PHILIPPA was thirty-six, and expecting to be a mother;
she is always queenly, when she is not bullying her husband.

THE BLACK PRINCE is a bright soldierly boy of seventeen.

JOHN OF GAUNT.

A COURT LADY.

PIERS DE ROSTY is a harsh, quick-tempered, arrogant tradesman
who has no intention of letting the despised English King get
the better of him, though he may hang him.

There are FIVE OTHER CONDEMNED MEN, but they have
little to do.

Production

The play is anti-romantic farce. It needs to be done straight-
forwardly and with spirit. There should be plenty of colour, and
heraldry must have abundant attention. The piece lends itself to
outdoor production, and was first performed at the Open Air
Theatre in Regent's Park.

There are the tents of the King and the Queen, and, if there is space for them, other tents too. Bright morning light. The costumes are of the mid-fourteenth century. The six Burghers should be modelled on Rodin's group at Calais.

The properties are those that go with the costumes and the period. There is nothing of a special character. There must be a double throne for the King and Queen.

A Note on Productions

It was given an open air production at Regent's Park on 17 July 1934, when *Androcles and the Lion* was also performed. It was revived at the Arts Theatre Club on 17 June 1951.

(46)
The Millionairess

A COMEDY IN FOUR ACTS
(1935–6)

The author says that this play 'does not pretend to be anything more than a comedy of humorous and curious contemporary characters'. In it he returns to the theme of the inequality created by poverty on the one hand and riches on the other, which always troubled him, and asks what it is that enables an individual to rise from poverty to riches and from obscurity to fame. Some people have a genius for being bosses, but in the preface he does not discuss what that mysterious personal force is. In the play he gives an answer: the ability to take chances, to venture into the unknown.

The preface is occupied with the discussion of the question: what are we to do with bosses, with those people of commanding ability in money making, in politics, in the church, and in everything else, the talented individuals? They cannot be 'liquidated' because without them civilization would go to pieces, but we must be delivered from their tyranny. Even the abolition of private property will not do it, for even then we shall be at the mercy of 'the decider, the dominator, the organizer, the tactician and the mesmerizer. . . .' The remedy, says Shaw, lies in the multiplication of talented persons 'to what may be called their natural majority limit, which will destroy their present scarcity value. But we must also eliminate the mass of ignorance, weakness and timidity which force them to treat fools according to their folly.' In other words, men and women in general must be educated sufficiently to distinguish merit when it exists and be made sufficiently intelligent and powerful to prevent their rulers from ruling, when those rulers cease to be 'efficient and successful'. He adds 'only a creed of Creative Evolution can set the souls of the people free'.

The play is in four acts. It opens in a solicitor's office in Lincoln's Inn Fields, and starts without any preliminaries with the Millionairess, Epifania Ognisanti di Parerga, interviewing the solicitor on the subject of making her will. This enables her to tell her story about her husband, Alastair Fitzfassenden, and her dead father, and that she intends to commit suicide. While they are talking, the husband, who happens to be the solicitor's friend, calls with a girl – the girl for whom he has deserted his wife. At the extended interview the conditions of the Millionairess's marriage with this man, a world-famous boxer and tennis player, are gone into more fully. She had married him because of his magnificent physical ability; but, alas, his physical ability lay only in his fists, and he had left her because he found that she was not his soul mate. It then appears that the Millionairess has a gentleman friend with whom she discusses subjects that are beyond her husband's mental grasp. After much discussion, the gentleman friend also arrives, and the orgy of disjointed domesticity rises to its height to fall away only that the act can end. 'I think I shall wait and see', says the solicitor, when left alone, which is all the audience can do.

The second act is at a riverside inn to which the Millionairess and her friend have come; they have a row, and the Millionairess, who is also a trained boxer, throws the man out of the room. There comes in a middle-aged Egyptian doctor with whom she develops a romance; he has to confess that he made a vow to his mother on her deathbed that if any woman wanted to marry him, and he felt tempted, he must hand her two hundred piastres (about thirty-five shillings), and tell her that she must go out in the world with nothing but that and the clothes she stood up in and earn her living for six months, or he would never speak to her again. The Millionairess, it seems, had also made a solemn promise to her father on his deathbed that she would only marry a man who, with no more than a hundred and fifty pounds, could in six months increase it to fifty thousand. They make the bargain and the act ends.

Act three is in a sweating den in the East End of London to which the Millionairess comes to earn her living; she soon gets control of the business and reorganizes it.

In the last act we are back at the riverside inn, now transformed into a smart hotel, where the Millionairess's husband and his girl are spending a week-end. It seems that the Millionairess had got a job at the inn as a scullery maid, and, before the proprietor knew where he was, she had secured control of it, rebuilt it, and put the late owner's son in charge as manager. Then arrives the solicitor, and the Millionairess's friend, still suffering from the injuries received in the lovers' quarrel. The Millionairess herself turns up and the domestic discussion is resumed, enabling a great variety of subjects, from divorce law to international politics, to be talked about. Then the Egyptian doctor arrives: he had given his £150 to the widow of a man with whom he worked some years ago who had made an important scientific discovery owned by the Imperial Metallurgical Trust. The Millionairess finds this to have fulfilled her father's conditions, and as she herself had fulfilled the conditions of the Doctor's vow, the solicitor is given his instructions.

Characters

EPIFANIA OGNISANTI DI PARERGA, the Millionairess, is a striking looking young woman, athletically built, exuberant, who carries the play on her shoulders; the playing demands great versatility.

JULIUS SAGAMORE is a smart young solicitor.

ALASTAIR FITZFASSENDEN, the Millionairess's husband, is a splendid athlete 'with most of his brains in his muscles'.

PATRICIA SMITH is a pleasant, quiet, self-possessed little woman.

ADRIAN BLENDERBAND is middle-aged, an imposing looking man, rather elegant.

THE DOCTOR is a serious, cultivated, middle-aged Egyptian, who speaks English well.

THE MAN is the owner of a sweatshop in the East End of London, old, thin, 'rat like'.

HIS WIFE is old, thin and worn out.

THE HOTEL MANAGER is young and smart.

Production

The leading actress is required to be a woman of marked personality, and technical accomplishment. All the other characters have to play up to her. The fable is fantastic, but the discussions are high spirited and greatly entertaining. Unless very well cast and directed the play will be found inconclusive and too loose in construction to be effective. It requires extremely smart and clear-cut playing, and must be produced in the style proper to its rhetorical writing, when its highly polished theatrical qualities will appear. In fact it requires actors of genius and an audience of connoisseurs.

A Note on Productions

The play was to be produced in the Malvern Festival in 1935, but was first produced (in German) at the Akademie Theater, Vienna, on 4 January 1936; first played in English at the King's Theatre, Melbourne, Australia, the following 7 March; and first played in England at Bexhill-on-Sea on 17 November the same year. It was intended for London production (with Edith Evans) in September 1940, abandoned on account of the blitz (the actress had played it on tour), and first appeared in London at the Q Theatre (with Sarah Tapping) on 29 May 1944, and at the New Theatre, London (with Katherine Hepburn) on 27 June 1952. The last mentioned production had ninety-eighty performances and was a great success; it was transferred to New York by the Theatre Guild, opening at the Shubert Theatre on 17 October. The play had previously been performed in America at the Country Playhouse, Westport, Conn., on 15 August 1938.

A film made by 20th Century Fox in 1960 based on an adaption by one hand and a script by another, which had the same title as the play, also some of the characters, a resemblance to some of the episodes, and a selection of the original lines, had no other relation to the play.

(47)
Cymbeline Re-finished

A VARIATION ON SHAKESPEARE'S ENDING
(1937)

This is a revision of the fifth Act of Shakespeare's play, clearing up what are considered to be confusions, and making 'a new ending for its own sake'. Eighty-nine lines of Shakespeare's play are retained, the remainder is Shavian blank verse. Shaw does not press his version upon those who have 'the courage and good sense to present the original word-for-word as Shakespeare left it, and the means to do justice to the masque'. With those words of his this piece can, in fact, be left. In a note presented to the audience when it was performed at the Embassy Theatre, Swiss Cottage, on 16 November 1937, Shaw admitted that 'I am a little ashamed'.

(48)
Geneva

ANOTHER POLITICAL EXTRAVAGANZA
(1938)

Originally called 'A fancied page of history', this play contains an excellent idea: to bring dictators to the bar of human justice to answer charges against them at the instance of the International Committee for Intellectual Co-operation; but the idea is not seriously carried out. Highly amusing, with many penetrating remarks, and admirable situations in the author's most effective manner, the play hardly leaves the level of fooling on which it starts, nothing is developed, not even the argument, and the audience is left at the end where it was at the beginning. One of the characters says in the middle of the long second act, 'We have been here less than an hour'. To which the answer is made, 'It seems to me twenty years'. Despite that self-admission, so deftly does Shaw write, so skilfully theatrical is his fooling, that the play is less boring on the stage than it may be to read, which is testimony in its favour.

There is a subtle secondary idea, more interesting than the

main one: the dictators actually appear before the Court, though there was no compulsion upon them to do so, and the Court itself did not expect them to come. The last words spoken by the Judge are, 'Not a farce, my friend. They came, these fellows. They blustered: they defied us. But they came. They came.' It is not unusual for Shaw to introduce an idea into his plays that he does not develop: it may be suspected that these ideas are probably what interested him more than the leading idea, and it is possible that it was for their sake that the play was written, though he lets the idea remain in embryo.

It should be remembered that the play is intended for an English audience, for its piquancy is in its whole-hearted onslaught upon national complacency.

The play consists of two short and two long acts. Its action starts at Geneva at the time of its writing. The Committee for Intellectual Co-operation has an office in charge of a girl secretary who constitutes the whole of its staff. She has nothing but quite useless work to do. To this office a Jew finds his way to lay a complaint of oppression against a ruler, and demands that the Committee should apply to the permanent court of International Justice at The Hague for a warrant. The girl, who doesn't understand anything about the matter, thinks it a good idea to write to the International Court; for it is the first piece of definite work she ever had to do. He is followed by a man who has a complaint against the Prime Minister of a Business Government, by a widow who wants a warrant for the murder of her husband against the President of the Earthly Paradise, by an Anglican Bishop who complains about Communism in his diocese, by a Russian Commissar who complains about the activities in Russia of the Society for the Propagation of the Bible in Foreign Parts, and by an American journalist who just looks in. The brilliant dialogue is on the level of farce.

In the second act, which takes place in the office of the secretary of the League of Nations, the secretary of the Committee has been sent for to tell her that her action in making demands to the International Court has resulted in extraordinary international complications. The British Foreign Secretary has been sent for, and the Senior Judge of the International Court also comes. This provides an opportunity for a discussion upon the functions of the International Court and of the League of Nations.

The third act was added after the war had started and was not part of the original English productions. It shows a restaurant overlooking the Lake of Geneva with the secretary who receives from the journalist the news of the abolition of Intellectual Co-operation by the International Court, also that the committee's secretary has been made a Dame of the British Empire and has netted £4,000 in suits for libel. Then appear the various other characters and there is talk about none of them having any idea of the sort of world they are living in: real human nature is in continual conflict with what ignorant human nature is supposed to be. The Judge says that the trial of the dictators has been fixed at The Hague. 'They will come', he declares. 'Where the spot light is, there will the despots be gathered.'

The fourth act is the Courtroom at The Hague. The Jew, the two secretaries, the betrothed of the girl secretary (for the sake of comic relief), the English Foreign Secretary, the man who complains against his government, the widow, and the Russian Commissar are there with the Judge. Then turn up Signor Bombardone (Mussolini), Mr Battler (Hitler) and General Flanco de Fortinbras (Franco), who defend themselves. A general argument takes place between all present, broken up by the report that the earth is doomed because its orbit has jumped.

Characters

BEGONIA BROWN, a young woman from Camberwell, the secretary of the Committee, a commonplace clerk, with no notion of her work, and the absurd action throughout is presented as she sees it.

A JEW, middle-aged, distinguished, with 'a blond beard and moustache, tophatted, frock-coated and gloved'.

A NEWCOMER, an obstinate-looking middle-aged man, looking like a provincial shopkeeper, but perhaps from the Dominions, who has no other name throughout.

A WIDOW, a 'Creole lady of about forty, with the remains of a gorgeous and opulent southern beauty', imposing in style and dress.

A JOURNALIST, a smart gay American.

A BISHOP, 'old, soft, gentle and rather infirm'.

COMMISSAR POSKY, very smart, and very Russian of course.

SECRETARY OF THE LEAGUE OF NATIONS, careworn, refined, about fifty.

SIR ORPHEUS MIDLANDER, the English Foreign Secretary, about fifty, very well dressed, 'genial in manner, quick-witted in conversation, altogether a pleasant and popular personality'.

THE JUDGE, a Dutchman, under forty, but 'very grave and every inch a judge'.

THE BETROTHED of Begonia, 'a cheerful young gentleman, powerfully built, with an uproarious voice', nephew of Sir Orpheus.

SIGNOR BOMBARDONE, dominant, brusque, every inch a man of destiny.

MR BATTLER, unsmiling, middle-aged, slim, erect, with a resolutely dissatisfied expression.

A DEACONESS, dressed as such, attractive and voluble.

GENERAL FLANCO DE FORTINBRAS, middle-aged, very smart, quite conventional.

Production

The play has to be treated as farce on an intellectual level, not in any way naturalistic. In the text, Sir Orpheus, Bombardone, Battler and Flanco are obviously intended to represent the persons of real life; but on the stage, when the play was done at Malvern before the war, all personal likenesses were avoided, the Foreign Secretary appeared in Court dress, and the others in romantic national costume. The result was to add to the dream-like quality of the piece as well as to the stage picture, which was all to the good. The play needs the most skilful speaking, and Begonia Brown carries a good deal of weight though the part can easily be overplayed: in fact, virtuosity is required throughout.

A Note on Productions

The play was first presented at the Malvern Festival on 1 August 1938, afterwards at the Saville and St James's Theatres, London, where it ran for a total of 237 performances. It was produced in Warsaw in Polish on 25 July 1939, the last performance being given after the war had started on 2 September 1939. It was given in Prague on 19 December 1947, and in Austria in March 1954. The first New York production was at the Henry Miller Theatre, New York, on 30 January 1940, by a company that had already toured it since the previous year in Canada and the United States.

(49)
In Good King Charles's Golden Days

A TRUE HISTORY THAT NEVER HAPPENED
(1939)

In this last completed play Shaw flouts the critics and the public by giving them what they complain of: talk but no 'action', a piece that seems never to be coming to an end, and discussion on matters that require thought. As so often with him the play has all the features of a *tour de force*. It is technically sparkling; for to maintain dialogue at the high level Shaw reaches, and for the time that the play occupies, is a feat that few dramatists could even attempt let alone expect to succeed in. Shaw's characters are historical personages, among the greatest of their time, and he exhibits them at the height of their powers.

His mind turns once again to the question of leadership. Newton, Kneller, Fox and Charles himself were leaders in their own spheres of science, art, religion and kingship, to say nothing of the women in the play who were mistresses in their own arts. Shaw states the problem, he presents people who are conscious of its implications, but he does not attempt to solve it. The dramatist's function as he saw it is not to solve problems but to get them faced. 'No, beloved,' says Charles, 'the riddle of how to choose a ruler is still unanswered; and it is the riddle of civilization.' But, as often before, Shaw does in an uncanny way indicate the direction in which an answer can be found, for he makes Charles say in the most significant passage in the play:

> I tell you again there are in England, or in any other country, the makings of half a dozen decent kings and councils; but they are mostly in prison. If we only knew how to pick them out and label them, then the people could have their choice out of the half dozen. It may end that way, but not until we have learnt how to pick the people who are fit to be chosen before they are chosen.

The play abounds in such passages, and the various persons are allowed to express themselves with due justice to their recognized opinions.

Newton is the scientist and, while Shaw is fair enough to him, he does not cease to hold him to ridicule, for Shaw is not on the side of the scientists. Kneller is introduced to expound the artist's conflict with the scientific man. The artist is the hand of God, '... the hand that can draw the images of God and reveal the soul in them, and is inspired to do this and nothing else even if he starves and is cast off by his father and all his family for it: is not his hand the hand used by God, who, being a spirit without body, parts or passions, has no hands?' Here speaks the true Shaw. Fox is the man of religion, who, before the earthly king, is the voice of the King of kings; Shaw treats him with great respect. Charles is the king who has to take great care to keep his head upon his shoulders, and undoubtedly Shaw holds him in great admiration, for he may be regarded as a portrait of Shaw, who was a king in his own sphere. The women are various types of feminine charmers, including the true wife, in Catherine, devoted to her husband.

The play, therefore, has characteristics that make it a work of high distinction. At moments, perhaps, the long first act, to which the brief second act is an epilogue, tends to flag, not because the dialogue fails so much as because it is difficult to maintain the necessary attention and mental alertness at so long a stretch. Shaw introduces a little knock-about fun, when Isaac Newton and the Duke of York have a scrap upon the floor; but he could do this once only, and invented little further relief, though he keeps the house-keeper handy, and re-arranges his characters so that we get a variety of combinations: Newton and Louise talking science and alchemy, Charles and James talking kingship, Newton and Kneller talking science and art. All the time the personal interests of the women impinge upon the intellectual talk of the men.

Characters

KING CHARLES II, aged fifty, very tall, highly polished, strongly authoritative in manner. The play is his: the characters as this intelligent man sees them.

MRS BASHAM, Isaac Newton's housekeeper, a middle-aged woman of distinct force of character.

SALLY, a young very presentable serving maid.

ISAAC NEWTON, aged thirty-eight, preoccupied, vain, and masterly in manner.

GEORGE FOX, aged fifty-six, a big man with bright eyes and a powerful voice, when he chooses to use it, a sympathetic character.

NELL GWYNN, attractive, practical, an obviously talented actress.

BARBARA VILLIERS, DUCHESS OF CLEVELAND, aged thirty-nine, a high born lady, who never forgets it for an instant, with every emphasis upon her personal attractions.

LOUISE DE KEROUAILLE, DUCHESS OF PORTSMOUTH, aged thirty, a Frenchwoman 'who retains her famous babyish beauty'.

JAMES, DUKE OF YORK, who is younger than the king, a very precipitate, headstrong and obstinate brother.

GODFREY KNELLER, aged thirty-four, a Dutchman, well dressed and arrogant.

QUEEN CATHERINE OF BRAGANZA, aged forty-two, born to be a queen, disappointed and troubled, but losing nothing of her queenly character.

Production

Historical high comedy demands to be done with exquisite style, with virtuosity in the extreme in its acting. The characters are well defined, strong personalities in their own right. There are two acts, the first the library in the house of Isaac Newton in Cambridge in the year 1680. The room is fully described in the text. In its original production there was an interval in the first

Act before the entrance of the Duke of York, to give relief to the audience. The second act is the boudoir of the Queen in Charles's house in Newmarket on the same day. The properties are described, they need to be correct, but not elaborate and are not especially difficult.

A Note on Productions

The play was first produced at the Malvern Festival on 12 August 1939. It was presented again at Streatham Hill Theatre on 15 April 1940 and afterwards toured, coming to the New Theatre 9 May 1940, when the performances were ended by the blitz. In both productions Cecil Trouncer was Isaac Newton, Herbert Lomax George Fox, Ernest Thesiger King Charles II, Eileen Beldon Nell Gwynn and Irene Vanbrugh Queen Catherine. Godfrey Kneller was played by Anthony Bushell, Bruno Barnaby and Alec Clunes. It was revived at the People's Palace, in the East End of London, on 23 October 1948 in the presence of the King and Queen and was revived again at the Malvern Festival in August 1949. It has not yet been given a professional production in America.

(50)
Buoyant Billions

A COMEDY OF NO MANNERS
(1947)

This 'intentionally unfinished comedy' would be a remarkable achievement by anyone practising the craft of Shakspeare. Had it been written by a young playwright it would have been hailed as a masterpiece, which it is not. This man of ninety-one said, 'I cannot hold my tongue nor my pen. As long as I live I must write.' With that strong appetite to write, Shaw produced a ripe work; ripeness dropping from the tree. 'A trivial comedy', he called it, which, indeed, it is except that it has wisdom. To generations brought up on Shaw it appeared a mere repetition of what he had done much better before, and it is true that some of the characters in his early plays appear again, if somewhat faintly, but the play gave delight, for it had much of the old energy, and the old message was still sounded: 'I don't want to be happy. I want to be alive and active.'

Junius has the desire to be a world-betterer, and argues with his father about it. He persuades him to send him on a tour to study the beneficent effects of the atom bomb. On his tour he arrives in Panama and discovers an Englishwoman living alone in a tropical forest. They engage in political, philosophical and personal discussions continued with an elderly native, until the lady ends the talk by attracting an alligator to them with her saxophone.

The third act is in the drawing room of the house in Belgrave Square, London, where lives Old Bill Buoyant, the Billionaire. A discussion takes place between the family of the billlionaire and his solicitor upon money, how it is made, taxed, and disappears, into which breaks in the young woman from Panama, who is the billionaire's firstborn. She introduces the theme of love. Then Junius appears because he wants to marry the young woman for the sake of her money. The act ends with them thinking it over. In the fourth and last act Old Bill Buoyant makes his first appearance and the question of the marriage is thoroughly discussed. He advises his daughter to marry the young man, but she is doubtful. After further discussion with the solicitor and members of the family, she decides to do so.

Characters

JUNIUS, the young man, through whose eyes the action takes place, is a version of Valentine in *You Never Can Tell*; he is in the early twenties.

HIS FATHER, an elderly, prosperous man of business.

SHE, the lady in the forest, is Clementina, daughter of the Billionaire, an extraordinary young woman who is attacked by the dangerous disease of love.

THE NATIVE, the lady's attendant, elderly, wise.

THE CHINESE PRIEST, who is in charge of the temple in the Buoyant House.

SIR FERDINAND FLOPPER, a middle-aged conventionally minded solicitor.

THE WIDOWER, a middle-aged son of the billionaire, who can play the cornet but do nothing else.

DARKIE, daughter of the billionaire, aged twenty, who displays plenty of confidence.

MR SECONDBORN, another son, a passionate mathematician, who earns nothing. Shaw's biographer, Archibald Henderson, thinks the playwright had him in mind in this character.

MRS SECONDBORN, his wife, an aggressive woman.

MRS THIRDBORN, wife of a further son.

FIFFY, the youngest son, aged seventeen, a raw adolescent.

OLD BILL BUOYANT, a grey-beard, like any other grey-beard, who is a clever speculator, devoted to the practice of meditation.

Production

It is a short play, although there are four acts named The World Betterer, The Adventure, The Discussion, The End. It requires to be treated lightly, gaily, but without any element of burlesque. Its qualities are entirely in the dialogue, which calls for good

321

speaking; the action is confused and inconclusive. Given good speaking, timing and point, it becomes a sparkling entertainment.

There are three settings. Act one, a well-furnished study. Act two, a jungle clearing in Panama, outside a wooden house on posts: there is an alligator. Act three is a London drawing room converted into a Chinese temple: the properties are described in the text. Act four is the same.

A Note on Productions

The play was written for the Malvern Festival but first produced in German at the Schauspielhaus, Zurich, under the title of *Zu viel Geld* on 21 October 1948, when it bewildered the audience. It was produced at the Malvern Festival on 13 August 1949, afterwards brought to the Princes Theatre, London, where it was given for eight weeks. Clementina was played with great gusto and tact by Frances Day. The critics treated the play with respect as the work of a very old man, but their attitude to his plays had hardly changed from what it always had been.

(51)
Shakes versus Shav

A PUPPET PLAY
(1949)

A tiny piece, hardly a play though included in the canon, written for tiny actors, lasting ten minutes. Shaw described it as 'the climax of my eminence', and in a note in the programme for the original performance declared that he had learnt part of his craft from puppets. It is a knockabout in blank verse. Shakes comes on in a rage, 'an infamous impostor to chastize' one who 'dares pretend here to reincarnate my very self . . . this fiend of Ireland'.

He demands of Shav 'Couldst thou write King Lear?' to which Shav answers, 'Couldst thou have written Heartbreak House?' The piece finishes with Shav saying:

> We both are mortal. For a moment suffer
> My glimmering light to shine.

Characters

The characters are SHAKES, SHAV, MACBETH, ROB ROY, CAPTAIN SHOTOVER and ELLIE DUNN.

Production

The piece was first performed by the Waldo Lanchester Marionette Theatre at Malvern on 9 August 1949. First presented in London at the Riverside Theatre, Festival Gardens, on 10 June 1951, afterwards at the Lyric Theatre, Hammersmith, on 1 December 1953. The voices of Shakes were recorded by Lewis Casson and of Shav by Ernest Thesiger.

(52)
Farfetched Fables

(1948)

This is a second-childhood piece in six short scenes to which Shaw added a preface, written the year after, of thirty-seven pages: six pages longer than the play. It is a sketch for a play rather than a completed work and opens with a talk on atomic bombs between a young man and a young woman in a public park. The second fable is in the War Office, and is ended by a gas attack. The third is at an Anthropometric Laboratory in the Isle of Wight, which had become a scientific centre for classifying people according to their secretions and reactions, otherwise a mad-house. The fourth shows the same place converted into a centre for Diet Commissioners. In the fifth it has been re-converted into a Genetic Institute, and in the sixth and last it has become a sixth form school, and concludes with the teacher advising her class to read the Book of Job. It is a satire upon science, the fables arising from the talk and behaviour of scientists.

Characters

There are twenty-three characters, all types of people rather than particular human beings.

Production

The six scenes offer opportunity for a scenic designer and for players who can speak well; but the opportunities are small. Done quickly and with spirit it can be made entertaining in the Shavian manner. It has not been publicly performed.

A Note on Productions

A private production was given at the Watergate Theatre, London, on 6 September 1950, and a public amateur performance by the People's Theatre, Newcastle-on-Tyne, on 13 January 1951.

(53)
Why She Would Not

A COMEDIETTA
(1950)

As Shaw admitted, he could not stop writing, and this last piece of work was started in the summer of 1950. It exists in a shorthand version, and a holograph manuscript is in the possession of an American collector. A typeset, fourteen-page proof by Shaw's printers, R. and R. Clark of Edinburgh, is in the Archibald Henderson Collection at the University of North Carolina. A typewritten version of sixteen pages was found among Shaw's papers and is in the British Museum. Shaw said of the play 'It's not worth finishing', though he seems to have intended it for the Standard Edition.

The play is concerned with a rich spinster, Serafina White, and a young man, Henry Bossborn, who encounters the lady in a wood one summer afternoon when she is being attacked by a tramp. He rescues her, and accompanies her home, when he tells her he is looking for a job. So he is introduced by her to her family firm. He is engaged on trial by the firm and succeeds so well that he gets control and becomes a rich man. He then persuades the lady to pull down her large old-fashioned house and to build a modern one. Having done so, she resents him, declaring she will be no further coerced. 'I will live my own life, not yours', she declares, and he says, 'Good day to you'. It is a familiar Shavian theme.

Characters

THE MAN is a rough looking fellow, a tramp pretending to be a guide.

SERAFINA WHITE is a young lady of about thirty.

HENRY BOSSBORN is a young artisan with an ambition for bossing others, indicated by his name.

REGINALD WHITE, grandfather of Serafina, is the chairman of the family firm.

JASPER WHITE is his son, not a boss by nature.

MONTGOMERY SMITH is head of the counting-house of the family firm.

There are also a NURSE-HOUSEKEEPER, two CLERKS, and three or four MEMBERS OF THE BOARD of the firm.

Production

The play is in five scenes, a wood, at the gates of a country house, a company's boardroom, the drawing room of the country house, and the lounge in a 1950 house. There is an interval of two years before the fourth scene and an unspecified interval between that and the fifth act. In its available form the piece is hardly playable, but its manner is that of the last three plays, fantastic and inconclusive. The play has not been produced. The British Museum version was printed in *The London Magazine* (August 1956).

Index

Plays

Characters

General